*Particles in the
Atmosphere and Space*

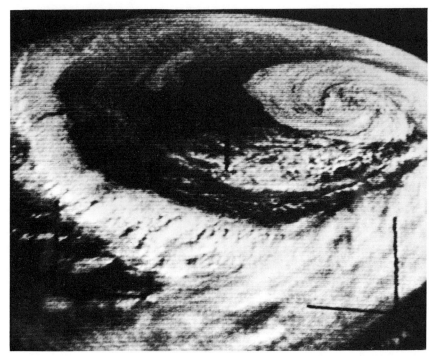

TIROS VI satellite photograph taken over the North Atlantic Ocean south-east of Nova Scotia on May 29, 1963. This is a spiral cloud array associated with a cyclonic vortex.

PARTICLES IN THE ATMOSPHERE AND SPACE

RICHARD D. CADLE
National Center for Atmospheric Research
Boulder, Colorado

REINHOLD PUBLISHING CORPORATION, *New York*

Copyright © 1966 by
REINHOLD PUBLISHING CORPORATION

All rights reserved

Library of Congress Catalog Card Number: 66-22808
Printed in the United States of America

Preface

This book really began seventeen years ago when I was asked to undertake a study of the chemistry of smog in Los Angeles, California. Since then I have had the opportunity and good fortune to undertake many basic and applied investigations of fine particles, especially when suspended in air. This has led me and my associates to activities such as flights through dust clouds formed by underground TNT explosions, participation in nuclear explosion tests, developing and applying high-speed photomicrographic equipment for photographing, *in situ*, ice particles in Alaskan ice fog, and sampling volcanic particulate effluents. In addition, we have conducted many laboratory experimental programs. Such experience has impressed on me the fact that fine-particle investigations involve as much art as science, and that the techniques applicable to one domain, such as smog, may also be applicable to a very remote domain, such as dust in a distant galaxy. Furthermore, I have been strongly impressed by the many ways in which particles from one source in an aerosol influence particles from another source in the same aerosol. One example is the action of freezing nuclei which have been added to a supercooled cloud; another is the agglomeration of particles formed by high-altitude nuclear explosions with natural aerosol particles.

Because of this interaction, and because many man-made particles are similar with respect to size and composition to natural aerosol particles, large parts of this book have been devoted to man-produced particles. Furthermore, man-made particles suspended in air are interfering to an increasing extent with our health and comfort.

This book, like the preceding one I have written entitled "Particle Size—Theory and Industrial Applications," is intended to be intermediate in scope between an introduction to the subject and an exhaustive treatise. It has been written especially for scientists and engineers who are not specialists in fine-particle science and technology, or who may be specialists in some phase of fine-particle behavior and wish to learn more about the nature of particles in our universe as a whole. No attempt has been made to provide an exhaustive review of the literature, and the references

v

to the original literature were selected as examples, because of their particular importance, or because of their historical interest. In addition, there are numerous references to reviews and to books dealing in detail with a subject treated in this book. This will permit a reader interested in a particular subject to obtain much more detailed information than could be presented here.

The world is flooded with books and a new one should only be written if there is some hope that it will satisfy some need. This book is intended to gather in one volume information concerning the fine particles in our universe, information that for the most part has been scattered through a voluminous literature covering such subjects as astronomy, air pollution, cloud physics, meteorology, radioactive fallout, and "space science." I feel that such a book should be useful if for no other reason than the wide spread in the location of the sources of particles reaching a given part of our universe. For instance, the particles in our atmosphere are produced in part by factories, by the breaking of bubbles in the oceans, and by the break-up of comets. It is helpful to consider in some detail all such sources if we are to understand the nature of particles in the Earth's atmosphere. Another example is dust on the lunar surface, which probably consists in part of original lunar material and in part of micrometeoroids which constantly rain down on our Moon's surface.

I am pleased to acknowledge the help of many persons in the preparation of this volume, many of whom supplied illustrative material. The latter are mentioned in the captions. In particular I wish to thank Dr. W. O. Roberts, Director of the National Center for Atmospheric Research, for encouraging me to write this book, and Dr. Eric R. Allen, Dr. E. A. Martell, and Mr. Paul Sears for reviewing portions of it.

R. D. CADLE

Boulder, Colorado
April, 1966

Contents

Chapter 1 **Introduction**

Fine particles in the atmosphere and space are of interest for at least three reasons. First, many types of such particles are of tremendous practical importance. The tragedy of the dust storms of the Great Plains of the United States during the 1930's is one example. The protection which must be afforded a space vehicle to minimize the likelihood that its surface will be penetrated by a micrometeoroid is another. Second, knowledge of the nature and behavior of the particles in the universe often provides information concerning various other aspects of the universe. For example, certain types of particles in our atmosphere such as radio-active fallout, pollens, and certain bacteria serve as tracers for the movement of air masses and tell us much concerning the dynamics of the atmosphere. Third is interest in the particles themselves as geological and cosmological phenomena. For instance, interplanetary particles seem to be largely responsible for the zodiacal light, and their presence raises questions concerning their nature and their source.

Throughout this book all three reasons are considered but not all kinds of particles. It is necessary to limit the size range considered, and this range has been rather arbitrarily chosen to be 0.05 to $10^4 \mu$ (5×10^{-6} to 1 cm). The lower end overlaps slightly the colloid range while the upper end overlaps somewhat the range in which direct measurement of individual particles without magnification is possible. It includes those particles in the lower atmosphere that maintain their identity and remain suspended for long periods of time, and larger particles such as raindrops, many hailstones, and most meteoroids.

DEFINITIONS OF PARTICLE SIZE

The terms "particle" and "particle size" are often highly ambiguous unless carefully defined. Ambiguity with respect to the term "particle" usually arises from the need to distinguish between aggregates and the "ultimate" particles constituting the aggregates. The phrase "particle size" as so often used is very indefinite and even when applied to spheres it may mean either radius or diameter.

1

Numerous definitions of particle size have been developed to avoid such ambiguity. The size may be defined either as a statistical property based on the measurement of each of a large number of particles in a powder or suspension, or in terms of some property of the suspension which is related to particle size. Measurements involving optical or electron microscopy and sieving are based on definitions of the first type while measurements of light scattering, which are used extensively in atmospheric and astronomical research, are based on the second type of definition.

A widely used statistical definition of diameter was proposed by Martin.[1] It is the distance between opposite sides of the particle, measured across the particle on a line bisecting the projected area. Some convention must be chosen with respect to the direction in which the diameters are measured. For instance, when the dimensions are measured with a microscope, it is convenient to use the direction parallel to the bottom of the field. Obviously the result of the measurement of a single irregular particle depends on the orientation of the particle, but by measuring large numbers of particles and combining the results statistically significant values are obtained.

Another very useful definition of diameter is that of a circle whose area is equal to the projected area of the particle. Special ocular micrometers (graticules) have been designed for making the comparison[2,3,4] and several types are commercially available.

For some purposes there are advantages to defining and naming particle size ranges. A system which is becoming generally accepted for particles suspended in the atmosphere defines three size ranges. Those with radii less than 0.1μ are called "Aitken nuclei" or "Aitken particles." Those having radii in the range 0.1 to 1μ are "large particles," and those having radii greater than 1μ are "giant particles." The term Aitken particles has resulted from the development and use of the Aitken nuclei counter.[5] This device is essentially an expansion-type cloud chamber in which water condenses on the particles in a sample of air. Usually most of the particles have radii smaller than 0.1μ. Particles in the size range 0.1 to 1μ radius are responsible for much of the decrease in visibility caused by photochemical smog and natural haze.

SIZE DISTRIBUTIONS

The particles in a suspension are never all exactly the same size, and in the atmosphere and space the distribution is usually very wide. Various methods have been used to present graphs and equations representing the distributions. It is useful to keep in mind the distinction between the size distribution of the particles in a sample and the size distribution of the particles in the original population of particles. Also, it is useful to distinguish between a population with fixed size limits at both extremes, and one in which no such limit (other than zero) exists at one or both ends. The latter type of population is especially common in nature.

When dealing with size data from the former type of population, or from the latter when only a specific size range is considered, it is helpful to classify the data into groups called classes which are defined by particle size limits called class boundaries. For convenience, the midpoint of each class interval is called the class mark, d_i, and i is the number of the interval. The number of particles in each class is the frequency, f_i, and n is the total number of particles.

A convenient device for representing classified data which is often used in atmospheric research is the histogram. It is a bar graph in which the abscissa represents the class intervals and the ordinate commonly represents the frequencies. The ordinates can represent properties of the particles other than frequencies, for example, total surface or weight in the class intervals.

Another method for graphically presenting particle size data, which is used extensively in industry but less often in atmospheric and space research, is the cumulative curve. This is obtained by plotting the percentage of particles having particle diameters greater than (or less than) a given particle size against particle size. These curves have the advantage over histograms in that the class interval is eliminated, and they can be used to represent data which are obtained in classified form having unequal class intervals, such as data obtained by sieving or by cloud-chamber techniques.[6] Special graph papers have been designed such that if the sizes are normally or log-normally distributed, the cumulative plots will be straight lines. Such paper is commercially available. Cumulative curves have the additional advantage in that the median diameter, corresponding to the 50 per cent point on the abscissa, is easily obtained, and so are the quartiles, corresponding to the 25 and 75 per cent points. Furthermore, the percentage represented by the abscissa may be that of surface or weight rather than that of number of particles.

Special methods of plotting have often been used for unusual types of data. For example, Junge[7,8] plots atmospheric aerosol size distribution data as $dN/d \log r$ per cm^3 against the radius r in microns on a log-log scale where N is the number of particles. This type of plot has the advantage that the concentrations as well as size distributions are indicated. The total number of particles per cm^3, ΔN, within the interval $\Delta(\log r)$ can be obtained readily from such plots, and the use of logarithmic scales is advisable because of the wide range of particle sizes and concentrations in the atmosphere.

DEFINITIONS OF MEAN SIZE

Numerous statistical methods are available for indicating the central tendency and spread of the sizes of a population of particles. These involve determining properties such as the various means (arithmetic, geometric, etc.), the standard deviation, and quartiles. The most common value for representing the central tendency of a set of measurements is the arithmetic mean or average value, which is defined as the sum of any group of values divided by the number of values in the group. For classified data the arithmetic mean is defined by the equation

$$\overline{d} = \frac{1}{n} \sum_{i=1}^{i=h} d_i f_i \tag{1.1}$$

where h is the number of class intervals.

A very convenient statistical property for indicating data spread is the standard deviation, defined by the equation

$$s = \left[\frac{1}{n} \sum_{i=1}^{i=h} (d_i - \overline{d})^2 f_i \right]^{\frac{1}{2}} \tag{1.2}$$

It is the square root of the average value of the squares of the deviations from the mean. When n is small it should be replaced by $n - 1$.

Numerous definitions of mean other than arithmetic mean are useful for various types of comparison. Many of these can be defined by the following equation for classified data:[9]

$$(\overline{d}_{qp})^{q-p} = \sum_{i=1}^{i=h} \frac{f_i}{n} d_i^q \bigg/ \sum_{i=1}^{i=h} \frac{f_i}{n} d_i^p \tag{1.3}$$

Thus, the arithmetic mean would be $\overline{d}_{10}$. Similarly, the mean surface diameter, which is the diameter of the particle whose surface is the arithmetic mean of the surfaces, is $\overline{d}_{20}$, and the mean volume or weight diameter is $\overline{d}_{30}$. The linear mean diameter is $\overline{d}_{21}$ and the surface mean diameter is $\overline{d}_{32}$.

The geometric mean, $\overline{d}_g$, is defined by the equation

$$\overline{d}_g = (d_1^{f_1} d_2^{f_2} d_3^{f_3} \ldots d_n^{f_n})^{1/n} \tag{1.4}$$

It is always less than or equal to $\overline{d}_{10}$, and the difference increases with increasing data spread.

The use of the median and quartiles for such purposes has already been mentioned. The mode, which is the size of maximum frequency, is also often used.

Although statistical information of the above types is often presented in connection with studies of particles in the atmosphere and space, it is not always appropriate. The size distribution of particles in the atmosphere and space is often studied between rather arbitrarily selected size limits. In such cases, plots of the original data, or regression lines and the standard errors of estimate may furnish the required information. Methods for calculating regression lines and standard errors of estimate are described in textbooks of mathematical statistics.

DISTRIBUTION FUNCTIONS

The mathematical expression which describes a distribution of data is known as a distribution function. One of the best known is the normal distribution:

$$f(d) = \frac{1}{s\sqrt{2\pi}} \exp\left[-\frac{1}{2}\left(\frac{d - \bar{d}}{s}\right)^2\right] \tag{1.5}$$

Such distributions are symmetrical about the arithmetic mean, and the mode, median, and arithmetic mean are identical. Normal distributions are completely determined by specifying the mean and the standard deviation.

Many size distributions are highly skewed, and can be represented by substituting some function of the diameter for the diameter in equation 1.5. The substituted function is often the logarithm of the diameter, in which case 1.5 becomes

$$f(d) = \frac{1}{\log s_g \sqrt{2\pi}} \exp\left[-\frac{1}{2}\left(\frac{\log d - \log \bar{d}_g}{\log s_g}\right)^2\right] \tag{1.6}$$

Here $\bar{d}_g$, as usual, is the geometric mean and s_g is the geometric standard deviation.

Exponential functions of the following form have been especially useful in astrophysics and in atmospheric research:

$$\frac{dN}{d(d)} = ad^c \tag{1.7}$$

The function is established by the values of the constants a and c. For instance, Steffens and Rubin[10] obtained a value of -4.5 for c for particles in Los Angeles smog. Junge,[7,8] plotting $dN/d \log r$ against r for particles in the natural atmosphere, obtained a slope of about -3 on a logarithmic scale over much of the size range. Since $dN/d \log r$ is identical to rdN/dr, this slope corresponds to a value of about -4 for c. Obviously, equation 1.7 is limited with regard to the size region it can represent since when c is negative, $dN/d(d)$ approaches infinity as d approaches zero.

Size distributions may have two or more modes. For example, coagulating aerosols may be bimodal.[11] Some multinomal distributions can be represented as the sum of two or more unimodal functions. Dalla Valle, Orr, and Blocker have proposed a general equation for representing bimodal particle size distributions.[12]

REFERENCES

1. Martin, G., Blythe, C. E., and Tongue, H., *Trans. Ceram. Soc. (Eng.)*, **23**, 61 (1924).
2. Patterson, H. S., and Cawood, W., *Trans. Faraday Soc.*, **32**, 1084 (1936).
3. Fairs, G. L., *Chem. Ind.*, **62**, 374 (1943).
4. May, K. R., *J. Sci. Inst.*, **22**, 187 (1945).
5. Aitken, J., "Collection of Scientific Papers," London, Cambridge Univ. Press, 1923.
6. Rich, T. A., *Geofisica*, **31**, 60 (1955).
7. Junge, C. E., in "Advances in Geophysics," V. IV, New York, Academic Press, 1957.
8. Junge, C. E., "Air Chemistry and Radioactivity," New York, Academic Press, 1963.
9. Mugele, R. A., and Evans, H. D., *Ind. Eng. Chem.*, **43**, 1317 (1951).
10. Steffens, C., and Rubin, S., in "Proceedings of the First National Air Pollution Symposium," Stanford Research Institute, Menlo Park, Calif., 1949.
11. Sinclair, D., "Measurement of Particle Size and Size Distribution," in "Handbook on Aerosols," U. S. Atomic Energy Commission, Washington, D. C., 1950.
12. Dalla Valle, J. M., Orr, C., Jr., and Blocker, H. G., *Ind. Eng. Chem.*, **43**, 1377 (1951).

Chapter 2 # The Troposphere

NATURE OF THE TROPOSPHERE

The troposphere is the lowest region in the atmosphere, extending from the Earth's surface up through the region of generally decreasing temperature to the tropopause, the altitude where the temperature ceases to decrease or may even increase. The troposphere is characterized by storms and turbulence, and receives much of its heat from the ground rather than by direct radiation from the Sun.

The particles in the troposphere are both "natural" and man-made, although it is often difficult and rather arbitrary to try to distinguish between them. For example, numerous of man's operations dump tremendous quantities of particles produced by combustion into the atmosphere. But numerous forest, brush, and grass fires do the same thing, and many of these are started by lightning.

SOURCES OF PARTICLES

Sea salt

Mason[1] has classified the mechanisms of formation of aerosols into four main groups. The first is the condensation and sublimation of vapor and the formation of smoke by both natural and man-made operations. The second is chemical reactions involving trace gases in the atmosphere. The third is the mechanical disruption and dispersal of matter at the Earth's surface, either as sea salt over the ocean or as various dusts, largely mineral, over the continents. The fourth is the coagulation of fine particles to form large particles which may be of highly mixed composition. A fifth category might be added, namely, the influx of extraterrestrial particles. Obviously, various combinations of these mechanisms can and do occur. For example, the fourth category can only take place following the operation of one of the other mechanisms. Also, the chemical reactions of category two may occur between trace gases and particles formed by other means.[2]

7

One of the most important individual types of solid fine particles in the atmosphere is ocean salt, which is mainly sodium chloride. Such particles are very important because they are very numerous, are widespread over both the oceans and continents, and play an important role in cloud formation. The concentrations of salt particles over the oceans may be as great as 100 particles per cm^3 but a concentration of one per cm^3 is more common. Even over the ocean there are many different types of particles in the atmosphere, and salt particles constitute a small percentage of the total. This is largely because continental aerosols can be carried long distances by the winds, even completely across oceans, as is described below. Also, there is some chemical reaction between salt particles and trace gases, and there is a continuous influx of extraterrestrial particles.

Pure sodium chloride crystals are hygroscopic, forming droplets, when the relative humidity exceeds about 75 per cent. Conversely, when the relative humidity drops below this figure, salt droplets evaporate completely to produce solid particles. At humidities between 75 and 100 per cent, water vapor condenses on or evaporates from a droplet containing dissolved sodium chloride until the vapor pressure of the droplet becomes equal to the partial pressure of water vapor in the air.

Most sodium chloride in the air started as droplets of sea salt which evaporated when the relative humidity fell below about 75 per cent. For many years it was believed that the droplets were formed as spray blown from the tops of breaking waves. Now it is well established that the droplets are mainly formed by the breaking of myriads of air bubbles as they reach the surface of the sea.[3,4,5,6] Most of the bubbles are produced by the breaking of small waves, but they may also be produced in other ways, such as by rain or snow falling on the water. Spray droplets are often formed by breaking waves but they are too large to remain in the air for long. Such particles are probably largely responsible for the high concentrations of salt in the air near the seashore. In fact, the heavy haze that is often observed along the coast when the surf is severe and there is a gentle breeze toward shore probably comes from this source. However, high coastal concentrations drop rapidly with increasing distance inland.

Bursting bubbles produce droplets in two size ranges. As the bubble bursts, a small jet rises from the bottom of the bubble. This jet quickly breaks up into droplets which are nearly all the same size and about one-tenth the size of the bubble. Thus, the size distribution of these droplets is largely determined by the size distribution of the bubbles. The smallest bubbles formed by small breaking waves are usually about 100μ in diameter, corresponding to droplets about 10μ in diameter. Since the concentration of salt in sea water is usually about 3.3 to 3.6 per cent by weight, the evaporated droplets produce particles that are about $\left(\dfrac{0.034}{2.1}\right)^{\frac{1}{3}} \times 10$ or about $2.5\,\mu$ in diameter.

Most airborne salt particles are not this large, and are produced in the second size range. Just before the bubble breaks, a thin film exists between the air of the bubble and the air of the open atmosphere. The breaking of this film produces a large number of very small droplets. Mason[7] has observed that the bursting of each such bubble produces 100 to 200 small droplets which evaporate to form particles with maximum diameters of about $0.3\,\mu$.

On the basis of calculations by Eriksson[8] which indicate that under steady-state conditions 0.3 per cent of the sea surface must be covered with whitecaps, Junge[9] estimated an order-of-magnitude production rate of one salt particle per cm^2 sec. He also suggests that a reasonable value for the average residence time of sea-salt aerosol particles over the ocean is 1 to 3 days.

The modal diameter for the log diameter vs. volume distribution of salt particles over the ocean varies from about 4 to $20\,\mu$, depending largely on wind velocity. The modal diameter for the log diameter vs. number distribution is a few tenths of a micron, and the spread between the two modal diameters demonstrates that the particle size distribution is very wide.[3,10]

Sea-salt particles are complex mixtures of the materials contained in solution and suspension in the sea. The major constituent is, of course, sodium chloride, but smaller amounts of other inorganic substances are present, particularly sulfates, carbonates, potassium, calcium, and magnesium. Organic substances are both dissolved and suspended in sea water. Furthermore, the ocean is probably covered with a layer of insoluble organic material that is usually only a few molecules thick. Such organic material would be incorporated to some extent in the sea-salt particles.

Neuman, Fonselius, and Wahlman[11] carried out an investigation of the organic carbon and nitrogen content of rain and snow samples from various places in Sweden. They defined organic nitrogen as nitrogen which is distilled as ammonia in the usual Kjeldahl procedure from which has been subtracted the free ammonia as determined by an alkaline distillation. Total nitrogen was defined as free ammonia nitrogen plus organic nitrogen. One test series involved analyzing the organic content of rain and snow collected at nine stations in Sweden over a period of four months. The geographical distribution of organic carbon was found to be quite constant over the sampling region and averaged about 160 mg carbon per square meter per month. A second test series consisted of analyzing rain and snow samples to determine the ratio of organic carbon to total nitrogen, and this ratio was also found to be quite constant, regardless of the sampling location. The free ammonia was between 25 and 100 per cent of the total ammonia, possibly indicating a varying degree of decomposition of the organic substances in the samples. The results suggest that there is a very extended source for the organic carbon in the atmosphere. Neuman *et al.* suggested that this source is the layer of organic material on the sea surface mentioned above. They also speculated that gaseous ammonia is introduced from the sea into the air, nitrogen-containing organic material first being introduced into the air on the droplets formed by breaking bubbles, followed by evaporation of the water and finally decomposition of the organic substances, liberating gaseous ammonia.

Sea-salt particles are for the most part so small that they penetrate far inland.[12,13] The limited data available indicate that there is little difference in the number concentrations of salt particles as far as 1000 miles inland and over the oceans. This suggests that the removal of such particles by rain is very small, as might be expected from theoretical considerations and from the results of laboratory experiments on the removal of very small particles by drops.

Over the oceans the sea-salt concentration in the air decreases with increasing altitude, but the size distribution remains essentially the same. Therefore, the removal process must be largely independent of size, and sedimentation must not be an important removal process, or if it is important, other factors must compensate for the classification according to size which would otherwise result. The removal is probably by precipitation, and the process must be similar to that for fine radioactive fallout particles, discussed later. As just mentioned, impaction by rain drops cannot be important because of the small size of the salt particles, unless the latter participate in cloud formation or diffuse to the cloud droplets.

Sodium and chloride ions associated with continental aerosols are not necessarily of marine origin. There is considerable evidence that much of the chloride associated with such aerosols is produced by various industrial processes. For example, Junge[14,15,16] collected particles in the "large" and "giant" size ranges with a cascade impactor and analyzed the samples for NH_4^+, Na^+, Mg^{++}, $SO_4^=$, Cl^-, NO_3^-, and NO_2^-. The water-soluble fractions of large particles collected in the vicinity of Frankfurt, Germany consisted largely of NH_4^+ and $SO_4^=$, but little ammonia was found in the giant particles. Chloride ions were found in both size ranges. When fresh maritime air arrived in the vicinity of Frankfurt, the Cl^- concentration decreased for the large particles and increased for the giant particles.

Junge[9] later obtained similar results on the east coast of the United

States in an essentially rural area. Again, NH_4^+ and SO_4^- were the main ions in the large particles, and the ratio of the two corresponded to a mixture of $(NH_4)_2SO_4$ and $(NH_4)HSO_4$. Na^+ and Cl^- ions were found in the giant particles, but hardly at all in the smaller "large" ones when the wind was from the ocean. Similar results were obtained in Miami, Florida and in Hawaii.

These results indicate that the sea-salt component of continental aerosol is largely associated with the giant particles. They are consistent with the finding mentioned above that the modal diameter for the log diameter vs. volume distribution of oceanic salt particles varies from about 4 to 20μ.

The giant sea-salt particles are of special interest since they play an important role in producing rain in nonfreezing clouds, as discussed later. Furthermore, they appear to play a role in rain formation even in clouds in middle latitudes whose tops extend above the freezing level. Thus, a knowledge of the distribution of such particles over both the land and oceans is of considerable importance. Toba[17] undertook a theoretical study of this problem, analyzing data from a number of publications.

As mentioned above, the size distribution of the sea-salt particles over the ocean, including the giant particles, remains almost invariant with changing altitude. Furthermore, a maximum in the concentration is sometimes found in the vicinity of 1500 ft above the surface of the sea, especially when the wind speed is low. Toba explains the decrease in concentration with height as a combination of sedimentation, eddy diffusion, and convection. He explains the concentration maximum as a result of the presence of a boundary layer several meters thick over the ocean surface, where the relative humidity changes rapidly with height. (Eriksson[8] has suggested that such maxima result from wind shear.)

Toba used data of Byers et al.[18] and of Junge and Gustafson[19] for the vertical distribution of giant sea-salt particles over continents. There appears to be an increasing concentration with increasing altitude through the first few hundred feet above which the concentration is fairly constant. Byers et al. suggested that the low concentration near the ground resulted from impaction of the particles on trees and other vegetation. Toba analyzed this type of distribution theoretically. He developed equations relating the ratio between the maximum and the ground concentrations to an efficiency of impaction by ground obstacles.

Forest fires, rocks, and soil

Another important source of tropospheric particles consists of grass, brush, and forest fires. Mason[6] has suggested that of the condensation nuclei which produce clouds, about one-tenth are sea salt, and the rest are mixed nuclei and the products of natural or man-made fires. Even a small fire introduces vast numbers of small particles into the atmosphere. It has been estimated that an average grass fire, extending over one acre, produces about 20,000 billion-billion (2×10^{22}) fine particles.[20] These particles range in composition from inorganic ash through carbon to complex tars and resins. If the particles were uniformly distributed through a column of air having a cross section of one acre and 10,000 ft in height, the number concentration of particles would be about two billion particles per cm^3. The concentration of condensation nuclei in a ventilated kitchen containing a large operating gas range was found[21] to exceed 5×10^5 nuclei per cm^3 while the outside air contained only about 25,000 nuclei per cm^3. Of course, most of these particles are very small, less than about $0.1\,\mu$ radius, and thus in the size range defining the so-called Aitken particles.

Smoke from forest fires can travel great distances as was demonstrated by the "blue Sun" which was observed in Edinburgh, Scotland, in September, 1950.[22,23] For a few hours on one day the Sun appeared to be a deep indigo blue. Meteorological considerations suggested that this appearance was a result of light scattering by smoke from forest fires in western Canada. Spectroscopic studies of the solar light during this period were made by the Royal Observatory in Edinburgh. The results were consistent with the theory of a forest-fire origin. The effective particle diameter for light scattering was about $1\,\mu$, although there must have been a fairly wide size distribution. That night the Moon also had a blue appearance, and it is interesting to speculate as to whether such phenomena were responsible for the phrase "once in a blue Moon."

Although combustion processes produce tremendous numbers of particles in the Aitken size range, they also produce larger particles, the "large" particles in the range 0.1 to $1\,\mu$ radius and "giant" particles that are larger than $1\,\mu$ radius. Most of the particles on a number basis have a diameter less than $1\,\mu$.

Particles of soil and rocks constitute an important portion of the particle loading of the atmosphere. Dust storms and sand storms such as those seen in "dust bowls" and in desert country dramatically emphasize this fact. A single dustfall in 1901 deposited an estimated two million tons of dust on the African desert and on Europe.[24] An estimated ten million tons of red dust from northwest Africa was deposited on England in 1903.[25] Another dramatic demonstration of atmospheric dust and sand consists of the beautiful and often weird rock forms that have been carved out by airborne particles in arid regions. Particles formed by the attrition of rocks are usually quite large, generally having diameters exceeding $1\,\mu$.

Minerals and other inorganic substances about 60% of total

- **Water-soluble fraction, about 15% of total**

  Elements identified by emission spectrograph:

Large amount (10%+)	Silicon, Aluminum, Iron
Small amount (1–9%)	Titanium, Calcium
1%	Magnesium, Barium, Sodium, Potassium
Very small amount (0.1–0.9%)	Lead, Zinc, Vanadium
0.1%	Manganese, Nickel
Trace (0.01–0.1%)	Tin, Copper, Zirconium, Strontium
0.001–0.01%	Boron, Chromium
0.001%	Bismuth, Cobalt

- **Water-insoluble fraction, about 45% of total**

  Substances identified by chemical means:

	(%)
SiO_2	14.3
Iron and Aluminum	7.8
Calcium (as Ca)	5.2
Fluoride (as F)	0.05
Sulfate (as H_2SO_4)	2.5
Ammonia	0.70
Nitrate (as HNO_3)	4.8
Chloride (as NaCl)	0.26
Nitrite	0.00
Sulfide	0.00
Sodium (as NaCl)	4.6

Organic compounds soluble in organic solvents, about 10%

Mainly hydrocarbons
Also small amounts of organic acids (0.27%), and aldehydes

Fibers, pollen, carbon and highly polymerized organic material, about 15%

Peroxides, 0.04%, (as H_2O_2)

Water and volatile organic substances (by difference), about 15%

Even gentle breezes are effective in raising mineral particles from surfaces. It is likely that such material is deposited from the atmosphere and then reentrained a multitude of times before it is washed into the ocean to become part of the ocean sediments. The contribution of mineral particles to the particle loadings of Los Angeles smog is shown in Table 2-1, which consists of the results of an analysis of airborne particles collected with an electrostatic precipitator. About 45 per cent on a mass basis of the collected material consisted of water-insoluble inorganic substances.

Volcanoes

Volcanoes, at times at least, have been an important source of fine particles in the atmosphere. One of the most famous eruptions was that of Krakatoa in 1883 in the East Indies, which produced explosion clouds 18 miles high and turned day into night in Batavia, 100 miles away. A more recent series of violent explosions was produced by the volcano Gunung Agung in Bali in 1963, which had long been inactive. Like the Krakatoa eruption, the Gunung Agung eruption injected particles into the stratosphere as well as into the troposphere, and apparently produced spectacular sunsets throughout the world. Figure 2-1 is a black and white copy of a color transparency of a sunset produced by high atmospheric particles, taken in Boulder, Colorado in October 1964. A streak through the sunset which was marked in the original but indistinct in the black and white copy is of interest since it may have been a shadow of one of the Rocky Mountains. The volume of fine ash thrown into the atmosphere by a powerful volcanic eruption has been estimated to be as much as 100 billion cubic yards.[26]

Meinel and Meinel[27] studied the late twilight glow, such as that shown in Figure 2-1, produced by the airborne ash from the Gunung Agung eruption. They observed two glows on at least one evening, one having a golden color which occurred at the horizon, and the other a faint lavender glow with a distinct boundary which could be seen against the darkening sky. On that evening (October 5, 1963) the movement of the Earth's shadow was timed through the layers. These times of transit were converted to heights, which were 22.3 km for the boundary of the brighter glow and 52.6 km for the fainter.

These authors pointed out that the appearance and intensity of the sunset glow changed from day to day and they suggested that a study of the appearance of the glow and height determinations over an extended period of time and from many places might be useful in the study of the circulation of the atmosphere.

Figure 2-1. The Rocky Mountains and clouds near Boulder, Colorado, silhouetted against sunlight scattered after sunset by particles high in the atmosphere. The background was salmon-red in the original color transparency. These particles may have been injected into the atmosphere by the Bali eruption of 1963.

Much less violent eruptions than those mentioned above may be very important contributors to the particle content of the atmosphere. This is probably especially true of the Hawaiian and Icelandic (rift) types. At times in the Earth's history such eruptions have poured out tremendous quantities of lava, such as the lavas of the Idaho and Columbia Plateaus in the United States. Such eruptions must also have emitted huge quantities of "fume." The relatively minor eruption of Kilauea, in Hawaii, in 1960 produced a haze that was followed by airline pilots as far as Wake Island, over 2000 miles away (Figure 2-2).

Huge gaps exist in our knowledge of the nature of particles formed by volcanoes. Some of them are merely finely divided lava, and may be in the form of spheres, dumbbells, pear-shaped objects, or hair ("Pele's" hair), much like some of the radioactive fallout particles described later. Some particles from certain types of eruptions are hollow, presumably as a result of gas emission by the particles while they are still molten. If the lava is basalt, they may be ferromagnetic. Other particles, especially those from explosive eruptions, are produced by attrition of the crater walls.

Figure 2-2. Flank eruption (1960) of Kilauea volcano, which destroyed the village of Kapoho, on Hawaii.

Particles collected from the stratosphere following the 1963 Bali eruption consisted largely of angular shards and relatively few small spheres.

Almost nothing is known, however, of the nature of the very small particles in the voluminous fume produced during and after many eruptions. Okita[28] has identified and determined the size distribution of aerosols from fumaroles in two of the craters of Mt. Tokachi in Japan. Most of the aerosol particles from Taisho crater were sulfur particles, presumably formed by the reaction

$$SO_2 + 2H_2S \rightarrow 3S + 2H_2O \qquad (2.1)$$

These particles were supercooled droplets that crystallized in about a day on a glass slide. The volcanic gas from the fumaroles at the Showa crater contained large numbers of hygroscopic particles tentatively identified as sulfuric acid. Particles in the gases from fumaroles, however, are not necessarily the same as those in volcanic fume.

During 1965, Halemaumau crater, the main vent of Kilauea volcano in Hawaii, was outgassing very strongly. This is unusual for Halemaumau except during an actual eruption and suggested that magma was very close to the surface. The fume had a strong odor of sulfur dioxide. That in the crater was bluish by scattered light, but as it rose, it became white, suggesting that the particles were hygroscopic and were absorbing water vapor as they rose.

On August 31 and September 1, 1965, Cadle sampled the particles in the fume, using both a filter composed of submicron-diameter polystyrene fibers and a Unico multi-stage impactor. The condition of Halemaumau on September 1 is shown in Figure 2-3. All of the particles collected with the impactor were on the third and fourth stages, which collected particles having mass median diameters of about 5μ and 3μ respectively, assuming that the particles had a density of 1. Almost no samples were collected on the impactor slides when away from the crater.

Examination of the impactor samples with a microscope revealed that they consisted of agglomerated droplets that remained liquid at a relative humidity of 30 per cent. They were found to be supersaturated aqueous solutions of a crystalline solid. Chemical tests showed that the solute contained NH_4^+ and $SO_4^=$. The crystalline solute was tinged yellow but, since it was soluble in water and insoluble in carbon disulfide, was not sulfur. Possibly some Fe^{+++} was present. A test with acidulated aqueous silver nitrate solution failed to reveal the presence of any Cl^-. The droplets were very hygroscopic as demonstrated by their growth when the impactor slide was placed on a "moist chamber" on the microscope stage.

Crystalline solute from the impactor slides was also studied with the electron diffraction feature of an electron microscope. Electron diffraction patterns were obtained for about 20 crystals and all corresponded to ammonium sulfate. No sodium chloride or sulfur particles were found.

Material collected on the fiber filter was examined with an electron microscope using a replica technique. Many of the particles observed were in the size range 1 to 10μ diameter, although there were also large numbers of smaller particles.

Ammonia has not previously been reported in the fume from Kilauea although it has been found at other volcanoes. In spite of the fact that these samples were handled with great care, the possibility that they were contaminated with atmospheric ammonia cannot be dismissed. Further studies of this kind, especially of the fume immediately above molten lava, are needed to establish whether ammonium sulfate is indeed an im-

(A)

(B)

Figure 2-3. The condition of Halemaumau crater on September 1, 1965: (A) view
from Uwekahuna bluff; (B) interior view.

portant component of the fume of erupting volcanoes. If it is, enormous amounts of ammonium sulfate must be emitted into the atmosphere at times by volcanic eruptions.

Optical phenomena produced by airborne volcanic dust have been described by van de Hulst.[23] In addition to brilliant sunsets, the particles may produce the "Bishop's ring," a reddish ring around the Sun and having a radius of about 30°. The quantitative studies of such phenomena suggest that the particles responsible are largely in the size range 0.1 to 1 μ radius, that is, in the range of Junge's "large" particles.

The suggestion has often been made that volcanic dust suspended in the atmosphere may affect the temperature at the Earth's surface to an important extent. Benjamin Franklin made such a suggestion in May, 1784, and he may not have been the first.[29] The expected effect would be cooling by a mechanism that might be called an inverse greenhouse effect. The dust particles are comparable in size to the wavelengths of visible light and scatter such light very effectively, reducing the amount of light which would otherwise reach the Earth's surface, be absorbed, and converted into heat. On the other hand, the particles have relatively little effect on infrared radiation, which is of long wavelength relative to the dust particle size. Since most of the electromagnetic radiation from the Earth's surface is infrared, the dust particles do not interfere with heat loss as radiation.

Humphreys[29] made an extensive study of the possibility that volcanism has affected and can change the Earth's climate by the above mechanism. His approach was based both on theory and available data concerning volcanic eruptions. He concluded that a major eruption could produce a temperature decrease over much of the world of 1°C or more. Even a change of 1°C may have practical significance since this is sufficient to shift isotherms on the Earth's surface by 160 miles and thus the latitude region within which certain crops can be successfully grown.

Meteoritic dust

Numerous investigators have been intrigued by the possibility that meteoritic dust has an influence on the behavior of the Earth's atmosphere. Most or all of the submicron-size extraterrestrial particles are vaporized and oxidized in the Earth's atmosphere, possibly to produce Aitken nuclei consisting of oxides and silicates. Larger objects may only partially melt, casting off droplets.

The amount of extraterrestrial material which meteoroids contribute to the Earth or even to the Earth's atmosphere cannot be precisely estimated from studies of meteors and meteorites alone if for no other reason than that the size of a tiny meteor streaking through the atmosphere is extremely difficult to estimate. Pettersson[30,31] has collected and studied samples of material from ocean sediments and from the atmosphere. The atmospheric samples were obtained by filtering large volumes of air and analyzing the collected particles for nickel. The sampling stations were on Mauna Loa and Haleakala in the Hawaiian Islands, locations where the atmosphere is nearly free of particles of terrestrial origin. Nickel is rare in terrestrial dust, and it was assumed that any nickel found on the filters was of meteoritic origin. Basalt, of which these mountains are composed, contains a few hundred parts per million of nickel, but presumably care was taken to avoid contamination from this source. The samples from ocean sediments were treated to obtain ferromagnetic spherules that appear to have been formed from the molten surface of meteorites as they passed through the Earth's atmosphere. Pettersson assumed on the basis of observations of dust from the Krakatoa eruption that particles of meteoritic origin would require about two years to pass from the atmosphere to the Earth's surface and estimated that about 1.4×10^7 tons of such particles are added to the Earth each year. It is of interest that the value, two years, for the residence time agrees reasonably well with estimates for the residence time of stratospheric radioactive fallout.

Although the amount of meteoritic particles mentioned above seems like a great mass of material, it would increase the Earth's mass by a factor of only 4×10^{-6} in one billion years. As discussed later, numerous other estimates have been made of the rate of influx of extraterrestrial material to the Earth.

Rosinski and Snow[32] have calculated the size distribution of particles produced by the condensation of the vapors emitted by meteors entering the Earth's atmosphere. The diameters of the particles were found to be approximately proportional to the size of the meteor, and for the most part to be less than 100A. Calculated median volume diameters ranged from 4.5 to 80A one minute after evaporation. Average concentrations of the condensed particles formed from meteor showers were found to be higher than the concentrations from the steady influx of sporadic meteors. Rosinski and Pierrard[33] suggest that water and nitric oxide are adsorbed on such particles, and that in the D-region of the ionosphere the adsorbed nitric oxide is ionized.

Biological materials

Biological materials are another important constituent of the atmosphere, especially because of their biological action. Obviously, the air contains a tremendous array of biological entities ranging in size from viruses to large birds. Most of the biological particles have diameters greater than 1μ, and this is true even of the viruses, the individual crystals of which may be very small but which are usually present in the atmosphere in clumps.

Such aerosol particles often travel great distances.[34] For example, fungi spores have been found above the Caribbean Sea 600 miles from the nearest possible source and pollen has been collected 1500 miles from the probable origin. Marine bacteria have been identified 80 miles inland, which is rather remarkable considering the low concentration of such bacteria in sea water (about 500 per cm^3). Presumably, such bacteria enter the atmosphere in the droplets formed by the breaking of bubbles.

Biological material is also found at very high altitudes. Spores of a number of molds were caught in a spore trap released from the balloon "Explorer II" at 72,500 ft and set to close at 36,000 ft.[35]

Biological material has at times been used for tracing air masses. In this regard, it is of interest that stratification of biological substances often occurs in the atmosphere. This almost certainly results from the rise of air masses from the lower troposphere into regions of wind shear.

The following quotation from Charles Darwin's "The Voyage of the Beagle"[36] seems particularly appropriate.

Generally the atmosphere is hazy; and this is caused by the falling of impalpably fine dust, which was found to have slightly injured the astronomical instruments. The morning before we anchored at Porto Praya, I collected a little packet of this brown-colored fine dust, which appeared to have been filtered from the wind by the gauze of the vane at the mast-head. Mr. Lyell has also given me four packets of dust which fell on a vessel a few hundred miles northward of these islands. Professor Ehrenberg finds that this dust consists in great part of infusoria with siliceous shields, and of the siliceous tissue of plants. In five little packets which I sent him, he has ascertained no less than sixty-seven different organic forms! The infusoria, with the exception of two marine species, are all inhabitants of freshwater. I have found no less than fifteen different accounts of dust having fallen on vessels when far out in the Atlantic. From the direction of the wind whenever it has fallen, and from its having always fallen during those months when the harmattan is known to raise clouds of dust high into the atmosphere, we may feel sure that it all comes from Africa. It is, however, a very singular fact, that, although Professor Ehrenberg knows many species of infusoria peculiar to Africa, he finds none of these in the dust which I sent him: on the other hand, he finds in it two species which hitherto he knows as living only in South America. The dust falls in such quantities as to dirty everything on board, and to hurt people's eyes; vessels even have run on shore owing to the obscurity of the atmosphere. It has often fallen on ships when several hundred, and even more than a thousand miles from the coast of Africa, and at points sixteen hundred miles distant in a north and south direction. In some dust which was collected on a vessel three hundred miles from the land, I was much surprised to find particles of stone above the thousandth of an inch square, mixed with finer matter. After this fact one need not be surprised at the diffusion of the far lighter and smaller sporules of cryptogamic plants.

Air pollution

Air pollution can be considered to consist of two general types, although this division is rather artificial. One is the widespread type of air pollution found in the atmospheres of many large cities and commonly called smog (Figure 2-4). The term "smog" is a combination of the words smoke and fog, and as originally applied to the dirty atmospheres of cities such as London and Pittsburgh was quite appropriate. Day has often been almost turned into night by fogs formed by condensation on particles of soot in the air of cities having a coal-burning economy. Now the term "smog" is also commonly applied, with less justification, to so-called photochemical smog. This is a type of city air pollution which owes many of its properties to photochemical reactions involving hydrocarbons, other organic substances, oxides of nitrogen, and atmospheric oxygen.

The other type is industrial air pollution, which refers to single-source or nearly single-source pollution emitted from a single factory or other industrial operation.

Figure 2-4. Smog over Denver, Colorado.

Obviously, this division is rather artificial. For instance, factory effluents may contribute to city smog.

A third type of air pollution, not considered in the above classification, is radioactive fallout. However, this type of contamination is sufficiently unique to be made the subject of a separate chapter.

Photochemical smog produces a much more hazy appearance in the atmosphere than smog derived from smoke. It is much more eye-irritating than the latter and produces a very specific type of plant damage often called "silvering." The unique character of photochemical smog was first discovered as a result of the observation that rubber goods in several cities in the western United States suffered severe cracking during periods of smog. Bartel and Temple,[37] noting that the cracking was typical of that produced by ozone in the laboratory, analyzed the air of the cities in question for ozone, using a method based on the oxidation of iodide to iodine. The air of these cities was found to contain much higher concentrations of ozone than those usually found in the uncontaminated atmosphere in middle latitudes. The fact that a large fraction of this oxidizing material was ozone was established by adsorbing gases from Los Angeles smog on silica gel at $90°K$, followed by spectroscopic examination of the gases desorbed at $195°K$.[38]

Haagen-Smit, Bradley, and Fox,[39] in 1953, found that ozone is produced in concentrations comparable with those in photochemical smog when mixtures of certain hydrocarbons, nitrogen dioxide, and air at concentrations found in smog, are irradiated with sunlight. Such photochemical reactions are now known to be responsible for many of the unpleasant properties of smog in many cities (Figure 2-5). The presence of ozone is characteristic of photochemical smog. During recent years relatively high concentrations have been found in many cities outside of the western United States, and photochemical smog is now recognized as being a very general nuisance. In fact, it is now being found in cities that have had a long record of the soot type of smog.

A major advance toward the control of photochemical smog was establishing automobile exhaust as the major source of hydrocarbons and an important source of oxides of nitrogen in the Los Angeles atmosphere.[40] Organic gases, in addition to hydrocarbons, such as various aldehydes and acids, undoubtedly also play a role in the photochemistry of this type of smog. They are emitted into the atmosphere not only by automobiles but also by almost all combustion of organic substances including backyard incineration and the burning of gas, fuel oil, and coal. Similarly, all such combustion produces oxides of nitrogen, largely by the "fixation" of atmospheric nitrogen. The important oxides of nitrogen for the pro-

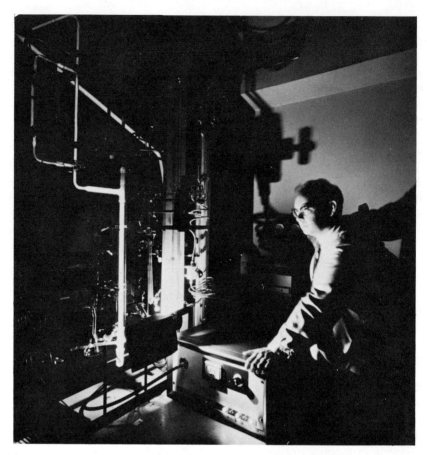

Figure 2-5. Apparatus for investigating reactions of atomic oxygen that occur in photochemical smog and in the natural atmosphere, National Center for Atmospheric Research, Boulder, Colorado. Atomic nitrogen is recombining to produce the Lewis-Rayleigh afterglow. In the next stage the atomic nitrogen is titrated with nitric oxide to produce atomic oxygen.

duction of photochemical smog are nitric oxide (NO) and nitrogen dioxide (NO_2).

Air pollutants are an important source of minor constituents, including particles, in the atmosphere but they usually go unnoticed except close to a source or when they accumulate. Atmospheric processes are usually quite effective in diluting and dispersing atmospheric contaminants. However, the presence of an atmospheric inversion is conducive to pollutant accumulation. Normally, the temperature decreases with increasing altitude to the tropopause but sometimes after a few hundred or a few thousand feet there is a rather sudden rise in temperature which, with increasing altitude, is followed by the more common decrease in temperature. The temperature increase is called an inversion. Since little mixing of air occurs through it, in effect a lid has been introduced over the area. If a city lies in a bowl or even a partially breached bowl produced by the terrain, an inversion within the bowl effectively traps the pollutants. Los Angeles County in California is a classic example. Mountains form three sides of the bowl and a gentle breeze from the ocean forms the fourth.

Photochemical reactions require the absorption of light by one or more of the reactants, and the absorption must ionize, decompose, or chemically activate the primary photochemical reactant. Several substances in photochemical smog absorb solar radiation of the wavelengths found near the Earth's surface, and of these nitrogen dioxide is probably the most important. It undergoes photochemical decomposition as follows:

$$NO_2 + h\nu \rightarrow NO + O \tag{2.2}$$

Most of the atomic oxygen produced by 2.2 reacts with the molecular oxygen, O_2, of the atmosphere to form ozone:

$$O + O_2 + M \rightarrow O_3 + M \tag{2.3}$$

where M is any third atom or molecule and is largely either molecular oxygen or nitrogen of the air. A small portion of the atomic oxygen may react with various organic substances to form free radicals, which are very reactive fragments of compounds and usually have very short lives:

$$RH + O \rightarrow R + OH \tag{2.4}$$

The ozone which is formed in reaction 2.3 will rapidly react with the nitric oxide found in 2.2:

$$NO + O_3 \rightarrow NO_2 + O_2 \tag{2.5}$$

If 2.2, 2.3, and 2.5 were the only reactions occurring in smog, a steady-state concentration of ozone of about three parts ozone per hundred million parts air by volume (pphm) would be attained.[41] This concentration is comparable to that normally in the uncontaminated atmosphere in middle latitudes whereas photochemical smog usually contains 15 to 100 pphm ozone.

At least two explanations for the higher ozone concentration seem possible. One is that some reaction in smog other than 2.5 removes nitric oxide. It is noteworthy that most of the oxides of nitrogen introduced into the atmosphere by various combustion processes are nitric oxide, and that during periods of photochemical smog, the oxides of nitrogen in the air at night are largely nitric oxide. However, during the morning the nitric oxide is almost entirely oxidized to nitrogen dioxide. This cannot result from oxidation by molecular oxygen in the air, which is much too slow. If the oxidation is by ozone, much more ozone must be produced than is indicated by the steady-state concentration which is observed. A compound or type of compound that is found in smog and in artificial smog produced in the laboratory is an organic nitrogen compound called PAN which may be peroxyacetyl nitrate.[42, 43]

$$H_3CCOONO_2$$
$$\underset{O}{\|}$$

It may be related to nitric oxide oxidation, but, if so, the mechanism is unknown.

The other postulated mechanism of ozone formation involves free radicals such as those formed by reaction 2.4. Such radicals add molecular oxygen of the air to form peroxy radicals and these in turn may react with more oxygen to form ozone:[41]

$$R + O_2 + M \rightarrow RO_2 + M \tag{2.6}$$

$$RO_2 + O_2 \rightarrow RO + O_3 \tag{2.7}$$

There is a little evidence to support this mechanism. When diacetyl is irradiated with visible light, it decomposes to form two acetyl radicals, and when this photolysis occurs in air, ozone is produced, possibly by

$$H_3C\!-\!\overset{O}{\underset{\|}{C}}\!-\!\overset{O}{\underset{\|}{C}}\!-\!CH_3 + h\nu \rightarrow 2H_3C\!-\!\overset{O}{\underset{\|}{C}} \tag{2.8}$$

$$H_3C\!-\!\overset{O}{\underset{\|}{C}} + O_2 \rightarrow H_3C\!-\!\overset{O}{\underset{\|}{C}}\!-\!O_2 \tag{2.9}$$

$$H_3C\!-\!\overset{O}{\underset{\|}{C}}\!-\!O_2 + O_2 \rightarrow H_3C\!-\!\overset{O}{\underset{\|}{C}}\!-\!O + O_3 \tag{2.10}$$

Hanst and Calvert[44] observed that the photochemical decomposition of diacetyl in oxygen produced acetic acid, but no peroxy acids. Such behavior might be found if ozone is formed by 2.10.

The ozone in photochemical smog is not directly responsible for its unpleasant properties, but it may be indirectly responsible for much of the plant damage it produces. Ozone reacts rapidly with a number of olefins,[45] and the reaction products produce plant damage typical of that produced by photochemical smog. However, the reaction products do not seem to produce much eye irritation or to contain much particulate material when the reaction involves concentrations of reactants comparable to those in smog.[46]

None of the above chemical equations accounts for the particulate material in photochemical smog, although several of these reactions must take part in the formation of such material. Schuck and Doyle[47] found that aerosol is formed when cyclohexene and nitrogen dioxide in air are irradiated. Prager et al.[48] observed particulate formation upon irradiation of 2,4,4-trimethyl-1-pentene and nitrogen dioxide in air. Numerous other scientists have studied aerosol production in such systems. Their results indicate that many, if not most, six-carbon and larger straight-chain, branched-chain, and cyclic olefins, as well as a number of aromatic hydrocarbons when present along with nitrogen dioxide in air, both in the parts per millions (ppm) concentration range, produce aerosols upon irradiation.[49]

The addition of sulfur dioxide to mixtures of air, hydrocarbons, nitric oxide, and nitrogen dioxide greatly increases the amount of particulate material produced upon irradiation.[47,50,51] The rate of sulfur dioxide disappearance is much greater than can be accounted for by the photochemical oxidation of sulfur dioxide alone, which is discussed later. Thus, the sulfur dioxide must be chemically involved in the NO—NO_2—hydrocarbon—O_2 reactions. Sizes of the particles resulting from the irradiation of such mixtures when sulfur dioxide is present are almost entirely below 1μ in diameter.

The particles produced when sulfur dioxide is present are almost entirely sulfuric acid droplets.[52] Since sulfuric acid is not a major constituent of photochemical smog, it is unlikely that sulfur dioxide contributes appreciably to its particulate content.

The composition of the particles in photochemical smog has been studied extensively. A detailed chemical and spectroscopic analysis is given in Table 2-1. A number of studies have been made of the organic material in photochemical smog, usually after collecting the particles on a filter operating at a high sampling velocity. The collected material has been extracted with a non-polar organic solvent. The infrared spectrum of this material has been found to bear at least a superficial resemblance to the spectrum of the particulate material produced by the reaction of ozone with certain olefins. Particles have also been collected from smog by impaction on microscope slides. Many of the particles consisted of dark brown, gummy, water-insoluble organic matter. Some consisted of droplets which were found to evaporate slowly over a period of several days while a rather tough film formed over the surface. Some were largely organic while others were largely aqueous.[53] Similar droplets were collected from automobile exhaust gases and from the smoke from burning wood. Probably they are quite generally produced by the combustion of organic material.

Hexagonal particles (plates) were occasionally collected on the slides. Judging from their low refractive index (slightly greater than 1.43) and stability to heat they may have been schairerite ($Na_2SO_4 \cdot Na(F,Cl)$) or pachnolite ($NaF \cdot CaF_2 \cdot AlF_3 \cdot H_2O$). Small quantities of fluorides were also found in samples of solutions condensed from photochemical smog in liquid-nitrogen traps and the particulate material collected with an electrostatic precipitator (Table 2-1). Acicular crystals are very common in material collected from photochemical smog and other polluted atmospheres as well. These are usually found to be gypsum ($CaSO_4 \cdot 2H_2O$).[53,54]

The concentrations of particles having diameters exceeding about 0.2μ in dense photochemical smog range from about 3000 to 10,000 particles per cm.[3] The size distribution in the range 0.2 to 10μ can be represented approximately by the distribution function

$$f(d) = ad^{-b} \qquad (2.11)$$

where a and b are constants and the value of b is about 4.

Smog in coal-burning communities, although it may include photochemical smog, differs in many ways from photochemical smog free of coal smoke. The former type contains a multitude of aromatic, aliphatic, and heterocyclic compounds produced by the partial combustion of coal, and the inorganic gaseous constituents are often present at considerably higher concentrations than in photochemical smog. The latter include sulfur dioxide, hydrogen sulfide, nitric oxide, nitrogen dioxide, hydrogen fluoride, carbon monoxide, and ammonia. If a sufficiently high concentration of hydrocarbons exists, ozone may be produced in such smog, but the measured concentrations tend to be much lower than those in photochemical smog. The low concentration may be real, but it is often only apparent, resulting from the difficulty of measuring the concentrations of a strong oxidizing agent in the presence of relatively large amounts of a strong reducing agent such as hydrogen sulfide.

There is a marked trend, at least in the United States, toward increasing use of petroleum products and a decreasing use of coal as a fuel. Air pollution legislation is resulting in more complete combustion of the coal that is used. A result is that as coal-produced smog diminishes, photochemical smog will increase or at least become more apparent unless effective measures are taken to reduce it.

Particles in the smog in coal-burning cities vary in nature with respect both to time and to city. This is largely because coal combustion is usually only one source of atmospheric contaminant in such places. These cities are usually highly industrialized, and the various industrial operations may contribute a variety of smokes, dusts, and fumes to the general pollution that are not produced by burning coal.

Smog which is actually a combination of fog and smoke is rather infrequent although when it does occur it may almost turn day into night. Most so-called smog in coal-burning communities, even in a city such as London, consists largely of an accumulation of pollutants beneath an atmospheric inversion. One of the most extensive studies of such smog has been undertaken by the "National Air Sampling Network" of the United States Public Health Service.[55-57] Established in 1953, it consists of about 185 urban and 51 nonurban sampling stations in all 50 states, Puerto Rico, and the District of Columbia. A large variety of smoggy and nonsmoggy conditions are represented, including photochemical smog.

Particles are collected by filtration through glass fiber filters and the collected material analyzed for weight concentration of particles, benzene-soluble organic material, and β-radioactivity. Some analyses are also made for NO_3^-, SO_4^-, Be, Mn, Pb, Sn, Fe, Cu, Li, V, Zn, Cr, Ni, Mo, Bi, Cd, and Sb. Table 2-2 shows total particulate matter, benzene-soluble organic matter, sulfate, and nitrate taken from the data of reference 57 for eight cities. The first four cities listed have mainly photochemical smog. It is noteworthy that the percentages of benzene-soluble organic matter and of nitrate were much higher and the percentages of sulfate

TABLE 2-2. PARTICULATE CONCENTRATIONS FOR SELECTED CITIES FOR 1958 (VALUES ARE ARITHMETIC MEANS.)

Station Location	A Suspended Particulate ($\mu g/m^3$)	B Benzene-soluble Organic Matter ($\mu g/m^3$)	% of A	C Sulfate ($\mu g/m^3$)	% of A	D Nitrate ($\mu g/m^3$)	% of A
Los Angeles	213	30.4	14.2	16.0	7.5	9.4	4.4
San Francisco	80	10.6	13.3	6.2	7.7	2.6	3.3
San Diego	93	12.2	13.1	7.7	8.3	4.2	4.5
Denver	110	11.0	10.0	6.1	5.5	2.3	2.1
New York	164	14.3	8.7	23.0	14.0	2.2	1.3
Pittsburgh	167	13.0	7.8	15.1	9.0	2.6	1.6
Cincinnati	143	13.7	9.6	12.2	8.5	2.6	1.8
Louisville	228	18.0	7.9	20.6	9.1	4.9	2.1

lower for the first four cities than for the second four. This is consistent with our concepts of the origin of photochemical smog.

Little is known concerning the size distribution of particles in smog other than the photochemical variety. The ultimate particles in coal smoke are largely of submicron size but such particles rapidly form aggregates of soot. Also, such smoke contains much larger particles of "fly ash" consisting of essentially inorganic cinder. When fog is present, a large weight percentage of the particles is in the size range characteristic of fog droplets, about 1 to 50μ in diameter.

Nader et al.[58] studied the size distribution of particles in the air of downtown Cincinnati, which has a long history of sooty smog. They used a "particle size analyzer" consisting of a miniaturized light scatter photometer and pulse height analyzer developed for field measurements for the Robert A. Taft Sanitary Engineering Center of the U. S. Public Health Service. Most of the particles were less than 2μ in diameter, and the mode of the size distribution was somewhere below 0.3μ. The authors concluded that this distribution is representative of Cincinnati air except when or where a high-output source drastically changes its composition.

The control of smog is very difficult for technical, political, and economic reasons. Usually it is not desirable to maintain a completely clean atmosphere since the cost in both money and limitation of individual action is generally exorbitant. Thus, a community afflicted with smog must decide to what extent it is willing to sacrifice money and convenience to clean up the atmosphere. The only method which has been found to be at all effective for controlling smog is control at the source. Many suggestions have been made with regard to methods for removing smog once it has formed, but the energy or logistic requirements are usually unreasonable.[59]

The effectiveness of control measures in many highly industrialized cities of the United States is well known. In such cities control has for the most part involved setting legal limits on factory emissions and providing effective enforcement. The elimination of backyard incinerators and of dump burning by "cut-and-fill" methods has also been helpful. Control of the grade of coal used in home furnaces, or the substitution of gas for coal as a fuel for home heating may considerably decrease the amount of atmospheric soot.

The control of photochemical smog is quite a different problem. Since most of the hydrocarbons in such smog, which play a major role in its formation, are emitted by automobiles, control at the source involves reducing the hydrocarbon content of automobile exhaust and of "blow-by," the gases emitted by the crank case. The latter are relatively easily controlled by recirculating the gases through the engine. Two general methods have been developed for decreasing the hydrocarbon content of exhaust gases. One uses a "flame afterburner" which is a high-temperature combustion chamber designed to burn the hydrocarbons. The other uses a "catalytic afterburner" which catalytically oxidizes the hydrocarbons at relatively low temperatures. Unfortunately, neither of these methods removes oxides of nitrogen and a satisfactory method for doing this remains to be discovered.

Industrial air pollution, as mentioned above, is the other type of air pollution. Almost any industrial activity is a potential or actual producer of air pollution. The pollutants may be solid, liquid, or gaseous. Because of the tremendous diversity of industrial operations, no attempt is made here to discuss particulate effluents from industries. Particle emission by several major industries has previously been discussed by Cadle.[60]

Chemical reactions

Airborne particles are both produced and altered by various chemical reactions. Many of these reactions are similar to those observed in smog. For example, atomic oxygen is produced by the photochemical decomposition by sunlight of nitrogen dioxide and ozone. Atomic oxygen reacts rapidly with any sulfur dioxide which may be present in the atmosphere to form sulfur trioxide, which in turn reacts rapidly with water vapor to form sulfuric acid droplets. The reaction takes place according to the equation

$$SO_2 + O + M \rightarrow SO_3 + M \qquad (2.12)$$

where M is any third molecule or atom. The value of the rate constant k in the rate equation

$$- d[O]/dt = k[O][SO_2][M] \qquad (2.13)$$

is

$$4.8 \times 10^{15} \, cm^6 \, moles^{-2} \, sec^{-1}$$

where M is O_2 or N_2, and the brackets refer to concentrations in moles/cm^3. The activation energy is zero, so k is independent of temperature.[61] The concentrations of atomic oxygen are too low in the troposphere, except possibly in some types of smog, for this reaction to be of importance when compared with other mechanisms for the oxidation of sulfur dioxide. However, the reaction may be of importance in the lower stratosphere, as discussed later.

Sulfur dioxide in sunlit air also undergoes photochemical oxidation to sulfuric acid:

$$2SO_2 + O_2 + h\nu \rightarrow 2SO_3 \tag{2.14}$$

$$SO_3 + H_2O \rightarrow H_2SO_4 \tag{2.15}$$

Sulfur dioxide absorbs solar radiation in the troposphere quite strongly in the wavelength range 2900 to 4000A. The energy associated with the photons of such radiation is much too low* to cause the sulfur dioxide to dissociate into SO and O. However, the SO_2 achieves an excited state upon absorption of the radiation and reacts much more rapidly with O_2 than it does in the ground or unexcited state.

Gerhard[62,63] has found that the reaction rate is proportional to the concentration of sulfur dioxide and amounts to about 0.1 to 0.2 per cent conversion per hour in bright sunlight. Other studies of this reaction were undertaken by Hall[64] and by Renzetti and Doyle.[50] Hall exposed tubes containing sulfur dioxide (56 to 230 mm Hg partial pressure) and oxygen (50 to 200 mm Hg partial pressure) to sunlight, and found that the rate of sulfur trioxide formation was directly proportional to the sulfur dioxide concentration and nearly independent of the concentration of oxygen. The reaction rate can thus be estimated from the equation

$$-\frac{d[SO_2]}{dt} \simeq k[SO_2] \simeq \Phi k_a[SO_2] \tag{2.16}$$

where Φ is the photochemical quantum yield, k is the observed photolysis rate constant, k_a is the absorption rate constant and brackets refer to concentrations.[65] Hall's value of k was 5×10^{-4} hr^{-1} for exposure to sunlight from 10 AM to 3 PM. He obtained one value for Φ, 0.036, using the 3130A line from a mercury arc lamp instead of the Sun. The Renzetti and Doyle data were obtained by irradiating a mixture of 0.2 to 0.6 ppm sulfur dioxide in air using medium-pressure mercury lamps. Leighton[65] estimated that their results corresponded to a value of k_a of 0.013 min^{-1}. Since the observed constant k averaged 0.0045 min^{-1}, Φ was about 0.3, an order of magnitude greater than that obtained by Hall. Gerhard and Johnstone,[63] who also used artificial radiation (a mercury sunlamp), obtained a value of k of 6.8×10^{-3} hr^{-1}, which Leighton estimated corresponded to a value of k_a of about 2 hr^{-1} and of Φ of 3×10^{-3}. They also made a few runs in sunlight, obtaining results suggesting a value of Φ of 10^{-2} to 10^{-3}.

---

*The energy for the dissociation of SO_2 into SO and O is about 135 kcal/mole, corresponding to a maximum wavelength for dissociation of 2100A.

Leighton has proposed the following mechanism for this reaction based on the formation of excited sulfur dioxide, SO_2^*:

$$SO_2 + h\nu \rightarrow SO_2^* \tag{2.17}$$

$$SO_2^* \rightarrow SO_2^{**} \tag{2.18}$$

$$SO_2^* + M \rightarrow SO_2 + M \tag{2.19}$$

$$SO_2^* + O_2 \rightarrow SO_4 \tag{2.20}$$

$$SO_4 + SO_2 \rightarrow 2SO_3 \tag{2.21}$$

$$SO_4 + O_2 \rightarrow SO_3 + O_3 \tag{2.22}$$

He has derived an expression based on these equations which, for high oxygen and low sulfur dioxide concentrations, predicts a photooxidation rate proportional to sulfur dioxide and independent of oxygen concentrations.

Sulfur dioxide oxidizes much more rapidly in aqueous solutions, as sulfurous acid, than in the gas phase. The oxidation is particularly rapid if the solution is alkaline[66] or contains the salts of certain metals such as manganese and iron.[67] Thus, fogs would be expected to promote the formation of sulfuric acid droplets in the troposphere, and this seems to agree with experience. Johnstone and Coughanowr[67] investigated the solution and subsequent oxidation of sulfur dioxide in air by aqueous drops containing dissolved catalysts. They used the theory for steady-state diffusion and chemical reactions in living cells developed by Rashevsky[68] to interpret and correlate their data. The differential equations applying to such cases are

$$D_i \left(\frac{d^2 c_i}{dr_1^2} + \frac{2}{r_1} \frac{dc_i}{dr_1} \right) + q = 0 \tag{2.23}$$

and

$$\frac{d^2 c_e}{dr_1^2} + \frac{2}{r_1} \frac{dc_e}{dr_1} = 0 \tag{2.24}$$

with the boundary condition that when $r_1 = r$,

$$D_i \frac{dc_i}{dr} = D_e \frac{dc_e}{dr} \tag{2.25}$$

where r_1 is the distance from the center of the spherical particle of radius r, c is the concentration of the reactant gas, q is the rate of the reaction of the dissolved gas with the material of the particle, D is the diffusion coefficient, and i and e refer to the interior and exterior of the particle.

These equations can be integrated for various types of steady-state reactions. Thus, when gas-phase diffusion is rapid relative to the rate of diffusion and reaction within the particle, and q is a first-order reaction, the steady-state rate, R_s, per unit area of particle surface is given by the equation

$$R_s = \frac{c_i D_i}{r} \left[\sqrt{k/D_i}\, r \coth \sqrt{k/D_i}\, r - 1 \right] \tag{2.26}$$

where k is the rate constant for the reaction. When $\sqrt{k/D_i}\, r$ is large, equation 2.26 reduces to

$$R_s = c_i \sqrt{D_i k} \tag{2.27}$$

If q is a zero-order reaction and the penetration of the reactant gas into the particle is small,

$$R_s = \sqrt{2 c_i D_i k} \tag{2.28}$$

When the rate of gas-phase diffusion is small relative to that of absorption by the particle, and the concentration of the gaseous reactant is high enough to remain essentially constant,

$$R_s = \frac{c_e D_e}{r} = \frac{p D_e}{R T r} \tag{2.29}$$

where R is the gas constant, T is the absolute temperature, and p is the partial pressure of the reactant gas. This equation is valid only when there is essentially no movement of the particle relative to the gas. These equations are applicable to many steady-state reactions involving aerosols.

Johnstone and Coughanowr[67] found that the rate of absorption of sulfur dioxide by stationary drops of dilute hydrogen peroxide was determined by gas-phase diffusion of the sulfur dioxide (equation 2.29). They found that the absorption of sulfur dioxide by drops of dilute solutions of manganese sulfate followed the steady-state rate equations for reactions controlled by liquid-phase diffusion and zero-order reaction (equation 2.28).

Junge[15] has shown that at least at one location (Frankfurt) there is a considerable difference in chemical composition between particles having radii between 0.1 and 1μ ("large" particles) and those larger than 1μ ("giant" particles). The former contained a high percentage of ammonium sulfate and the latter a much lower percentage of ammonium sulfate, but a relatively high percentage of sodium chloride. Possibly, as Junge suggests, the giant particles were produced in particulate form, largely as sea salt, while the large particles were formed by coagulation between molecular complexes of ammonium sulfate produced from the gaseous phase and solid particles having radii exceeding 0.1μ. However, it also seems possible that the sulfate was produced by the oxidation of sulfur dioxide in fog droplets which contained dissolved ammonia. The results indicate that ammonium sulfate particles may be formed in large quantities in regions where combustion is producing both sulfur dioxide and ammonia.

A reaction that might be expected to be important but actually is extremely slow, if it occurs at all, is the reaction of ozone with sulfur dioxide to form sulfur trioxide. The reaction is very slow even when the relative humidity is high.

The sizes of the sulfuric acid droplets produced by any of the above reactions will be determined by the amount of sulfuric acid per drop and by the relative humidity. At equilibrium the vapor pressure of the water in the drops will equal the partial pressure of the water vapor in the air.

When sulfur dioxide dissolves and oxidizes in droplets that contain dissolved sodium chloride, the sulfuric acid produced may cause hydrogen chloride to be emitted from the droplet, especially as the droplet dries. If the amount of sodium chloride exceeds the amount of sulfuric acid on a molar basis, evaporation of the water will result in a solid particle consisting largely of mixed sodium chloride and sulfate. Such particles have often been collected from the atmosphere.

In addition to sulfate, nitrate is formed in sea-salt particles. Particularly high nitrate contents have been found in particles exceeding 1μ in diameter collected over coastal areas of the northeastern part of the United States.[16] Such particles seem to result from the reaction of sea-salt particles with nitrogen dioxide (NO_2) in the air, and the concentrations of nitrate in the particles are very high when the NO_2 concentration is especially high, due to air pollution.

Robbins, Cadle and Eckhardt[69] studied this reaction in the laboratory by preparing mixtures of reactant vapors and aerosols in air in a 10 m^3 chamber. Samples were collected by filtration from the air in the chamber and analyzed for nitrate and chloride. The NO_2 reacted rapidly with the sodium chloride crystals (or droplets, when the humidity was high) to form nitrate but no nitrite. The first step in the reaction appears to be the hydrolysis of NO_2 to form nitric acid (HNO_3) vapor:

$$3NO_2 + H_2O \rightarrow 2HNO_3 + NO \qquad (2.30)$$

This is followed either by adsorption of the HNO_3 on the relatively dry sodium chloride particles at relative humidities less than about 75 per cent or, at higher humidities, dissolving of the HNO_3 in aqueous droplets containing sodium chloride. Interaction then occurs between the nitric acid and the sodium chloride, followed by desorption of the hydrogen chloride, either immediately following the reaction or during subsequent evaporation of the droplets. Results were also obtained which demonstrated that the reaction between NO_2 and NaCl to form nitrosyl chloride (NOCl) and sodium nitrate, often suggested as a possible primary step in the formation of chlorine or hydrogen chloride in the atmosphere, is very slow compared with the process described above.

Many plants evolve organic gases and many of these absorb the near-ultraviolet solar radiation that reaches the troposphere. Such gases may undergo photochemical oxidation to produce high molecular-weight compounds which condense from the atmosphere to form aerosols. The reactions would be expected to be very similar to those of drying oils in oil-based paints. Went[70] ascribes summer heat haze to such reactions and points out that a more or less dense haze exists all year over the Amazon basin, the jungles of northern Colombia, and the highlands of southeastern Mexico, and that in the summer a haze covers most of the United States. Possibly these reactions explain the fact that the atmosphere absorbs more sunlight in summer than in winter and why the night sky is so much clearer in winter.

Such reactions bear a resemblance to those occurring in photochemical smog. The haze of such smog usually increases in intensity during the morning, reaches a maximum at or shortly after noon, and then usually decreases. Darwin,[36] during his famous voyage on the ship "Beagle," observed a similar phenomenon in Brazil.

During this day I was particularly struck with a remark of Humboldt's, who often alludes to "the thin vapour which, without changing the transparency of the air, renders its tints more harmonius, and softens its effects." This is an appearance which I have never observed in the temperate zones. The atmosphere, seen through a short space of half or three quarters of a mile, was perfectly lucid, but at a greater distance all colours were blended into a most beautiful haze, of a pale French grey, mingled with a little blue. The condition of the atmosphere between the morning and about noon, when the effect was most evident, had undergone little change, excepting in its dryness. In the interval, the difference between the dew point and temperature had increased from $7°.5$ (sic) to $17°$.

PARTICLE SIZE DISTRIBUTIONS

Numerous studies have been made, particularly by Junge and his co-workers, of the concentrations and size distributions of natural aerosols.[9,15,16,71] Junge has found it convenient to plot atmospheric aerosol size distribution data as $dN/d \log r$ per cm^3 against the radius r in microns on a log-log scale where N is the number of particles. Typical plots for

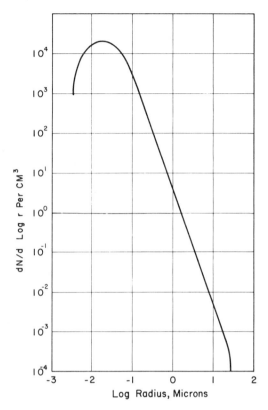

Figure 2-6. Particle size distribution in continental air (U. S. Air Force, "Handbook of Geophysics," New York, Macmillan, 1960).

continental and marine aerosols are shown in Figures 2-6 and 2-7. This method of plotting presents particle concentrations as well as size distributions. For airborne particles over continents, the slope of the curve is about -3 throughout much of the distribution, so $dN/d \log r$ is approximately inversely proportional to r^3. Since $dN/d \log r$ is identical to $r dN/dr$, the number of particles per unit volume per unit of particle size is approximately proportional to r^{-4}. Note that particles smaller than about 1μ radius are present in very much larger concentrations over the continents than over the oceans. The main reason is that the average rate of production per unit area of land is greater than that per unit area of the seas.

The data shown in Figures 2-6 and 2-7 are averages and the variations about them, as might be expected, are extremely large. This is true both

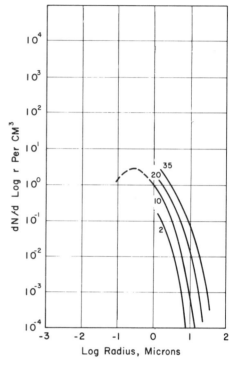

Figure 2-7. Particle size distribution in maritime air. Numbers on curves refer to air speed in miles per hour (U. S. Air Force, "Handbook of Geophysics," New York, Macmillan, 1960).

with respect to time and location, and with respect to the concentrations and the shape of the size distribution curve. Obviously, the plot for the smoke above a forest fire might be vastly different than that for air in a desert sand storm. Variations in concentrations of Aitken particles in mountain regions between 0 and 155,000 particles per cm³ have been reported.[72] Large variations of course also occur in contaminated atmospheres. For example, dense Los Angeles smog, which is photochemical in origin, may contain 3×10^3 to 10×10^3 particles per cm³, largely in the size range 0.1 to 1μ radius. Such smog, superimposed on the natural distribution represented by Figure 2-6, would considerably change the appearance of the size distribution.

A theoretical explanation for the similarities among size distributions of natural aerosols measured at different times and places has been developed by Friedlander.[73] The explanation is independent of the initial size distribution and of the mixing proportions, and is based on a similarity transformation of the equation describing the kinetics of a coagulating, settling aerosol. It assumes that the upper end of the size distribution approaches a quasi-stationary state such that the rate at which matter enters by coagulation equals the net rate at which matter is lost by sedimentation. This theory enables one to estimate the rate at which matter is transferred from the lower to the upper end of the size distribution.

Hidy[74] has reviewed the theory of coagulating particles undergoing Brownian motion, and in particular examined the effects of heterogeneity of particle size, and of particle motion in a rarefied medium, using numerical solutions of the coagulation equations. Of particular interest from the standpoint of atmospheric particle size distribution is his conclusion that a "self-preserving" distribution function develops after a sufficiently long time and was found to be independent of the initial distribution. However, it did vary with the ratio of the mean free path of the medium, such as air, to the radius.

Twomey and Severynse[75] studied the size distributions of natural aerosol particles having radii of less than 0.1μ. "Decay" (coagulation) rates were determined by collecting air samples in large metallized "Mylar" bags and passing them through the particle size measuring device called a diffusion battery. The results suggested that most natural airborne particles are initially about 0.01μ in radius, but rapidly grow out of this region by agglomeration. The mode in the distribution occurred for particles with radii of about 0.08μ. It is suggested that this is about the region where atmospheric particles have the longest existence since they are not rapidly removed by gravitation, are too small to be effectively washed out by rain, but are large enough to remain relatively unaffected by diffusion. When the data were plotted in the manner employed by Junge, described above, the slope for particles of larger than 0.1μ radius was -2 to -2.5 rather than -3.

CLOUD PHYSICS

Condensation

Most clouds form when moist air rises and expands. The expansion produces cooling, and where sufficient cooling has occurred, condensation of the water vapor forms cloud droplets. In the absence of condensation nuclei, the partial pressure of water vapor in the air would have to be about four times that necessary to achieve saturation in order for condensation to occur. However, the particles described in previous sections serve as condensation nuclei, and little if any supersaturation is required (Figure 2-8). Hygroscopic particles serve as condensation nuclei at humidities below saturation.

(A)

Figure 2-8. The author's wife demonstrating the action of condensation nuclei and the low concentration of such nuclei in marine air. (A) Steam is coming from a crack in the floor of the caldera of Kilauea volcano in Hawaii. (B) A burning match provides a high concentration of condensation nuclei.

It is in their role as condensation nuclei that the sizes of the nonvolatile tropospheric particles are of greatest importance. As the following discussion will show, the sizes of the volatile water droplets in a cloud also play a major role in their behavior.

The equilibrium vapor pressure of a liquid having a curved surface is slightly greater than that for the same liquid having a plane surface. A droplet of water will evaporate unless it is in a slightly supersaturated atmosphere. The equilibrium vapor pressure is given by the following equation:

$$\ln \frac{p^1}{p} = \frac{2M\sigma}{r\rho RT} \tag{2.31}$$

where M is the molecular weight of the liquid, p and p^1 are the vapor pressures above a plane and curved surface, respectively, σ is the surface tension, ρ is the density of the liquid, R is the gas constant, and T is the

(B)

Figure 2-8 *Continued*

absolute temperature. When the surfaces are charged, the equation becomes

$$\ln \frac{p^1}{p} = \frac{M}{R \rho T} \left(\frac{2\sigma}{r} - \frac{q^2}{8 \epsilon \pi r^4} \right) \qquad (2.32)$$

where q is the quantity of charge and ϵ is the dielectric constant.

The effect of curvature is very small unless the droplet radius is less than about 0.1μ, but droplets smaller than this evaporate rapidly, even in a slightly supersaturated atmosphere. Such droplets can only act as condensation nuclei when the atmosphere is sufficiently supersaturated that the partial pressure of the water vapor in the air exceeds the vapor pressure of the droplet. According to one theory of self-nucleation,[76] aggregates of water molecules containing about 80 molecules are formed by a series of bimolecular collisions. The vapor pressure of such an aggregate is sufficiently low that it can serve as a condensation nucleus at a supersaturation of at least 4.2.

Condensation nuclei can be considered to act by catalyzing the formation of aggregates of water molecules, which in turn act as nuclei. The condensation nuclei serve to decrease the work of formation of the aggregates.[76] The work of formation W of water droplets during self-nucleation is given by the equation

$$W = \frac{16}{3} \frac{\pi \sigma^3 V_B}{[kT \ln (p^1/p)]^2} \tag{2.33}$$

where V_B is the volume per molecule of the droplet and k is Boltzmann's constant. In this case, p^1/p is the degree of supersaturation. When this is unity, that is, when the atmosphere is just saturated with water vapor, W is infinite and self-nucleation cannot occur. The effect of condensation nuclei can be accounted for by multiplying W by a factor f which is a function of the contact angle θ between the growing aggregate of water molecules and the surface of the foreign particle. When the surface is flat,

$$f = \frac{(2 + \cos \theta)(1 - \cos \theta)^2}{4} \tag{2.34}$$

Note that when a droplet just touches the surface, θ is 180° and f is unity, in which case the unmodified equation for self-nucleation, 2.33, applies. As θ decreases to zero, the factor decreases to zero, so as θ decreases, the amount of supersaturation required to obtain mist or fog likewise decreases.

As a "rule of thumb," the amount of supersaturation required for an insoluble, wettable particle to act as a condensation nucleus will be slightly less than that calculated from equation 2.31 or 2.32 for a droplet of the same size as the particle; the amount of supersaturation will be slightly greater than that calculated for an insoluble, nonwettable particle. Thus, in general, the smaller the particle the less effective it will be as a condensation nucleus.

Several equations have been proposed for the equilibrium vapor pressure (p_s^1) at the surface of a droplet of solution. The following was proposed by Mason:[6]

$$\frac{p_s^1}{p} = \left[\exp \frac{2\sigma M}{\rho^1 rTR} \right] \left[1 + \frac{imM}{M^1 \left(\frac{4}{3} \pi r^3 \rho^1 - m \right)} \right]^{-(\rho/\rho^1)} \tag{2.35}$$

where ρ^1 is the density of the solution, m is the mass of solute, M^1 is the molecular weight of solute, and i is van't Hoff's factor. The latter depends on the chemical nature and the degree of dissociation of the solute. For sodium chloride, i varies from 2.0 for very dilute solutions to about 2.9 for saturated solutions.

Equation 2.35 is made up of two terms, one accounting for the effect of surface curvature and the other for the vapor-pressure lowering caused by the presence of the solute. As a result of the operation of these two factors, the equilibrium relative humidity (or supersaturation) for a droplet containing a fixed mass of solute increases at first with increasing droplet radius (increasing dilution), reaches a maximum, and then decreases, asymptotically approaching zero supersaturation for infinite r. The radius r_c in cm corresponding to the maximum is given by the approximation[1]

$$r_c = (8 \times 10^5 \, mT/M')^{\frac{1}{2}} \tag{2.36}$$

When a droplet of a solution exceeds the critical radius and is maintained in an atmosphere exceeding the supersaturation in equilibrium with the droplet, it may grow indefinitely. The larger the mass of sodium chloride in the particle, the smaller is the supersaturation corresponding to r_c. When $m = 10^{-15}$ g, $r_c = 0.62 \mu$ and the supersaturation is about 0.13 per cent.

Many atmospheric particles are composite, being composed in part of water-soluble and in part of water-insoluble material. Such particles probably behave as condensation nuclei in much the same manner as the completely water-soluble particles except that the radius will be larger for a given concentration of the soluble material in solution.

Cloud droplet size distribution

Typically, cloud droplets range in size from 1 to 50μ in diameter with a number median diameter of about 5μ. The measured size distributions are quite irregular, but usually the plots of droplet concentration vs. droplet radius are skewed as shown in Figure 2-9. Determining the size distribution of cloud droplets with accuracy is difficult, and smaller droplets may be missed. Thus, the skewed appearance may represent experimental error rather than a natural phenomenon. This seems especially likely since the sizes of particles precipitated from aqueous solution by cooling or by chemical means are usually normally distributed.

A number of methods have been used to determine the particle size distribution of cloud droplets. The most common type is some variety of impactor, in which a fraction of the cloud is moved at high velocity against a collecting surface. The momentum of the particles tends to carry them to the surface rather than follow the air stream as it is deflected. There are several problems in applying this technique. The impaction (collection) efficiency varies with the droplet size, decreasing with decreasing size. The collection efficiency as a function of droplet size

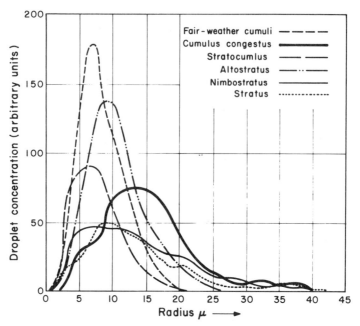

Figure 2-9. The droplet-size distributions of various cloud types.[82]
(*Courtesy of Springer-Verlag*)

must be known to correct for this effect. If the impaction is violent, the drops may shatter. If large numbers are collected per unit area of surface, the drops may coalesce. The collected droplet will evaporate unless effective precautions are taken. Several ingenious methods have been developed to overcome these difficulties. A technique which has been used extensively involves covering the collecting surface, usually a microscope slide, with a layer of oil. The layer must be sufficiently thick that the droplets become immersed in the oil, which inhibits evaporation and coagulation.

Another method takes advantage of the fact that the collection efficiency of a cylinder for small particles increases with decreasing cylinder diameter. A set of rotating cylinders of differing size is placed in a moving cloud or moved through the cloud. The total weight of water collected on each cylinder is determined and the droplet size distribution is calculated from the collection efficiencies of the cylinders at the air flow rate existing during the collection. Schaefer[77] has designed and built several instruments of this type for use at the summit of Mt. Washington in the eastern United States. He used porous cylinders made of cotton or alumina so that the collected droplets soaked into the material. Thus, the gain in weight of the cylinders represented the amount of water collected.

Another impaction method involves covering the collecting surface with a layer of soot or magnesium oxide which is thicker than the drops to be collected. The impacting drops produce holes in the coating which are slightly larger than the drops and remain after the latter have evaporated.

Electrostatic precipitation has also been used. One method[78] involves charging the drops by ionization and then precipitating them into a cell containing oil with a strong electric field. The instrument consists of a wire 20 cm long stretched along the axis of a horizontal bakelite tube 4 cm in diameter. A rectangular hole is made in the center of the bottom of the tube and a plastic cell containing a thin layer of oil is placed in this hole without touching the tube. Wires at ground potential are stretched across the bottom of the cell and an intermediate "grid" wire at $-2kV$ crosses the top of the cell. The axial wire carries a charge of $-14kV$. The droplets are ionized by the axial wire and accelerated toward the grid wire. Their momentum carries them past the grid wire and into the oil with the aid of the small potential difference between the grid wire and the ground wires at the bottom of the cell.

Various optical methods have also been used. Some depend on measuring the properties of the scattered light. For example, an average size can be estimated from the angular diameters of the corona rings observed about a point source of light shining through the cloud and a crude estimate of the width of the size distribution can be made from the width of the rings.[79,80] McCullough and Perkins[81] used a photomicrographic method for determining cloud droplet size from an aircraft. A rotating mirror or prism kept the images stationary on the film.

The liquid-water content of clouds may be expressed either in terms of mass of water per unit mass or volume of air, or in terms of the number of particles per unit volume. The water content of a small cumulus cloud is usually only a few tenths of a gram per m^3 and is almost always less than 1 gram per m^3. Higher concentrations than 1 gram per m^3 are observed in cumulonimbus clouds. The number concentrations are usually of the order of tens or hundreds per cm^3.

The liquid-water content is usually not constant throughout a cloud. In a cumulus cloud it is low near the base, increases with increasing height, and then may decrease again before the top is reached.[83,84] Similarly, the mean droplet size is small near the base of the cloud, increases to a maximum value with increasing height in the cloud, and then may decrease.

From our knowledge of the concentrations of condensation nuclei of various sizes, of the influence of size on effectiveness, of the degree of supersaturation achieved in clouds, and the number concentrations of cloud droplets, it is evident that particles in the size range 0.1 to 1μ radius are especially important to cloud formation and growth. On the other hand Aitken nuclei, unless they agglomerate to form larger particles, must be quite unimportant with respect to the initial formation of clouds.

Rain formation

Superficial thought concerning the problem of the manner in which rain is produced by rain clouds may suggest that the problem is simple. Either the droplets will continue to grow in much the way in which they were formed until they rain out, or they simply grow by collision. Actually, the droplets are limited in size by the amount of water vapor available, and while coalescence of cloud droplets is an important mechanism of rain formation, especially in the tropics, the mechanism of such coalescence is not obvious.

Probably the earliest widely accepted and theoretically sound mechanism of rain formation involves a preliminary formation of ice crystals. According to this theory, at temperatures between -40 and $0°C$, non-aqueous particles are present in the cloud which serve as freezing nuclei. Water vapor condenses on such particles to form ice and evaporates from the droplets as the condensation lowers the partial pressure of water vapor in the air. If there are fewer freezing nuclei than cloud droplets, the resulting ice crystals will be much larger than the droplets. Such crystals will fall at different rates, being of different sizes; because they are all quite large, impaction can occur. The result is growth into snow flakes which melt to form rain if the temperatures are above freezing at lower altitudes. Water droplets tend to supercool to between -20 and $-40°C$ in the absence of freezing nuclei.

At one time it was thought that this was the only mechanism of rain formation. Now it is realized that this cannot be so since rain often forms in clouds that do not extend up into regions of freezing temperatures.

The ice-crystal theory of rain formation is the basis of the weather-modification experiments undertaken by Langmuir, Schaefer, and their co-workers.[85-88] The assumption is made that rain fails to fall from many clouds because there are too few solid particles present which can serve as freezing nuclei at the temperatures existing in the clouds. Thus, by introducing proper nuclei it should be possible to effect the formation of rain in such clouds.

The selection of particulate material which is highly effective for relatively low amounts of supercooling, and which is easily dispersed in finely divided form, is obviously required. Relatively simple experimental systems have been designed to determine the effectiveness of freezing nuclei. The central feature of a very simple arrangement is a horizontal commercially available quick-freeze cabinet which opens at the top. The temperature in such a cabinet is thermostatically maintained constant, so various degrees of supercooling can be achieved and maintained. A fog can be created in such a cabinet by introducing moisture-laden air. The resulting supercooled fog droplets are not very effective for scattering light, and when a beam of light shines through the fog, a rather weak Tyndall beam is produced. However, when ice crystals form, they are sufficiently large and irregular in shape that the individual crystals can be seen shimmering in rather spectacular fashion.

Numerous variations and elaborations of this technique have been employed. Photometric observation of the scattered light from the Tyndall beam can replace visual observation. Sophisticated auxiliary equipment can be used for producing and metering the freezing nuclei and water vapor introduced into the cabinet. The freezer itself can be replaced with some sort of cloud chamber, such as a variation of the Wilson cloud chamber.

Another technique which has at times been used for studying the effectiveness of freezing nuclei, especially those of natural origin, involves observation of the freezing points of droplets condensed on the suface of a cold metal plate exposed to the particles. The metal surface may be placed in a cold chamber, but cooled independently of the chamber, and the droplets or crystals on the surface observed with a microscope.

Vonnegut,[89,90] using the former technique, found that silver iodide crystals are particularly effective freezing nuclei. He theorized that substances having crystal structures similar to that of ice should be effective as freezing nuclei and selected silver iodide on that basis. Since silver iodide is rather expensive, many investigations have been made in attempts to find substitutes. A great many substances exhibit some effect, and a few crystalline substances are almost as effective as silver iodide.

Many studies have been made of the mechanism of freezing nucleation. It is evident that crystal structure is important but not necessarily the controlling factor. Silver iodide, like common ice, is in the hexagonal crystalline system, and so are the very effective lead iodide and cupric sulfide. However, monoclinic silver sulfide and cubic silver oxide appear to produce a higher threshold temperature for freezing than the hexagonal cadmium iodide. Ice crystals seem to form preferentially on active sites on the nuclei. These sites are usually imperfections, particularly steps formed during growth or cleavage.

Many soils, sands, and clays are effective as freezing nuclei at temperatures between -20 and $-10°C$, and such materials probably act as natural freezing nuclei for rain formation.

According to Mason,[1] when silver iodide crystals are placed in saturated air which is then expanded so that supersaturation occurs, only water condenses on the crystals at temperatures exceeding $-4°C$. At temperatures between -4 and $-12°C$, ice crystals form on specific sites on the silver iodide if the air is supersaturated with respect to liquid water. At lower temperatures, crystals are formed on the nuclei even when the air is undersaturated with respect to liquid water so long as it is supersaturated with respect to the vapor pressure of ice. This behavior suggests[1] that when the nuclei are larger than 1 or 2μ in diameter, condensation followed by freezing occurs on active sites at temperatures not much below $0°C$, provided there is sufficient supersaturation. At lower temperatures, ice can form directly from the vapor phase. Aitken nuclei, which require considerable supersaturation before condensation can occur, must not behave as freezing nuclei in natural clouds unless they are greatly supercooled or the nuclei diffuse to the supercooled droplets. Similar results have been obtained with several other chemical species, such as lead iodide and cupric sulfide.

If silver iodide particles are exposed to ultraviolet light or even intense sunlight, they lose much of their effectiveness. Metallic silver is liberated and the surface characteristics are changed. Similarly, many organic vapors are adsorbed on silver iodide and decrease the nucleating action.[91,92] Poppoff and Sharp[91] investigated the effect of amines, ammonia, and alcohols on the nucleation of supercooled water droplets by silver iodide. All of the gases tested inhibited nucleation, and it was found that the vapor concentrations required for inhibition increased with droplet temperature decrease. Furthermore, it was shown that the adsorption of these inhibitors on freezing nuclei was reversible, and was probably physical adsorption of the Van der Waals type instead of an irreversible chemisorption.

Poisoning of freezing nuclei may often occur, particularly when the nuclei are produced by combustion processes which may also produce tarry materials. For example, a study was made in the author's laboratory of the concentrations of condensation nuclei, freezing nuclei, and water vapor in the exhaust gases of an F80 jet aircraft.[93] A rather elaborate freezing nuclei meter was constructed (Figure 2-10). It consisted essentially of three expansion chambers, each equipped with a light-extinction

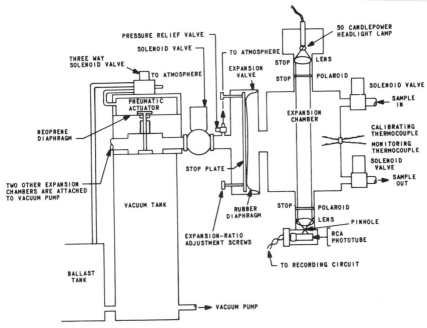

Figure 2-10. Schematic drawing of freezing nuclei meter.[93] (*Courtesy of the American Meteorological Society*)

photometer. The gas drawn into the sampling probe was divided equally among the three chambers. The initial temperature in the chambers was below freezing, and each chamber had a different expansion ratio, so that the cloud in each chamber was supercooled to a different degree. The temperatures after expansion were -10, -18, and $-30°$C.

Although the exhaust gases were found to contain large concentrations of condensation nuclei, no freezing nuclei were detected in the jet exhaust. This result was confirmed using a home freezer adapted as a nuclei detector. Since the air drawn into the jet engine contained freezing nuclei, but none were detected, it is highly probable that one or more of the components of the jet exhaust strongly inhibited freezing nucleation.

Silver iodide is insoluble in water but forms a colloidal suspension in solutions of sodium iodide in acetone. One type of silver iodide nuclei generator operates by forming a finely divided spray of such a colloidal suspension by forcing it through a nozzle with hydrogen, butane, or propane, and igniting the spray.[94] The temperatures are sufficiently high to vaporize the silver iodide which cools to form a smoke consisting of very small silver iodide particles. They are mostly in the size range 50A to 1500A.[6] Another type of generator burns small pieces of coke which have been impregnated with a colloidal suspension of silver iodide in a sodium iodide-acetone solution. A stream of air is passed through the coke bed to provide a forced draft.

Silver iodide nuclei are often generated for research purposes by coating a coil of resistance wire such as nichrome with silver iodide and slowly vaporizing the fuzed crystals by passing a current through the wire.[91,95] Birstein[95] found that the concentration of particles he produced in this manner was about 10^5 to 10^6 particles per cm^3 and that the diameters, determined by electron microscope measurements, ranged from about 0.004 to 0.4μ with a mean (arithmetic?) of about 0.08μ.

All of these methods produce a preponderance of very small particles with diameter means below 0.1μ. It seems likely, therefore, that silver iodide particles less than 0.1μ diameter are effective freezing nuclei. If this is so, it seems likely that Aitken-size particles, although not important as condensation nuclei in the natural atmosphere, may be important as freezing nuclei. However, this conclusion is rendered somewhat uncertain by the fact that these nuclei-generating methods produce some particles that have diameters exceeding 0.1μ, and it is possible that the larger particles are responsible for most of the nucleation. Mügge[96] has described field work by Georgii, undertaken near Frankfurt, Germany, which suggests that in very high cloud tops the Aitken nuclei participate in the freezing process below $-30°C$. It is also of interest to note in this regard that the concentrations of naturally occurring freezing nuclei vary from about 1 per liter at $-13°C$ to about 1000 per liter at $-25°C$, and that 1 to 10 ice crystals per liter are sufficient to produce continuous precipitation.[97]

Numerous organic substances also possess the ability to nucleate supercooled water to form ice. For example, some steroids can nucleate ice crystals at temperatures as high as $-1°C$ when the steroids are purified by thermal recrystallization.[98,99] One of the amino acids nucleates ice at $-4.5°C$ and several organic substances such as phloroglucinol and α-phenazine have been suggested for use in cloud seeding. Fukuta[99] investigated metaldehyde $(CH_3CHO)_4$, which is a cyclic tetramer of acetaldehyde, as a possible cloud seeding agent. Under suitable conditions it was found to be capable of producing ice crystals at $-0.4°C$. The nucleating ability as judged by the amount of supercooling required depends on the method of preparation, dispersal, and particle size. Fukuta recrystallized the metaldehyde from ethanol, ground the crystals, and fractionated them according to size by air sedimentation. He retained for study only those particles less than 13μ in diameter. He observed that at $-2°C$ a large proportion of the crushed crystals (10^6/gram) produced nucleation whereas the onset of ice formation using the same technique was $-4°C$ for ground silver iodide and $-3.5°C$ for ground α-phenazine. The nucleating action of metaldehyde was explained on the basis of its molecular and crystal structure. Fukuta[100] has also suggested that the freezing-nucleating ability of certain organic substances can be enhanced by spraying solutions of them in suitable organic solvents. This enhancement results from the cooling of both the solvent and the ambient air. Ten solvents were tested, and the organic nuclei were 1,5-dihydroxyphenazine, and phloroglucinol, both of which had been found to act as freezing nuclei at temperatures above $-5°C$. Fukuta found that spraying a suspension of insoluble freezing nuclei in a volatile organic liquid also enhanced the nucleating action as a result of the evaporative cooling.

Langer et al.[101] investigated 32 organic compounds as possible cloud-seeding agents. The following substances produced "complete nucleation": phloroglucinol at $-2°C$, trichlorobenzene at $-12°C$, D($+$)-raffinose at $-14°C$, trimesic acid at $-15°C$, and melamine at $-15°C$. They concluded that the activity of organic freezing nuclei is determined by the configuration of electric link-dipole moments in the molecule.

Parungo and Lodge[102] determined the ice nucleating ability of a series of substituted phenols and benzoic acids. Two methods were employed for determining the activity: the maximum temperature for which freezing occurred, as determined on a cold-stage microscope, and the relative number of ice nuclei formed at a fixed temperature in a cold chamber. These scientists concluded that activity generally varied with the potential strength of a hydrogen bond between the hydroxyl or carboxyl group and a water molecule. They suggested that a "free-energy relationship" exists between molecular structure and nucleating power.

Ice crystals themselves are probably the best freezing nuclei. However, it is logistically difficult to seed clouds directly with ice crystals. A better approach is to produce the ice crystals directly in the clouds, and this can conveniently be accomplished using dry ice (solid carbon dioxide). As a small particle of the dry ice falls through a supercooled cloud of water droplets, large numbers of ice crystals are produced. Langmuir[103] calculated that a piece of dry ice about 5 mm in diameter would produce about 10^{16} ice crystals before evaporating.

Cloud seeding with silver iodide or dry ice has usually been used in attempts to increase the amount of rainfall. The nuclei are introduced into clouds which are considered to be appropriate subjects for seeding, either using silver iodide smoke generators on the ground, or airborne smoke generators or dry ice dispensers.

The effectiveness of cloud seeding as a means of increasing rainfall remains highly controversial. There is little doubt that some additional rain can be produced in this manner under some conditions. It is likely that the situation which is most promising for increasing precipitation is that in which large air masses rise over mountainous regions, expanding and cooling adiabatically. The resulting clouds may be deficient in freezing nuclei, which can be supplemented by generators on the ground in the region of rising air. Mason[1] suggests that the continuous generation of silver iodide nuclei on the windward side of a mountain range might produce light but persistent snow on the lee side.

Cloud seeding has also been used or suggested for other types of weather modification. Several attempts have been made to determine whether hurricanes can be modified by seeding with dry ice or silver iodide.[104-107] The results suggest that certain features, at least, of hurricanes can be modified in this way. For example, it has been shown that a supercooled cumulus cloud in a hurricane may increase greatly in both height and diameter in a few minutes after seeding (Figure 2-11).

The possibility of overnucleating storm clouds has also been suggested. If the concentration of ice crystals formed in such a cloud is sufficiently large, none of them would be able to grow to such a size that they could settle from the cloud as precipitation. Thus, in principle, it is possible to prevent hail, lightning, and tornados by overseeding incipient thunderstorms. Numerous papers have been published describing field experiments, and some success has been claimed.

An interesting and often annoying phenomenon related to freezing nucleation is the formation of ice fog. As the name suggests, it is a fog consisting of ice crystals and occurs over populated regions in very cold climates. It is particularly well known at Fairbanks, Alaska and neighboring airbases. In all cases investigated, the water vapor producing the fog is produced by human activities such as the operation of electric power plants, heating furnaces, and automobiles. An aircraft taking off can create a dense, local ice fog. Usually such fogs form only at temperatures below $-40°C$. This temperature is essentially that for self-nucleation, so there must be few particles in such atmospheres that are very effective as freezing nuclei.

As mentioned earlier, ice crystal formation is not the only mechanism of rain development in clouds. The condensation process does not permit growth to raindrop size since the number concentrations of cloud droplets are too large and the amount of available water vapor too small for this to happen. Rain and drizzle formation in clouds whose temperatures are entirely above freezing must be the result of collisions between cloud droplets followed by coalescence. The collisions are almost certainly largely the result of differences in settling rates among the droplets of different size. Furthermore, only fairly large droplets can take part in such a process.

Langmuir[108] investigated the collection of droplets by falling drops, introducing the dimensionless parameter K defined as

$$K = L/R = \frac{2}{9} r^2 \rho U/R\eta \tag{2.37}$$

where L is the range which the droplet of radius r would have if projected into air at the velocity U, η is the viscosity of the air, and R is the radius of the collecting drop. Langmuir defined the collection efficiency E as the ratio of the capture cross section to the cross-sectional area of the collecting drop. For high Reynolds numbers,

$$E_h = K^2 / \left(K + \frac{1}{2}\right)^2 \tag{2.38}$$

and for Reynolds numbers much smaller than 1000,

$$E_e = [1 + \left(\frac{3}{4}\right) \ln 2K/(K - 1.214)]^{-2} \tag{2.39}$$

Langmuir proposed the following empirical equation for intermediate values of the Reynolds number, Re:

$$E = [E_e + E_h (\text{Re}/60)]/[1 + (\text{Re}/60)] \tag{2.40}$$

These equations have been found to be quite satisfactory when there is a large size difference between the drops involved. However, both theoretical considerations and experimental results indicate that the Langmuir equations are much less satisfactory when the drops are nearly the same size.

Hocking[109] has theoretically considered the latter situation for drops sufficiently small for Stokes' equation to apply. His definition of E was essentially that of Langmuir. He determined the forces on the drops from the solution of Stokes' equation for two moving drops, making allowance for their mutual interaction. A series of differential equations of motion resulted which were solved by a Runge-Kutta method of step-by-step integration using an electronic computer.

Picknett[110] confirmed Hocking's finding that there is a critical drop size below which coalescence does not occur. He found experimentally that when the drop radius was 40μ, droplets smaller than 2μ were not collected and when the drop radius was 30μ, droplets smaller than 4μ were not collected. From Figure 2-12 we see that if the larger droplet has a radius of 30μ, the smaller, slower-settling droplet must have a radius no smaller than about 6μ, while if the larger has a radius of about 20μ, the

(A)

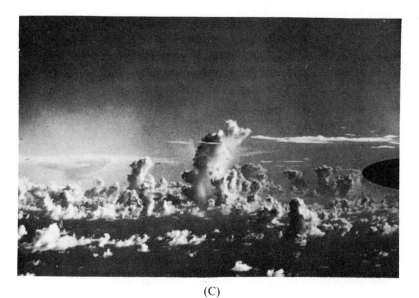

(C)

Figure 2-11. The effect of seeding a cumulus cloud with silver iodide: (A) 6 minutes before seeding; (B) 1 minute after seeding; (C) 7 minutes after seeding; (D) 11 minutes after seeding. (*Courtesy Dr. R. H. Simpson*)

(B)

(D)

Figure 2-11 *Continued*

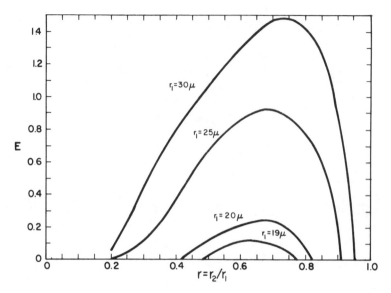

Figure 2-12. The collision efficiency for drops of radius $r_1 \mu$ colliding with a droplet of radius $r_2 \mu$.[109]

smaller must have a radius of about 8μ. If the smaller droplet is smaller than the critical size, it will not impact on the larger one but will be carried around it instead. Probably the larger droplets are usually formed initially by condensation on large hygroscopic nuclei.

A related problem is the collection of solid, nonwettable particles by larger drops as a result of the difference in settling rate. Such particles are collected much less efficiently than miscible droplets.[111,112] This situation has been investigated theoretically by Pemberton,[113] who derived a non-dimensional number, the penetration factor, which is used in a mathematical formula for the condition for the retention of the particle by the drop. The equations of motion of a particle moving according to Stokes' law in the velocity field due to the potential flow around a sphere were also derived. The penetration factor is defined as

$$Z = \left(\frac{2W}{m}\right)^{\frac{1}{2}} \Big/ u \qquad (2.41)$$

where u is the terminal velocity of the drop, m is the mass of the particle, and W is the total amount of work done by the particle against the surface tension of the drop.

Pemberton solved the differential equations of motion for a number of values of Z, using a computer, and plotted the collection efficiency against a dimensionless particle parameter for various values of Z.

Such studies somewhat underestimate the effectiveness of rain for removing wettable particles from the atmosphere. Greenfield[114] has pointed out that if the particles are actually suspended in the clouds, coagulation with cloud droplets may occur which in turn are swept up by rain. Thus, even submicron-size particles can be removed.

A number of attempts have been made to produce rain from cumulus clouds by spraying them with water or various aqueous solutions. Spraying into the tops of such clouds has been found to be quite ineffective, especially when the spray droplets have been large, since at best one hopefully large raindrop will be produced for each spray drop introduced. As pointed out by Mason, this approach could only be effective if the resulting raindrops break up to form new droplets which in turn are large enough to carry on the impaction process. However, rainclouds thick enough for this to occur will usually produce rain naturally.[1]

Cloud seeding with water can be improved by introducing droplets of about 70μ diameter into the base of a growing cloud. Since the air in such a cloud mass is rising, growth can occur as the droplets rise with the growing cloud and later as they settle through the air mass. Bowen[115] has described the results of cloud seeding experiments based on this idea. The water was dispersed from an airplane equipped with spraying devices which produced a median diameter of about 50μ. A cloud was selected for seeding if it was growing and if it was one of a number of similar clouds which could be used as controls. The results were quite encouraging, especially for clouds that were more than 5000 ft thick at the time of seeding. Other experiments, carried out in the United States and in the Caribbean, have been less encouraging.

A similar approach is to substitute hygroscopic particles for the water droplets. Such particles, if a few microns in diameter, form aqueous droplets which are large enough to grow by impaction. Since the water is furnished from water vapor in the cloud, a considerable saving in weight is effected. Since droplets are somewhat easier to disperse than particles, a concentrated solution of the hygroscopic substance can be substituted for the relatively pure substance. For example, the solubility of sodium chloride in water at room temperature is about 36 parts per 100 parts by weight of water. A number of cloud seeding experiments have been undertaken using dry or aqueous solutions of sodium chloride. The results can be summarized as being encouraging but inconclusive.

Hail

Hail usually forms in the large convective storms that frequently occur over land in the middle latitudes. Conditions favorable for the occurrence of such storms include[116]

(1) conditional and convective instability;

(2) abundant available moisture in the lower levels;

(3) regions of strong winds in both lower and upper levels, usually veering with height;

(4) a mechanism for converting the potential energy associated with the instability to kinetic energy.

Hail is usually associated with thunderstorms, and large hailstones generally are produced only by thunderstorms. However, convective storms that do not produce lightning may produce hailstones that are usually small.

Hailstones range in size from less than one cm to several cm diameter, the median diameter being about 1.5 cm. A hailstone 13.8 cm in diameter, about the size of a grapefruit, has been reported to have fallen in Nebraska.[1]

Hail is formed when ice crystals, produced by condensation of vapor as described above, become sufficiently large so that in settling they collide with supercooled water droplets. The droplets are nucleated by the ice and freeze either immediately or after spreading over the surface of the growing hailstone. The term settling in this case is a relative one, since the growing hailstone may be surrounded by rapidly rising air, and the stone may actually be rising, but less rapidly than the ambient air and the supercooled droplets.

When a hailstone becomes sufficiently large, it will settle from the turbulent cloud system, falling to the ground. However, a thunderstorm has a complicated structure and at least some of the hailstones may settle part way to the ground and then be swept up again several times before reaching the ground.

The density of hailstones varies markedly, from about 0.1 to 0.8 gram/cm^3. This variation has been attributed to the rate of freezing. If impaction of supercooled droplets by growing hailstones occurs at sufficiently low temperatures, the droplets may freeze before they can spread over the hailstone, and soft, low-density stones will be formed. At higher temperatures freezing may be sufficiently slow that onion-like structures and higher densities are produced.

REFERENCES

1. Mason, B. J., "Clouds, Rain, and Rainmaking," Cambridge, Cambridge University Press, 1962.
2. Cadle, R. D., and Robbins, R. C., *Discussions Farad. Soc.,* **30**, 155 (1960).
3. Woodcock, A. H., *J. Meteorol.,* **10**, 362 (1953).
4. Kuelman, F., Dombroski, N., and Newitt, D. M., *Nature,* **173**, 261 (1954).

5. Moore, D. J., and Mason, B. J., *Quart. J. Roy. Met. Soc.*, **80**, 583 (1954).
6. Mason, B. J., "The Physics of Clouds," Oxford, Clarendon Press, 1957.
7. Mason, B. J., *Nature*, **174**, 470 (1954).
8. Eriksson, E., *Tellus*, **11**, 375 (1959).
9. Junge, C. E., "Air Chemistry and Radioactivity," New York, Academic Press, 1963.
10. Woodcock, A. H., *Tellus*, **9**, 521 (1957).
11. Neumann, G. H., Fonselius, S., and Wahlman, L., *Int. J. Air Poll.*, **2**, 132 (1959).
12. Crozier, W. D., Seeley, B. K., and Wheeler, L. B., *Bull. Am. Meteorol. Soc.*, **33**, 95 (1952).
13. Twomey, S., *J. Meteorol.*, **12**, 81 (1955).
14. Junge, C. E., *Tellus*, **5**, 1 (1953).
15. Junge, C. E., *J. Meteorol.*, **11**, 323 (1954).
16. Junge, C. E., *Tellus*, **8**, 127 (1956).
17. Toba, Y., *Tellus*, **17**, 131 (1965).
18. Byers, H. R., Sievers, J. R., and Tufts, B. J., "Artificial Stimulation of Rain," London, Pergamon Press, 1957.
19. Junge, C. E., and Gustafson, P. E., *Tellus*, **9**, 164 (1957).
20. Neuberger, H., *Mech. Eng.*, **70**(3), 221 (1948).
21. Amelung, W., and Landsberg, H., *Bioklimatische Beiblätter*, **1**, 49 (1934).
22. Wilson, R., *Roy. Astron. Soc., Occasional Notes*, **2**, 137 (1952).
23. van de Hulst, H. C., "Light Scattering by Small Particles," New York, Wiley, 1957.
24. Hellmann, G., and Meinardus, W., *Meteorol. Z.*, **19**, 180 (1902).
25. Shaw, W. N., "Manual of Meteorology," 2nd ed., Cambridge, Cambridge Univ. Press, 1936.
26. Köppen, W., and Geiger, R., "Handbuch der Klimatologie," V. 1, Part B, Berlin, Gebrüder Borntraeger, 1936.
27. Meinel, M. P., and Meinel, A. B., *Science*, **142**, 582 (1963).
28. Okita, T., *J. Meteorol. Soc. Japan*, **40**, 181 (1962).
29. Humphreys, W. J., "Physics of the Air," New York, Dover, 1964.
30. Pettersson, H., *Nature*, **181**, 330 (1958).
31. Pettersson, H., *Scientific American*, p. 123, February, 1960.
32. Rosinski, J., and Snow, R. H., *J. Meteorol.*, **18**, 736 (1961).
33. Rosinski, J., and Pierrard, J. M., *J. Atm. Terr. Phys.*, **26**, 51 (1964).
34. Jacobs, W. C., "Compendium of Meteorology," T. F. Malone, Ed., Boston, Mass., Am. Meteorol. Soc., 1951.
35. Rogers, L. A., and Meier, F. C., *Nat. Geog. Soc. Contrib. Papers, Stratosphere Ser.*, **2**, 146 (1936).
36. Darwin, Charles, "The Voyage of the Beagle," New York, Bantam Books, 1958.
37. Bartel, A. W., and Temple, J. W., *Ind. Eng. Chem.*, **44**, 857 (1952).
38. Stanford Research Institute, "The Smog Problem in Los Angeles County," Menlo Park, Calif., 1954.
39. Haagen-Smit, A. J., Bradley, C. E., and Fox, M. M., *Ind. Eng. Chem.*, **45**, 2086 (1953).
40. Magill, P. L., Hutchison, D. H., and Stormes, J. M., "Proceedings of the Second National Air Pollution Symposium," Stanford Research Institute, Ed., Menlo Park, Calif., 1952.

41. Cadle, R. D., and Johnston, H. S., "Proceedings of the Second National Air Pollution Symposium," Stanford Research Institute, Ed., Menlo Park, Calif., 1952.
42. Stephens, E. R., Scott, W. E., Hanst, P. L., and Doerr, R. C., *J. Air Poll. Control Assoc.*, **6**, 159 (1956); *Proc. Am. Petrol. Inst.*, **36**, III, 288 (1956).
43. Stephens, E. R., Darley, E. F., Taylor, O. C., and Scott, W. E., *Int. J. Air and Water Pollution*, **4**, 79 (1961).
44. Hanst, P. L., and Calvert, J. G., *J. Phys. Chem.*, **63**, 71,2071 (1959).
45. Cadle, R. D., and Schadt, C., *J. Am. Chem. Soc.*, **74**, 6002 (1952).
46. Cadle, R. D., and Magill, P. L., *AMA Arch. Ind. Hyg. Occ. Med.*, **4**, 74 (1951).
47. Schuck, E. A., and Doyle, G. J., Report No. 29, Air Pollution Foundation, San Marino, Calif. (Oct. 1959).
48. Prager, M. J., Stephens, E. R., and Scott, W. E., *Ind. Eng. Chem.*, **52**, 521 (1960).
49. Altshuller, A. P., and Bufalini, J. J., *Photochem. and Photobiol.*, **4**, 97 (1965).
50. Renzetti, N. A., and Doyle, G. J., *J. Air Pollution Control Assoc.*, **8**, 293 (1959); *Intern. J. Air Pollution*, **2**, 327 (1960).
51. Schuck, E. A., Ford, H. W., and Stephens, E. R., Report No. 26, Air Pollution Foundation, San Marino, Calif. (1958).
52. Endow, N., Doyle, G. J., and Jones, J. L., *J. Air Pollution Control Assoc.*, **13**, 141 (1963).
53. Cadle, R. D., Rubin, S., Glassbrook, C. I., and Magill, P. L., *Arch. Ind. Hyg. Occ. Med.*, **2**, 698 (1950).
54. Sumi, L., Corkery, A., and Monkman, J. L., "Atmospheric Chemistry of Chlorine and Sulfur Compounds," Monograph No. 3, American Geophysical Union, 1959.
55. U. S. Public Health Service Publication No. 637. GPO, "Air Pollution Measurements of the National Air Sampling Network," Superintendent of Documents, Washington 25, D.C., 1958.
56. Zimmer, C. E., Tabor, E. C., and Stern, A. C., *J. Air Poll. Control Assoc.*, **9**, 136 (1959).
57. Am. Ind. Hyg. Assoc., "Air Pollution Manual, Part I . . . Evaluation," Detroit, 1960.
58. Nader, J. S., Ortman, G. C., and Massey, M. T., *Am. Ind. Hyg. Assoc. J.*, **22**, 42 (1961).
59. Cadle, R. D., and Wohlers, H. C., *Air Repair*, **1**, No. 4, 30 (1952).
60. Cadle, R. D., "Particle Size," New York, Reinhold, 1965.
61. Cadle, R. D., and Powers, J. W., "Some Aspects of Atmospheric Chemical Reactions of Atomic Oxygen," Paper presented at CACR Symposium, Visby, Sweden, August, 1965.
62. Gerhard, E. R., "The Photochemical Oxidation of Sulfur Dioxide to Sulfur Trioxide and Its Effects on Fog Formation," Engineering Experiment Station, Univ. of Illinois, Urbana, Ill., 1953.
63. Gerhard, E. R., and Johnstone, H. F., *Ind. Eng. Chem.*, **47**, 972 (1955).
64. Hall, T. C., Jr., "Photochemical Studies of Nitrogen Dioxide and Sulfur Dioxide," Doctoral Thesis, Univ. of California at Los Angeles, 1953.
65. Leighton, P. A., "Photochemistry of Air Pollution," New York, Academic Press, 1961.
66. Junge, C. E., and Ryan, T. G., *Quart. J. Roy. Meteorol. Soc.*, **84**, 46 (1958).
67. Johnstone, H. F., and Coughanowr, D. R., *Ind. Eng. Chem.*, **50**, 1169 (1958).

68. Rashevsky, N., "Mathematical Biophysics," Chicago, Univ. of Chicago Press, 1938.
69. Robbins, R. C., Cadle, R. D., and Eckhardt, D. L., *J. Meteorol.*, **16**, 53 (1959).
70. Went, F. W., *Scientific American*, p. 63, May, 1955.
71. Junge, C. E., "Advances in Geophysics," V. IV, New York, Academic Press, 1957.
72. Landsberg, H., "Atmospheric Condensation Nuclei," *Ergebn. Kosm. Phys.*, **3** (Leipzig Akademische Verlagsgesellschaft) p. 207 (1938).
73. Friedlander, K., *J. Meteorol.*, **17**, 479 (1960).
74. Hidy, G. M., *J. Colloid Sci.*, **20**, 123 (1965).
75. Twomey, S., and Severynse, G. T., *J. Atm. Sci.*, **20**, 392 (1963); **21**, 558 (1964).
76. LaMer, V. K., *Ind. Eng. Chem.*, **44**, 1270 (1952).
77. Schaefer, V. J., "Demountable Rotating Multicylinders for Measuring Liquid Water Content and Particle Size of Clouds in Above or Below Freezing Temperatures," G. E. Research Lab. Report, Contract No. W33-038-AC-9151, 1945.
78. Pauthenier, H., and Brun, E., *Compt. Rend.*, **212**, 1081 (1941).
79. Köhler, H., *Meddel. Met.-Hydr. Anst. Stockholm*, **2**, No. 5, 58,96,106,189 (1925).
80. Cadle, R. D., "Particle Size Determination," New York, Interscience, 1955.
81. McCullough, S., and Perkins, P. J., "Flight Camera for Photographing Cloud Droplets in Natural Suspension in the Atmosphere," NACA Res. Memo E50K01, 1951.
82. Diem, M., *Met. Rundschau*, **1**, 261 (1948).
83. Warner, J., and Newnham, T. D., *Quart. J. Roy. Met. Soc.*, **78**, 46 (1952).
84. Warner, J., *Tellus*, **7**, 449 (1955).
85. Langmuir, I., *Science*, **112**, 35 (1950).
86. Schaefer, V. J., *Science*, **104**, 457 (1946).
87. Schaefer, V. J., *Bull. Am. Meteorol. Soc.*, **29**, 175 (1948).
88. Schaefer, V. J., *Ind. Eng. Chem.*, **44**, 1381 (1952).
89. Vonnegut, B., *J. Appl. Phys.*, **18**, 593 (1947).
90. Vonnegut, B., *Chem. Rev.*, **44**, 277 (1949).
91. Poppoff, I. G., and Sharp, G. W., *J. Meteorol.*, **16**, 288 (1959).
92. Birstein, S. J., "Geophysics Research Paper No. 32," Air Force Cambridge Research Center, 1954.
93. Poppoff, I. G., Robbins, R. C., and Goettelman, R. C., *Bull. Am. Meteorol. Soc.*, **39**, 144 (1958).
94. Vonnegut, B., *Bull. Am. Meteorol. Soc.*, **33**, 420 (1952).
95. Birstein, S. J., *Bull. Am. Meteorol. Soc.*, **33**, 431 (1952).
96. Mügge, R., in "Simposio Internazionale Sulla Fisica della Nubi e Relative Applicazioni all' Agricoltura," Asti, Italy, April, 1958, Atti, 1958.
97. aufm Kampe, H. J., and Weickmann, H. K., *J. Meteorol.*, **8**, 283 (1951).
98. Head, R. B., *Nature*, **191**, 1058 (1961).
99. Fukuta, N., *Nature*, **199**, 475 (1963).
100. Fukuta, N., *J. Atm. Sci.*, **22**, 207 (1965).
101. Langer, G., Rosinski, J., and Bernsen, S., *J. Atm. Sci.*, **20**, 557 (1963).
102. Parungo, F. P., and Lodge, J. P., Jr., *J. Atm. Sci.*, **22**, 309 (1965).
103. Langmuir, I., "General Electric Research Laboratory First Quarterly Progress Report, Meteorological Research," 1947.
104. Simpson, R. H., and Malkus, J. S., *Science*, **142**, 498 (1963).

105. Malkus, J. S., and Simpson, R. H., *J. Appl. Meteorol.*, **3**, 470 (1964).
106. Riehl, H., *Science*, **141**, 1001 (1963).
107. Simpson, R. H., and Malkus, J. S., *Scientific American*, **211**, No. 6, 27 (1964).
108. Langmuir, I., *J. Met.*, **5**, 175 (1948).
109. Hocking, L. M., *Q. J. Roy. Met. Soc.*, **85**, 44 (1959).
110. Picknett, R. G., in "Aerodynamic Capture of Particles," New York, Pergamon, 1960.
111. McCully, C. R., Fisher, M., Langer, G., Rosinski, J., Glaess, H., and Werle, D., *Ind. Eng. Chem.*, **48**, 1512 (1956).
112. Oakes, B., in "Aerodynamic Capture of Particles," New York, Pergamon, 1960.
113. Pemberton, C. S., in "Aerodynamic Capture of Particles," New York, Pergamon, 1960.
114. Greenfield, S. M., *J. Met.*, **14**, 115 (1957).
115. Bowen, E. G., *Quart. J. Roy. Meteorol. Soc.*, **78**, 37 (1952).
116. Newton, C. W., *Meteorological Monographs*, **5**, No. 27, 33 (1963).

Chapter 3 # The Stratosphere and Mesosphere

NATURE OF THE STRATOSPHERE

The stratosphere is the region of the atmosphere immediately above the troposphere (Figure 3-1). The altitude of demarcation between the two is known as the tropopause, and is usually a region occupying a narrow altitude range. The stratosphere is a region of nearly uniform or rising temperature, extending upward to about 50 km. Thus, the tropopause is generally defined in terms of temperature. Dobson[1] defines the tropopause essentially as follows:

Where and when the stratosphere starts as an abrupt change from falling to rising temperature with increasing altitude, the tropopause is the height at which this change occurs.

When the stratosphere starts as a sharply defined change from a rapidly decreasing temperature to a fall of less than 2°C per km, the tropopause is the height of that change.

When no abrupt change exists, the tropopause is the height where the rate of fall of temperature first drops to 2°C per km, provided it does not exceed this value at slightly higher altitudes.

This definition is useful but admittedly artificial, since it assigns a precise altitude to that which is actually a region. For example, judging from cloud formations at the tropopause observed from aircraft, the tropopause may often have a layered structure.

The temperature of the stratosphere is generally controlled by radiation while that of the troposphere is largely governed by mixing and convection. The stratosphere is largely free of the rain storms so characteristic of the troposphere, although large thunderstorms may penetrate the tropopause into the lower stratosphere. In general, the stratosphere is less turbulent than the troposphere, although severe stratospheric turbulence has been observed by high-flying aircraft. Also, the stratosphere is generally much dryer than the troposphere. Very high-speed

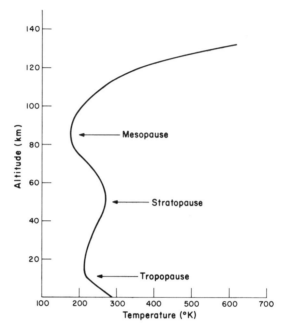

Figure 3-1. Schematic diagram of air temperature
as a function of height. Based on U. S. Standard
Atmosphere, 1962.

winds are common in the stratosphere. Speeds above 150 mph are not
unusual and they sometimes exceed 400 mph.

The stratosphere has a large scale circulation that plays an important
role in the distribution of worldwide radioactive fallout. Properties of
the stratosphere relating to this circulation are discussed in Chapter 4.

PARTICLE SIZE DISTRIBUTION

The variation of particle concentration and size distribution in the
stratosphere has been investigated by several workers. Rosen[2] studied the
vertical distribution of dust from 0 to 30 km. Particles were counted and
sized using a photoelectric particle counter of the type developed by
Gucker and O'Konski.[3] It was essentially a dark field microscope
equipped with a light source and a photomultiplier as a detector. As usual
for such devices, the stream of air being sampled was of such a size that
no more than one particle was likely to be in focus at a given moment.
Thus, the pulse height was a function of particle size and refractive index.

The output from the photomultiplier was fed into a two-channel pulse height discriminator, yielding a rough indication of both the particle concentration and size distribution. One channel counted all particles with diameters greater than about 0.55μ and the other all particles with diameters greater than 0.75μ.

Two balloon flights were made with this instrument, both about 20 miles north of Minneapolis and at about sunrise. The data from both flights suggested that there is a peak particle concentration in the stratosphere at a pressure of about 0.1 atm, corresponding to an altitude of about 16 km. Above this height the concentration expressed as particle number per unit weight of air remained nearly constant, that is, there was a nearly constant "mixing ratio." Rosen suggested that the particle concentration vs. height "profile" might have been perturbed by dust from the Bali volcanic eruption mentioned earlier.

As Rosen points out, if a particle source is above the atmosphere, the mixing ratio and size distribution will be independent of altitude, while if the source is in the lower atmosphere or at the Earth's surface, the mixing ratio and size distribution will be altitude dependent in the stratosphere. On this basis Rosen concludes that the source of the particles above the maximum must be at least above 85 km and estimates a mass downward flux of particles 0.5 to 2μ diameter of $4 \times 10^6 \rho$ metric tons per year over the Earth where ρ is the average density of the dust particles.

Junge, Chagnon, and Manson[4] made a theoretical and field study of stratospheric aerosols up to 30 km altitude, and Junge[5] investigated the vertical profiles of Aitken nuclei in the upper troposphere and stratosphere. These studies involved the use of balloon-borne Aitken nuclei counters, which are actually modified Wilson cloud chambers. The counters were designed to meet the following requirements: (a) be operable to pressures as low as 0.01 atm, (b) provide good coverage of the low-concentration range from zero to a few hundred particles per cm^3, and (c) provide automatic recording. Junge et al.[4] used a photographic method of recording the number of droplets produced by each expansion. At low atmospheric pressures the expansion chamber was pressurized since otherwise the water droplets remained so small that photography was difficult.

A typical set of results is shown in Figure 3-2. In general, the particle concentrations dropped slowly and irregularly with increasing altitude in the troposphere. At a few kilometers above the tropopause, the concentration became a few particles per cm^3 and maintained about this order of magnitude to the peak elevation reached by the balloon. Examination of a number of such profiles suggests that low values of 1 per cm^3 are

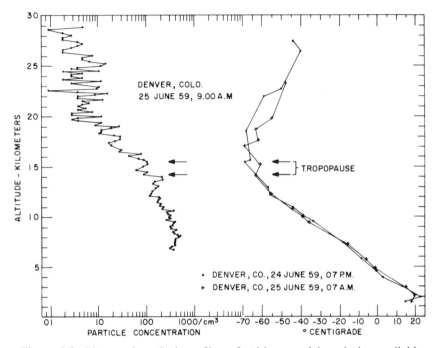

Figure 3-2. Measured vertical profiles of Aitken nuclei and the available temperature soundings closest in space and time.[4] (*Courtesy of the American Meteorological Society*)

probably more representative of the higher altitudes than the 1 to 10 shown in Figure 3-2. Most of the profiles exhibited considerable vertical structure. For example, in one there was a layer at 8 km, about 500 m thick, having quite sharp boundaries, for which the particle concentration was about an order of magnitude greater than that immediately above or below the layer. In another there was a layer at an altitude of 10 km of similar thickness having a concentration about an order of magnitude less than that in the troposphere. This suggested an intrusion of stratospheric air. Layer structure was also observed in the lower stratosphere but not so marked as in the upper troposphere. The theoretical treatment suggested the presence of a coagulation-diffusion equilibrium, an effective particle diameter of 0.08μ, and an eddy-diffusion coefficient at the tropopause of 1500 cm^2/sec.

Junge and co-workers[4] also determined vertical profiles for particles larger than 0.1μ radius. A balloon-borne air sampler was developed for this purpose which collected solid particles from the air with inertial jet impactors. The samples were deposited on a small area of a gum-coated slide, and because successively narrower jets were used, the particles were classified according to size. The collected samples were evaluated with a microscope. The results of flights with impactors, like those obtained by Rosen using counters, indicated a peak in the particle concentration in the stratosphere between 16 and 22 km. Thus, the profiles for particles exceeding 0.1μ radius were quite different from those for the Aitken nuclei.

The concentrations at any given altitude in the stratosphere were found to vary little with time over a period of more than a year. The size distribution was such that dN/dr was essentially inversely proportional to r^3 for the size range 0.1 to 1μ radius. The results are summarized in Figure 3-3.

Judging from the fact that the concentrations of particles smaller than 0.1μ radius decreased rapidly with increasing altitude it seems likely that

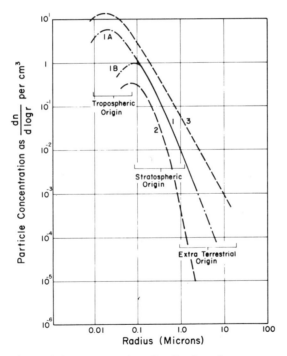

Figure 3-3. Average size distribution for stratospheric aerosols. Curve 1A is for the lower stratosphere and 1B for altitudes above 20 km. Curves 2 and 3 are estimated confidence limits.[4] (*Courtesy of the American Meteorological Society*)

these are mainly of tropospheric origin. It is unlikely that particles much smaller than $0.01\,\mu$ will exist independently for long in the stratosphere because of their high rate of coagulation with larger particles.

The existence of the concentration peak at 16 to 22 km for particles of 0.1 to $1\,\mu$ radius, suggests that such particles may be formed by chemical reactions in the stratosphere or troposphere, followed by growth by coagulation.

Although few data were obtained by Junge *et al.*[4] for particles larger than $1\,\mu$ radius, there seemed to be considerable fluctuation in the concentrations of such particles with time. The times required for such particles to fall from 100 km to the lower stratosphere are short compared with meteorological processes in the stratosphere. Thus, it seems very likely that they are of extraterrestrial origin. This conclusion agrees with that reached by Rosen on the basis of the variation of the concentration of such relatively large particles with altitude, as mentioned above.

Several more vertical profiles of Aitken nuclei in the stratosphere have been described and discussed by Junge.[5] The nuclei counter was the same as that used in the previous study.[4] Together with the results described above, data from 7 flights were obtained covering the period of June 1959 to August 1960. To explain his results he proposed the following equation, which disregards horizontal gradients and transports in the atmosphere and considers only vertical processes:

$$D\,\frac{\partial^2 N}{\partial z^2} - aN - HN^2 - u\,\frac{\partial N}{\partial z} = 0 \qquad (3.1)$$

where D is the eddy-diffusion coefficient, N is the nuclei concentration, a is a coefficient of the removal rate by washout, H is the coagulation coefficient, u is the gravitational sedimentation velocity, and z is the altitude, all, of course, in consistent units.

The first term gives the local change in particle concentration by eddy diffusion. The second gives the rate of removal as a result of rain and snow, and assumes that this rate is proportional to the concentration and that the coefficient a is constant with time and altitude. Actually, in the stratosphere it will be zero or nearly zero. The third term is the rate of change of concentration due to coagulation, and the last term gives the removal rate by sedimentation. This equation represents a tremendous oversimplification in addition to neglecting horizontal motion. The last two terms are based on the assumption that the particles are all the same size, which of course is grossly incorrect. Nonetheless, such an equation is useful for correlating data and for demonstrating the processes affecting particle concentrations in the atmosphere.

CHEMICAL COMPOSITION

Numerous studies have been made by Junge and his co-workers of the chemical composition of the particles in the size range 0.1 to 1μ radius that are found at about 20 km. The earliest results were obtained with impactors during balloon flights mentioned above.[4] The total weights of material collected were very small, and were estimated to be 0.08 microgram on one stage of the impactor and 0.4 microgram on another.

The samples were analyzed using an electron microprobe analyzer. A very narrow electron beam is focused on a particle or surface to be analyzed, whereupon the surface fluoresces, emitting x-rays whose wavelengths are determined with a sensitive x-ray spectrometer. The wavelengths correspond to the elements in the particle or surface. Thus, the elements rather than the compounds making up the sample are determined. The electron beam is produced by an incandescent tungsten filament and accelerating gun. The beam is focused with electron optics similar to those in an electron microscope to form an electron probe about 1μ in diameter. The sample must be mounted on a conducting surface to avoid electrostatic charging by the electron beam.

This device has been found to be very useful for identifying particles collected from the atmosphere. Junge et al.[4] collected samples on aluminum or germanium, which had to be very pure so that fluorescence of impurities would not interfere with interpretation of the x-ray spectra. The aluminum used was about 99.99 per cent aluminum and the germanium contained less than 1×10^{-10} part impurities per part germanium. Analyses could be made with this method for all elements, except the inert gases, with atomic numbers between those of aluminum and uranium, although elements having atomic weights greater than that of zinc were difficult to detect because of low excitation efficiency and a high noise level.

Only silicon, sulfur, and iron were detected among the stratospheric particles in the size range 0.1 to 1μ radius, and of these only sulfur was present to an appreciable extent. The particles were very hygroscopic, suggesting that they were soluble salts, probably sulfates. No nickel was detected, which indicates that little of this particulate material was of extraterrestrial origin. Junge et al. concluded that sulfate is an important, if not the most important, constituent of such particles. This study did not indicate the nature of the cation, although it seemed likely that it was sodium or ammonium.

Junge[6] has found that sulfates are important constituents of extremely clean tropospheric air as indicated by the fact that samples of ice from the central part of the Greenland ice cap contained an order of magnitude more sulfate than other common tropospheric constituents such as chloride, sodium, calcium, and potassium. Presumably, this sulfate was scavenged from the atmosphere by precipitation and accumulated in the ice. Junge theorizes that this sulfate was formed by the oxidation of hydrogen sulfide and sulfur dioxide, since these are known to be present throughout the troposphere. Junge *et al.* suggest, therefore, that hydrogen sulfide and sulfur dioxide enter the stratosphere at the equator where it is oxidized by the action of O_2 and sunlight or by ozone.

Atomic oxygen would also be an important oxidant in the stratosphere, as shown by Cadle and Powers.[7] The resulting sulfur trioxide would react rapidly with water vapor to form sulfuric acid which would presumably undergo further reactions to form the sulfate salts. The concentrations of gaseous sulfur compounds in the troposphere seem to be sufficiently high that such an explanation is reasonable.

The reaction of atomic oxygen with sulfur dioxide was investigated using a high-velocity flow system. Atomic oxygen was produced in most of the experiments by subjecting molecular nitrogen to a microwave discharge and titrating the atomic nitrogen produced with nitric oxide:

$$N + NO \rightarrow N_2 + O \qquad (3.2)$$

The endpoint of the gas titration was indicated by the disappearance of the N_2^* (Lewis-Rayleigh) and NO^* afterglows. The "air afterglow," which results from the slow reaction

$$NO + O(+M) \rightarrow NO_2^*(+M) \qquad (3.3)$$

was produced by adding a slight excess of nitric oxide (Figure 2-5). The intensity of this glow is proportional to the atomic oxygen concentration and was measured along the reaction tube with a photomultiplier tube to determine the rate of atomic oxygen disappearance as a result of reaction with the sulfur dioxide. Initial rates and rate constants for the reaction were calculated from the resulting data. The reaction of atomic oxygen with sulfur dioxide could also be carried to completion, using an excess of sulfur dioxide and the amount of sulfur dioxide remaining after reaction determined by gas chromatography. The rate constant, k, was then calculated using the integral equation

$$\ln \frac{[SO_2]_1}{[SO_2]_2} = k \int_{t_1}^{t_2} [O]dt \qquad (3.4)$$

where the brackets refer to concentrations and t is reaction time, calculated from the flow rate.

The rate constants determined in these two ways were nearly the same, namely, 4.8×10^{15} cm^6 mole^{-2} sec^{-1}, based on atomic oxygen reaction and 3.4×10^{15} cm^6 mole^{-2} sec^{-1}, based on the reaction of sulfur dioxide. As mentioned in Chapter 2, the rate constant is nearly independent of temperature and is a three-body reaction:

$$SO_2 + O + M \rightarrow SO_3 + M \qquad (3.5)$$

The rate constant was also found to be nearly the same for M $= O_2$ or N_2.

Now, if we know the values of [O] and [M] at any place in the atmosphere, we can estimate the lifetime of the sulfur dioxide existing at that place at any moment by calculating $\tau(SO_2)$. This is defined as $[SO_2]/d[SO_2]/dt$ and is thus the time required for all of the sulfur dioxide existing at any moment to react if the reaction is first-order in sulfur dioxide, and $d[SO_2]/dt$ does not change with time. Values of $\tau(SO_2)$ for reaction 3.5 were calculated from the first of the two values of k given above, values of [O] taken from the Handbook of Geophysics,[8] and values of [M] for various heights taken from the U. S. Standard Atmosphere (1962).[9]*

The results, presented in Table 3-1, demonstrate that although the concentrations of atomic oxygen in the lower stratosphere are not well known, it is likely that any sulfur dioxide reaching the stratosphere will be

TABLE 3-1. VALUES OF $\tau(SO_2)$ FOR THE REACTION OF SULFUR DIOXIDE WITH GROUND-STATE ATOMIC OXYGEN

Altitude (km)	$\tau(SO_2)$ (sec)
10	8.7×10^6
15	1.2×10^6
20	2.1×10^5
30	2.0×10^4
50	9.0×10^4

oxidized rapidly compared with the time required for the sulfur dioxide removed to be replaced from the tropopause, probably about a year. Thus, this reaction may contribute to the particulate sulfate in the stratosphere. The maximum concentration of these particles at about 20 km may result from the combined effects of increasing concentration of atomic oxygen and decreasing concentration of sulfur dioxide with increasing altitude, but of course other explanations are possible.

Not much is known concerning sulfur dioxide concentrations in the

*The calculations were made from the relationship $\tau(SO_2) = k^{-1}[O]^{-1}[M]^{-1}$.

atmosphere, except near the Earth's surface. Judging from results quoted by Junge,[10] a typical concentration over continents, except close to sources of air pollutants, is 10 microgram/m³ and over oceans is 1 microgram/m³. However, the variations are large. The majority of the sulfur in the lower atmosphere is gaseous and most of this is sulfur dioxide.

The concentration of sulfur dioxide of 1 microgram/m³ at STP corresponds to a mole fraction of about 10^{-9}. Note that if the mole fraction of sulfur dioxide entering the air is this high, reaction 3.5 will not appreciably affect either the concentration of atomic oxygen or of ozone.

Martell[11] has suggested that if sulfates are prevalent in the upper troposphere, it is not necessary to assume that they are formed in the stratosphere. An alternative explanation of a stratospheric sulfate layer is that the sulfates are produced in the troposphere and form layers in the stratosphere by a combination of horizontal and vertical air movements. However, this seems merely to transfer the problem of atmospheric chemical reactions from one atmospheric domain to another. Martell has proposed another alternative, namely, that sulfate particles in the Aitken size range are transported slowly and vertically into the stratosphere as air is slowly exchanged vertically between the troposphere and stratosphere. According to this hypothesis, agglomeration of the particles as they are transported upward in the stratosphere results in growth into the size range 0.1 to 1μ radius, and finally depletion results in a decreasing concentration after the maximum concentration is reached at about 20 km. Eventually, it may be possible to test this hypothesis by determining particulate sulfate concentrations as a function of both particle size and altitude in the upper troposphere and the stratosphere.

Another possible source of sulfate particles is volcanic eruptions which at times inject tremendous quantities of sulfur compounds into the high troposphere and stratosphere. However, major eruptions are rather infrequent events and to the author's knowledge no such eruptions had occurred during the five years prior to the investigation reported by Junge.

Fenn, Gerber, and Wasshausen,[12] apparently stimulated by Junge's work, measured the amounts of sulfate and ammonium ions in airborne particles above the Greenland ice cap. Measurements were made during the period June through August 1961 at Camp Century, which is about 135 miles east of Thule Air Force Base, Greenland. Concentrations of airborne particles were determined using an Aitken-type nuclei counter and a Casella impactor in order to cover a size range of about 10^{-3} to 5μ. Samples for chemical analysis were also collected with the Casella impactor, which had to be run for about 10 hours at 15 liters/min to collect enough sample for this purpose. All of the samples apparently were collected fairly close to the ground.

The concentrations of the large particles, collected with the Casella impactor, varied from less than 1 particle per cm^3 to about 5 particles per cm^3. Fenn concludes that since all the particles were collected on the fourth stage of the impactor they could not have been larger than 1.5μ diameter. This conclusion may be correct, but Casella impactors, unless modified, tend to leak. A result is that most of the particles are collected on the last stage even when quite large particles are present.

The concentrations of Aitken nuclei were much more variable, ranging from almost zero to about 1500 per cm^3.

The sulfate concentrations were quite constant. Assuming a particle size of 1μ diameter and a density of 2, a sulfate particle concentration of about 0.6 particle per cm^3 of air was estimated. Since the average concentration of large particles was 1.5 particles per cm^3, on the average about 40 per cent of the total aerosol mass consisted of sulfate particles. The concentrations of ammonium ion varied considerably. The ammonium ion/sulfate ion weight ratio varied from unity to about 1/30, which can be compared with the stoichiometric ratio 1/2.67 for $(NH_4)_2SO_4$ and 1/5.3 for $(NH_4)HSO_4$. If the sources of the particles over Greenland and in the "sulfate layer" in the stratosphere are similar, it seems likely that a high percentage of the latter particles are ammonium sulfate.

Junge and Manson[13] continued the stratospheric aerosol studies, using recovered rod impactor samples obtained during aircraft flights at the 20 km level from 63°S to 72°N during March to November 1960. These studies were undertaken as part of the High Altitude Sampling Program of the Department of Defense (HASP). Interpretation of the results of the balloon studies was hampered by the fact that samples were obtained from a small volume of air taken at a specific time and location, whereas the results obtained during participation in HASP were from a large number of latitudes in the northern and southern hemispheres. The results showed that the sulfate layer extends over a large part, if not all, of the Earth, and is constant in time and space. Analyses of collected particles were made using the electron microprobe technique, x-ray fluorescence, vacuum spectrometry, and chemical methods. Again the results demonstrated the predominance of sulfate, and about one-fourth of the amount of ammonium ion corresponding to the stoichiometric ratio for $(NH_4)_2SO_4$.

MOTHER-OF-PEARL CLOUDS

Another interesting phenomenon occurring in the stratosphere is the occasional formation of "mother-of-pearl" clouds, sometimes called nacreous clouds. These are observed over the North Atlantic and Scandinavian countries in the winter at altitudes between 25 and 30 km. They probably consist of ice particles at concentrations of a few per cm^3. They are only observed at night when lower clouds and haze are obscured by the Earth's shadow. Mother-of-pearl clouds derive their name from the beautiful iridescence they display. Apparently these clouds are associated with the standing, "mountain," waves that are produced in the lee of mountain ranges. Such waves are responsible for producing the common lenticular clouds often observed in the troposphere behind mountain ranges. As mentioned earlier, clouds are very rare above the tropopause because of the extreme dryness of the stratosphere. Those thunderstorms that penetrate into the stratosphere carry their own moisture with them. This dryness is demonstrated by the fact that aircraft commonly form contrails of condensed engine exhaust moisture in the upper troposphere, but seldom produce contrails of appreciable duration in the stratosphere, the droplets and ice crystals evaporating almost as soon as they are formed.

Mason[14] has suggested that mother-of-pearl clouds are lenticular clouds at great heights. When air flowing over the mountains rises, it cools as a result of expansion, the temperature falls below the dew point, and lenticular clouds are formed. The return of the air to lower levels, as the air passes the crest of the wave, warms the air and the cloud droplets evaporate. Thus, the lenticular clouds represent the wave crest. Mason also suggests that high-level wave clouds are unlikely to form unless the wind speed increases with height. If this is so, the lifetime of the individual cloud particles may be no more than minutes although the clouds themselves may last much longer.

It is of interest that while Mason implies that lenticular clouds, including the mother-of-pearl clouds, are formed throughout the region from the lower troposphere to about 30 km, Dobson[1] states that the latter clouds appear only within a rather narrow altitude range around 27 km. Probably the reason that they are generally observed only in northern latitudes and in the winter is that only in such regions and times are the combined requirements of a mountainous terrain and a sufficiently cold stratosphere to produce condensation fulfilled.

NATURE OF THE MESOSPHERE

Just as the tropopause is the region of demarcation between the troposphere and the stratosphere, the stratopause divides the stratosphere from the mesosphere. For purposes of this book, the stratopause is defined as the region at about 50 km where the rising temperature gives way to a falling temperature with increasing altitude. The mesosphere is then defined as the region of falling temperature between about 50 and 80 to 85 km, followed by the mesopause and the thermosphere, a region of rising temperature at least to 200–300 km and usually the outermost defined region of the earth's atmosphere. The thermosphere is often considered to blend with the solar corona.

A different definition of the stratosphere and mesosphere is sometimes used. The stratosphere is roughly defined as the nearly isothermal region above the tropopause and the stratopause is the region in which this isothermal region gives way to a rising temperature. The region defined above as the stratopause is called the mesopeak in this system of nomenclature.

Other systems have been used for classifying atmospheric regions. For example, the atmosphere below the ionosphere, starting at 60 to 80 km, has been termed the lower atmosphere, while the ionosphere itself is divided into various regions. Also, an exosphere, ozonosphere, and chemisphere have been defined.

NOCTILUCENT CLOUDS

Little is known about the concentrations and identity of particles in the mesosphere. The results obtained by Rosen,[2] described above, suggest that the mixing ratio for particles larger than about 0.6μ diameter is constant above about 20 km to a height which is undetermined, but probably extends into the mesosphere. These particles are probably of extraterrestrial origin.

Most of the little we do know about the particles which occur in this region comes from studies of "noctilucent" clouds.[15-20] The clouds are observed during the summer at twilight in far northern and southern latitudes; they are light blue and in structure resemble an inverted ocean complete with waves (Figure 3-4). These clouds apparently always occur at the mesopause, between the mesosphere and thermosphere, at about 250,000 ft. The nature of the particles constituting these clouds and the mechanism of the cloud formation have long been a mystery. Three hypotheses have been proposed. The first is that they are ice clouds formed by self-nucleation. This is supported by the fact that the mesopause represents a region of minimum temperature, and that the temperature is lowest in the summer. The second hypothesis suggests that these clouds consist of nonvolatile solid particles and is based on correlations that have been observed between meteor showers and occurrence of the clouds. The third hypothesis is that the clouds consist of particles of ice which have condensed on nonvolatile solid particles in much the way that clouds of ice particles are formed in the troposphere.

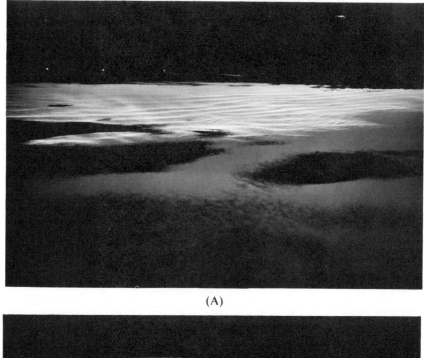

(A)

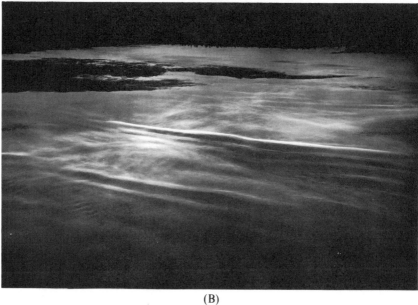

(B)

Figure 3-4. Photographs of noctilucent clouds taken (A) at Grande Prairie, Alberta and (B) at Watson Lake, Canada. (*Both photographs by Benson Fogle*)

This last hypothesis has received considerable support from the results of a sampling program, using rocket-borne particle collectors.[18-20] The approach was to sample the particles from a noctilucent cloud and also to sample the atmosphere at the same altitude in the absence of such a cloud. The particles were captured on collecting surfaces carried in the nose cones of Nike-Cajun rockets (Figure 3-5). Four types of collection surfaces were used: (1) a nitrocellulose film, 200A thick, shadowed with aluminum; (2) a nitrocellulose film coated with fuchsine (magenta); (3) a 1μ thick coating of indium on lucite; and (4) a calcium surface protected with a film of paraffin and silicone oil. A blank was provided by mounting a plastic plate 0.5 mm above the collecting surface and over about 5 per cent of the surface. The covered area was shielded from particles having a ballistic trajectory but was accessible to small contaminating particles. A protective outer shell prevented particle collection during the rocket ascent until an altitude of 75 km was reached. The shell was then opened and particles collected to an altitude of 98 km when the front

Figure 3-5. Collector device used to sample particles in noctilucent clouds. An outer nose cone covered this device before launch and was ejected at about 75 km. (*Courtesy of AFCRL*)

of the rocket was closed. No sampling was attempted during the descent. Four flights were attempted and two were successful, one into a noctilucent cloud and the other when no clouds were visible. Between 10^2 and 10^3 more particles were collected from the noctilucent cloud than when such a cloud was absent, and these were solid particles.

The particles had an exponential size distribution, that is, the number of particles greater than the given diameter varied as kr^{-p} where p was between 3 and 4. Almost no particles were found smaller than 0.05μ radius and it is suggested that this is a property of the particles themselves rather than a result of the collection and measurement conditions. Electron micrographs showed that a halo on the collecting surface surrounded about 20 per cent of the particles from the noctilucent cloud, which suggested that these particles had been imbedded in some substance, presumably ice, which later evaporated (Figure 3-6). No such halos were observed around the particles collected from the cloudless atmosphere.

Attempts were made to analyze the particles using neutron activation. The results seemed to indicate that the particles contained iron and nickel,

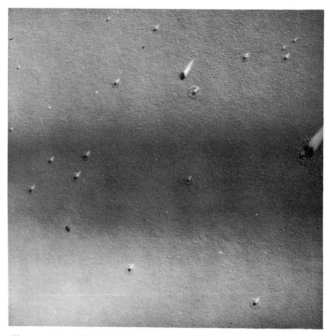

Figure 3-6. Electron micrograph of noctilucent cloud particles. (*Courtesy of AFCRL*)

suggesting an extraterrestrial origin. For the most part the particles varied in size from 0.05 to 5μ diameter, which agrees with the sizes of the particles estimated from measurements of the intensity and polarization of light from the clouds.

Witt and Bolin[21] measured the degree of polarization of the light scattered by noctilucent clouds and concluded that the effective mean radius of the cloud particles was 0.10 to 0.15μ.

All of these results seem to agree with the third hypothesis. There is still a mystery, however, concerning the source of the unusually high concentration of extraterrestrial particles at the time and altitude of noctilucent cloud formation. Kellogg[22] points out that a particle of 0.1μ radius could only remain at the 250,000 ft level if there were an upward motion of the air of about 1 m/sec, and suggests that this may be one reason for the seasonal character of noctilucent clouds.

Charlson[23] has proposed a simple noctilucent cloud model. He suggests that particles of dust (of cosmic origin, for example) fall through a layer of the atmosphere which is supersaturated with respect to ice. These particles become coated with ice, and the thickness of the coating is of importance with respect to the optical properties and the mass "budget" of the system. He concludes that an updraft of tens of centimeters per second is necessary to maintain a noctilucent cloud.

ROCKET EXHAUST

The possibility that the mesosphere and thermosphere could be seriously contaminated by the exhaust from very large rockets, such as those to be used to effect landings of men on the Moon, has often been suggested. For example, the NOVA system for manned moon exploration is to use 1500 tons, 500 tons, and 250 tons of fuel in the first, second, and third stages, respectively. The extent of contamination has been examined semiquantitatively by Kellogg[22] and by Pressman et al.[24] The latter workers concluded that with an accelerated space program using large boosters, sufficient gases and particles would be injected into the atmosphere to produce marked changes in such parameters as upper atmosphere temperature, electron density, and airglow. Kellogg reached quite a different conclusion, by assuming that any change less than the natural fluctuations must be insignificant. He states, "...it is unlikely that rockets will do much to affect this apparently large burden of aerosols in the upper atmosphere, except locally and for short periods." He goes on to emphasize that even the tenuous upper atmosphere is quite massive and quickly purges itself of new material released in it.

PROBING WITH OPTICAL RADAR

The possibility of studying the composition of the upper atmosphere by optical radar (laser probing) has intrigued many investigators. For example, Young[25] has made calculations which indicate that the upper atmosphere can be probed by optical radar to reveal the altitude and density of metastable species in the atmosphere, and that the technique might be useful for the geophysical exploration of auroras, airglows, solar flares, and meteor trail phenomena.

Fiocco and Smullin[26] have detected scattering layers in the upper atmosphere with optical radar. The equipment consisted of an RCA-designed ruby laser delivering pulses of about 50 nsec duration and 0.5 joule at a wavelength of 6940A, a transmitting telescope, a receiving telescope, and a photometer utilizing a 20A-wide interference filter and a cooled EMI 9558 A photomultiplier. The experiments were carried out during June and July 1963 at Lexington, Massachusetts.

The results showed Rayleigh molecular scattering up to 50 to 60 km, but at greater heights, up to 140 km, very weak echoes were obtained which were ascribed to airborne particles. The latter echoes came from two main regions, 60 to 90 km (often about 80 km, corresponding to the mesopause) and 110 to 140 km (often about 120 km). It is of considerable interest that the lower echoes (80 km) came from about the height of noctilucent clouds. Possibly the higher echoes (120 km) correspond to the region of meteoric breakup. Fiocco and Colombo[27] developed the hypothesis that the existence of a scattering layer in the thermosphere at an altitude between 110 and 140 km is due to meteoric fragmentation and developed a model for such fragmentation. They suggested that in its flight through the atmosphere the cross-sectional area of a meteoroid increases due to progressive fragmentation. Thus, the atmosphere would act as a "filter," and the average size distribution of micrometeoroids would vary with the height. Fiocco and Colombo added their estimate of the influx of extraterrestrial material to the large number of such estimates which have been made, suggesting a total influx to the Earth of 6×10^4 tons per day. Fiocco[28] showed that a marked correlation existed between the occurrence of optical radar echoes and the occurrence of the ionospheric phenomenon known as sporadic E or as the sporadic E region. He concluded that the correlation could be considered to be additional evidence that the optical radar echoes were caused by extraterrestrial incoming particles and that sporadic E may sometimes be related to the same cause, although the characteristics of the particles involved in the two phenomena may be different. Fiocco emphasized that the positive correlations were established for only one set of observations, obtained during a period of high meteoric activity.

In this connection it is of interest that considerable controversy has occurred concerning the origin of sodium vapor in the atmosphere, which has been identified by its emission in the airglow and seems to have a maximum concentration at about 80 km. The sources usually suggested are meteoroids or sea salt. For example, Hunten[29] has described the results of measurements of the twilight emissions of sodium, potassium, and lithium which permitted the amounts and vertical distributions of these atoms to be determined in some detail. The sodium/potassium ratio suggested a marine origin for these atoms. Lithium concentrations varied sporadically, suggesting an extraterrestrial origin for this element.

REFERENCES

1. Dobson, G. M. B., "Exploring the Atmosphere," Oxford, Clarendon Press, 1963.
2. Rosen, J. M., *J. Geophys. Res.*, **69**, 4673 (1964).
3. Gucker, F. T., Jr., and O'Konski, C. T., *Chem. Rev.*, **44**, 373 (1949).
4. Junge, C. E., Chagnon, C. W., and Manson, J. E., *J. Meteorol.*, **18**, 81 (1961).
5. Junge, C. E., *J. Meteorol.*, **18**, 501 (1961).
6. Junge, C. E., *J. Geophys. Res.*, **65**, 227 (1960).
7. Cadle, R. D., and Powers, J. W., "Some Aspects of Atmospheric Chemical Reactions of Atomic Oxygen," Paper presented at CACR Symposium, Visby, Sweden, August, 1965.
8. Miller, L. E., "Atmospheric Composition," in "Handbook of Geophysics," 2nd Ed., New York, Macmillan, 1960.
9. "U. S. Standard Atmosphere, 1962," Superintendent of Documents, U. S. Government Printing Office, Washington, D. C.
10. Junge, C. E., "Air Chemistry and Radioactivity," New York, Academic Press, 1963.
11. Martell, E. A., Paper presented at CACR Symposium on Atmospheric Chemistry, Circulation, and Aerosols, Visby, Sweden, August 18–25, 1965.
12. Fenn, R. W., Gerber, H. E., and Wasshausen, D., *J. Atm. Sci.*, **20**, 466 (1963).
13. Junge, C. E., and Manson, J. E., *J. Geophys. Res.*, **66**, 2163 (1961).
14. Mason, B. J., "Clouds, Rain, and Rainmaking," Cambridge, Cambridge University Press, 1962.
15. Witt, G., *Tellus*, **14**, 1 (1962).
16. Ludlam, F. H., *Tellus*, **9**, 341 (1957).
17. Hesstvedt, E., *J. Geophys. Res.*, **66**, 1985 (1961).
18. Hemenway, C. L., and Soberman, R. K., *The Astronomical Journal*, **67**, 256 (1962).
19. Soberman, R. K., *Sci. Amer.*, **208**, No. 8, 50 (June, 1963).
20. Skrivanek, R. A., and Soberman, R. K., in "Cosmic Dust," *Ann. New York Acad. Sci.*, **119**, Art. 1, 98 (1964).
21. Witt, G., and Bolin, B., paper presented at CACR Symposium on Atmospheric Chemistry, Circulation, and Aerosols, Visby, Sweden, August 18–25, 1965.
22. Kellogg, W. W., *Space Science Reviews*, **3**, 275 (1964).
23. Charlson, R. J., paper presented at CACR Symposium on Atmospheric Chemistry, Circulation, and Aerosols, Visby, Sweden, August 18–25, 1965.

24. Pressman, J., Tank, W., Connell, J., Brown, H. K., Reidy, W., Dalgarno, A., Millman, S., and Warneck, P., "Modification of the Earth's Upper Atmosphere by Missiles," Final Report, Contract 5 D-112, Geophysics Corporation of America Report No. 62-18-G, Bedford, Mass., 1962.
25. Young, R. A., *Discussions Faraday Soc.*, **37**, 118 (1964).
26. Fiocco, G., and Smullin, L. D., *Nature*, **199**, 1275 (1963).
27. Fiocco, G., and Colombo, G., *J. Geophys. Res.*, **69**, 1795 (1964).
28. Fiocco, G., *J. Geophys. Res.*, **70**, 2213 (1965).
29. Hunten, D. M., paper presented at CACR Symposium on Atmospheric Chemistry, Circulation, and Aerosols, Visby, Sweden, August 18–25, 1965.

Chapter 4 Radioactive Fallout

MECHANISMS OF FALLOUT FORMATION

Air bursts

Aside from a few isolated incidents, hazards from airborne nuclear radiation are very modern phenomena. The history of such hazards can be considered to have started with the first man-made nuclear explosion, at Alamogordo, New Mexico, in 1945.

Most of the hazards from airborne radiation originate in particles rather than gases. The particles vary in size from a few Angstroms to boulders which are thrown from craters. It is convenient to classify radioactive particles according to the mechanism by which they were formed. The following scheme is useful, although it can be criticized on several grounds.

A. Production from deliberate nuclear explosions
  1. Fission devices
     (a) Underground and surface explosions in silicate soils
     (b) Underground and surface explosions in coral (calcium carbonate) soils
     (c) Surface and underwater explosions
     (d) Air bursts
  2. Fusion devices
     a, b, c, and d as above
     (e) "Clean" weapons
     (f) "Salted" weapons
B. Accidental production
  1. Runaway reactors
  2. Damaged reactors
  3. Accidental detonation of nuclear weapons

The basic principles of fission and fusion (thermonuclear) reactions have been discussed elsewhere in detail[1-3] and need not be repeated here.

First, let us consider the mechanism of particle production by the explosion of fission devices.   Such explosions produce a multitude of nuclides ("fission products") which vary somewhat in composition, depending upon the fissionable material (uranium 235, uranium 238, plutonium 239) and neutron speed.   Most of the fission products are found in two groups according to atomic weight, one group having an abundance peak for an atomic weight of about 95 and the other having a peak for an atomic weight of about 140[2].

The fission products formed by a nuclear explosion may be divided into two categories, namely, those produced directly by fission, the primary products, and secondary products which are produced by decay of the primary products.   These secondary products or daughters consist of nuclides which have been produced at various stages of the radioactive disintegration series of the primary products.   Since these primary nuclides may be liquids, solids, or gases at ordinary temperatures and have half-lives varying from fractions of a second to thousands or millions of years, the properties of the disintegration series to a considerable extent influence the condensation of the nuclides as the fission products cool following the explosion.   An example is the series

$$_{54}Xe^{140} \xrightarrow{\text{16 sec}} {}_{55}Cs^{140} \xrightarrow{\text{66 sec}} {}_{56}Ba^{140} \xrightarrow{\text{12.8 days}} {}_{57}La^{140} \rightarrow {}_{58}Ce^{140} \text{ (stable)}.$$

Since xenon is a gas, it cannot condense, but as it disintegrates to form solid products these will condense either along with other fission products and bomb debris or on particles that have already formed.   Such delayed condensation may give rise to "fractionation" which is a change in the ratio of a primary nuclide (or its daughters) to one or more other nuclides relative to the ratio immediately after the explosion.

In addition to the fission products, radioactive nuclides are produced by the capture of neutrons by stable nuclides.   The neutrons are produced in the fission process, and this capture leads to the formation of a new species called a compound nucleus, which is in a highly excited state.   This excitation energy may be emitted as gamma radiation.   Charged particles may also be ejected as a result of neutron capture.   A particularly common reaction is that with nitrogen

$$_{7}N^{14} + {}_{0}n^{1} \rightarrow {}_{6}C^{14} + {}_{1}H^{1}$$

The subscripts refer to atomic number and the superscripts to atomic weight.   The carbon 14 is radioactive, decaying by the reaction

$$_{6}C^{14} \rightarrow {}_{7}N^{14} + {}_{-1}e^{0}$$

The neutrons can also react with various bomb materials, producing new nuclides.

The composition of the fission-product mixture for various types of nuclear explosions and various times following the explosion has been calculated by a number of researchers, starting with Hunter and Ballou in 1951.[4-7]

Most explosions are the result of the sudden, violent release of gases. The gases may initially be cool, as when a balloon bursts or the diaphragm of a shock tube is punctured. Or they may be very rapidly heated at the same time that they are formed, in which case the heat will greatly contribute to the violence of the explosion.

Chemical explosions result from the release of gaseous explosion products which are heated by the chemical energy produced. The energy from nuclear explosions results from the conversion of mass to energy, and this is possible because of a "peculiarity" of the series of all the known elements arranged according to atomic weight. Nuclides in intermediate positions are lighter in relation to the numbers of protons and neutrons that constitute them than nuclides such as U^{235} or H^1 near or at the ends of the series. This results from the higher binding energy of the protons and neutrons in the nuclides in intermediate positions. Thus, the splitting up or fission of a nuclide such as uranium 235 releases energy, and so does the combination or fusion of the very light nuclides to form heavier ones.

Fusion weapons, the so-called hydrogen bombs with yields in the range equivalent megatons of TNT, are triggered by fission explosions and thus produce fission products much as do the lower-yield fission bombs.

When a bomb of the fission or fission-fusion type explodes, a great amount of energy is liberated in a very small period of time. The fission products and weapon parts attain temperatures comparable to those in the center of the sun, namely, several tens of millions of degrees, and are completely vaporized. Furthermore, since these gases at the moment of explosion occupy the same volume as the unexploded bomb, tremendous pressures are developed. They are probably more than a million times atmospheric pressure.

These extremely hot gases radiate large amounts of energy of very short wavelength, largely in the x-ray region. The surrounding air strongly absorbs radiation of these wavelengths, producing a very hot and very luminous "fireball."

The actual processes are much as follows.[1] A radiated photon is absorbed by an atom, molecule, or ion, raising it to a highly excited state. When the excited species returns to the ground state, a photon is emitted having the same frequency as the first (it can be considered to be the same photon). The emitted photon will generally move in a different direction from the first one, until it, in turn, is absorbed and re-emitted. The result is a "random walk," and an expansion of radiation away from the explosion point much slower than the velocity of light.

During the earliest stages of the expansion of the gaseous bomb residues, the mean free path of the photons is large compared with the diameter of the volume of expanding gas. Energy is rapidly transferred by radiation within this volume, and a uniform temperature is maintained. The volume within the "fireball" at this stage is called the isothermal sphere. If the ambient air has an appreciable density, that is, if the altitude is not extremely high, the radiation emitted by the isothermal sphere is absorbed by the surrounding air, which becomes very hot.

While these events are occurring, a shock front is being produced. The vaporized bomb products expand violently as a result of the very high pressure, and in a few microseconds have produced a shell of debris which is expanding at a rate of several hundred miles per second and has an initial temperature of about a million degrees C. This expanding shell acts as a piston, initiating a compression wave which rapidly becomes a shock front.

So long as the mean free path of the radiation in the hot gas is sufficiently great that transfer of energy by radiation is more rapid than that by mass motion, the shock front lags behind the expanding surface of the fireball. However, as the fireball expands and the temperature within the fireball decreases, the mean free path decreases both in absolute terms and relative to the size of the fireball. The shock front then overtakes the expanding radiation front and moves ahead of it. By this time the temperature has dropped to about 300,000°C, and in the case of a 20-kiloton explosion when about 0.1 millisecond has elapsed since the explosion occurred. The expanding shock front compresses the air and raises its temperature, producing incandescence. The fireball now consists of two concentric parts. The inner part is still isothermal and is surrounded by the outer shell, produced by the shock wave. The outer shell has a somewhat lower temperature than the isothermal sphere.

As the fireball grows at a rate determined by the rate of travel of the shock front, the temperature drops. The hot, incandescent air has been opaque, but finally the outer portion of the fireball cools and becomes sufficiently transparent that the incandescent isothermal sphere once more becomes visible. The development of this condition is known as breakaway. Following breakaway, the visible fireball (still defined by the radius of the shocked air) continues to grow, but more slowly, as shown in Figure 4-1.

The temperature of the interior of the fireball decreases steadily, but the apparent surface temperature passes first through a minimum and then

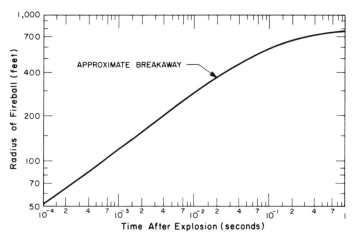

Figure 4-1. Variation of radius of luminous fireball with time in a 20-kiloton explosion[1] (from "The Effects of Nuclear Weapons").

through a maximum before it finally steadily declines. This behavior for a 20-kiloton bomb is shown in Figure 4-2. The behavior of the apparent surface temperature results from the fact that at breakaway, radiation from the isothermal region penetrates the outer surface of the fireball, and this occurs to an increasing extent as the outer portion of the fireball cools and becomes more transparent. Figure 4-2 also shows a discrepancy between the "observed" temperatures as indicated by measurements of surface brightness and surface temperatures calculated from the shock velocity. This difference results from attenuation of the radiation between the outer surface of the fireball and the observer, which is caused by various compounds such as nitrogen dioxide.

Temperature of course plays a very important role in the formation of radioactive particles by nuclear explosions. Somewhat less obvious is the fact that the way in which temperature varies with time is also important. One reason for this is that the time which has elapsed before condensation starts to occur is an important factor in determining the amount of fractionation. The times required for the various events described above to occur are functions of the energy yield of the explosion. These functions are described as scaling laws. For example, the scaling law for the time for thermal minimum is given by the approximation

$$t_{min} \approx 0.0025 W^{\frac{1}{2}} \qquad (4.1)$$

where t_{min} is time in seconds and W is kilotons TNT equivalent. Similarly, the time at which the maximum temperature occurs in an air burst is

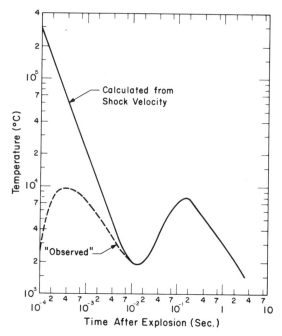

Figure 4-2. Variation of apparent fireball surface temperature with time in a 20-kiloton explosion[1] (from "The Effects of Nuclear Weapons").

given by the expression $0.032W^{1}$. The minimum and maximum radiating temperatures are almost independent of the energy yield. Freiling[8] gives the following scaling law for the maximum temperature, T_{max}:

$$T_{max} \approx 8900W^{-0.03} \qquad (4.2)$$

The boiling points of many metals and their oxides are in the vicinity of 2500 to 3000°C, and since their vapor pressures decrease rapidly with decreasing temperature, the fission products and other vaporized bomb debris would be expected to condense when the fireball temperature decreases into this range. According to Freiling, the temperature drops to $3300W^{-0.03}$ degrees Kelvin at a time $15t_{max}$.

When the explosion is an air burst, that is, when the burst occurs below 100,000 ft, but at a sufficient height that the fireball does not touch the Earth's surface, the fallout at first consists essentially only of fission products and other bomb debris but rapidly agglomerates with natural aerosol particles. The first step in the fallout production when the fireball cools sufficiently to become supersaturated is nucleation. This involves the formation of stable clusters of atoms or molecules and is immediately followed by condensation of vapor on the nuclei. As large numbers of droplets are formed, coagulation can occur.

Magee[9] has developed a theory of particle formation which applies to air bursts. His development is based largely on the nucleation and condensation processes and leads to the equation for particle size distribution

$$n(r)dr = \frac{n_T}{r} \exp\left(-\frac{r}{r'}\right) dr \tag{4.3}$$

where n_T is the total number of particles and r' is the mean particle radius. According to this theory, r' is the ratio of the radial growth rate of a particle to the logarithmic growth rate of the nucleation rate.

Another theory has been developed by Stewart,[10] who includes coagulation and condensation in his treatment. He arrived at the log normal distribution

$$n(r)d(\ln r) = \frac{n_T}{\sqrt{2\pi}} \exp\left[-\frac{1}{2}\left(\ln \frac{r}{\underline{r}}\right)^2\right] d(\ln r) \tag{4.4}$$

where $\underline{r}$ is the modal radius and is given by the equation

$$\underline{r} = \frac{v_B N_0 T_c}{Kn}\left(\frac{k}{2\pi mA}\right)^{\frac{1}{4}} \tag{4.5}$$

where

v_B = molecular volume in the liquid phase
N_0 = initial number of atoms per unit volume
T_c = absolute temperature at the time of condensation
K = $4kT/9\eta$($\approx 3 \times 10^{-9}$)
η = viscosity of air
n = concentration of nuclei
k = Boltzmann's constant
m = molecular mass
A = $7500°K$

Stewart concluded that the modal particle size for an air burst or high surface burst would be about 0.2μ diameter. He assumed a fireball radius of 500 ft and an iron content of 25 tons. He concluded that it would be very unlikely that a particle would attain a size as large as a few hundred microns diameter in the short time available for growth.

Freiling has compared Magee's and Stewart's equations with experimental particle size information for air bursts. The data agree fairly well, within the size range for which reliable data were obtained, with both the

Magee and Stewart equations. The values for the parameters obtained are $n_T = 1.86 \times 10^6$, $\underline{r} = 0.072\mu$ (Stewart), and $n_T = 2195$ and $r' = 1.8\mu$.

Freiling suggests that the fractionation resulting from the interaction of the radioactive fission products ("radionuclides") with the growing particles can be thought of in two ways: first, with respect to the fractionation index, which is the "ratio of two extremely different radionuclides," and second, the interpolated behavior of the other products. Since the fractionation index is the result of very different properties of two mass chains, it can hopefully be treated by a very simple approximation. This approximation is that a high-boiling-point nuclide will be distributed among the particles according to their volume (or d^3), a volatile radionuclide will be distributed according to the surface of the particles (or d^2). It is based on the assumptions that most of the bomb material condenses and solidifies before the more volatile nuclide condenses, and that the particles remain immersed in the vapors during the entire condensation period.

The fractionation index for a given particle size was calculated for the Magee and Stewart size distributions as applied to the particle size data mentioned above. It was calculated to be log $(0.18r)$ and log $(1.1r)$, respectively. The former expression would require 100μ radius particles to account for the measured degree of fractionation. Some of the intermediate fractionating pairs of radionuclides may also be analyzed in this manner, but others require a more detailed treatment. Freiling did not undertake such a detailed treatment, but indicated that it might involve considerations of collisions between growing particles and vaporized fission products "which lead to incorporations of the products in the carrier material with certain efficiencies (accommodation coefficients) and probabilities of escape." It might also be necessary to include refinements such as consideration of gas-phase diffusion and diffusion in the particle, and elaboration of condensation theory to take into account depletion of the volatile material as condensation progresses and the inhomogeneous development of the fireball.

Freiling tested these ideas with data gathered from the radiochemical analyses of fractionated samples from a large number of air bursts, the yields of which varied by a factor of several hundred. The logarithm of the ratio of total Sr^{89} present in a sample to the total Zr^{95} was taken as the fractionation index. Strontium 89 is produced by the series

$$_{35}Br^{89} \xrightarrow{\text{4.4 sec}} {_{36}Kr^{89}} \xrightarrow{\text{3.2 sec}} {_{37}Rb^{89}} \xrightarrow{\text{15 min}} {_{38}Sr^{89}} \xrightarrow{\text{51 days}} \ldots$$

whereas zirconium 95 is formed by the series

$$_{36}Kr^{95} \xrightarrow{\text{short}} {_{37}Rb^{95}} \xrightarrow{\text{short}} {_{38}Sr^{95}} \xrightarrow{\text{0.7 min}} {_{39}Y^{95}} \xrightarrow{\text{10 min}} {_{40}Zr^{95}} \xrightarrow{\text{65 days}} \ldots$$

All of these are beta emitters, progressing along the series by emitting one electron at a time and thereby increasing by unity in atomic number. The precursors of Sr^{89} are gaseous (mainly as krypton) for much longer times than are required for the fireball to cool to temperatures at which condensation can occur, so it is the "volatile" nuclide, whereas the precursors of Zr^{95} are all solids except for an extremely short time immediately after the explosion. The Sr^{89}/Zr^{95} ratio had a range of about 100 fold. Logarithms of other ratios of radionuclide fractions were plotted against this index. Freiling reached the following qualitative conclusions on the basis of these plots:

(1) The relative volatility indicated by the results bears both similarities to and differences from that shown in high-yield surface bursts, probably reflecting the identity of the nuclide compounds and differences in the carrier materials.

(2) The order of decreasing volatility was the following: Cs^{137}, Sr^{89}, Cs^{136}, Cd^{115}, U and Ag nuclides, Ba^{140}, Y^{91}, Ce^{141}, Mo^{99}, Pu and rare earth nuclides, and Zr nuclides.

The physics, chemistry, and meteorology of fallout has been reviewed by Björnerstedt and Edvarson.[11] They state that for "reasonable" concentrations of vapor in the fireball, a 20-kiloton explosion will produce a particle size distribution with a median diameter of less than a micron. However, the particle growth rate increases with time, so the median diameter might be expected to increase with increasing explosion-energy yield.

Surface bursts

A nuclear explosion in which the fireball touches the surface may be considered to be a surface burst. Some authors differentiate between surface and tower bursts in which an experimental device, usually of low yield, is exploded from the top of a tower, but this distinction is rather artificial.

The intense heat of a surface burst vaporizes soil and other material in the vicinity. These vapors are taken up in the fireball. According to "The Effects of Nuclear Weapons" if 1 per cent of the energy of a 1-megaton burst is expended in this manner, about 4000 tons of vaporized soil will be added to the fireball.

The rise of the fireball and the negative phase of the shock wave produce a violent wind which blows inward toward and up into the fireball. This lifts tremendous amounts of particulate material into the fireball and scours out a crater. The cratering may be implemented by fracturing of the rock or compacted soil by the shock wave. The shock wave will to some extent be "coupled" with the soil, travelling downward through the earth. The negative phase of this shock wave and also components of the wave that are reflected back to the Earth's surface by major inhomogeneities in the Earth's upper crust will help loosen the soil.

The size of the crater varies greatly with the energy yield of the explosion, the height above the ground at which it occurs, and the nature of the soil or rock. The statement is made in "The Effects of Nuclear Weapons," "It is believed that for a 1-megaton weapon there would be no appreciable crater formation unless detonation occurs at an altitude of 450 feet or less."

Surface bursts on or over water have effects similar to those over soil. Large quantities of water are vaporized and drawn up into the fireball, and additional amounts may be swept up by the inrush of air. If the explosion occurs over the ocean or other body of salt water, the salts will be vaporized and eventually become part of the fallout.

The formation of fallout during the cooling of a surface-burst fireball apparently is much more complex than that during the cooling of the fireball from an air burst. As the fireball cools, condensation of the vapor of a particular material will occur when the partial pressure of the vapor exceeds the vapor pressure of the liquid (or solid, in the case of sublimation). Some supersaturation may take place, but this is probably not an important factor in fallout formation. Thus, if each substance condensed independently of the other substances condensing from the fireball, the time and temperature of condensation would be determined largely by the combined factors concentration and vapor pressure-time relationship. The vapors will not condense completely independently of each other. Instead, there will be a considerable tendency for the materials present in large concentrations to cause the simultaneous condensation of less concentrated or more volatile substances, just as many stages are required in a still to achieve acceptable separation of many mixtures. Nonetheless, there will be considerable fractionation as a result of relative concentration and volatility as well as a result of the nature of the decay series.

The amount of rock and soil which is drawn into the fireball from a surface burst must increase with decreasing distance of the explosion location from the surface. When sufficiently large amounts of such material are introduced into the fireball, only part of the material is vaporized. The cooling vapor may condense on the nonvaporized particles or form separate particles as a result of self-nucleation. In the latter case, agglomeration with the nonvaporized material may occur. If this material is in liquid form, solution or partial solution of the condensed fraction may occur. If the unvaporized particles are solid, the condensation or agglomeration may enclose the particle in a coating of highly radioactive material. Even the unvaporized particles are usually radioactive as a result of neutron activation of some of their constituents.

Adams, Farlow, and Schell[12] made a detailed study of the nature of fallout particles and reached a number of conclusions concerning the production mechanism. They assumed that air is engulfed by the fireball, which is undoubtedly true if earth can be "drawn in." Thus, the fireball contains oxygen by the time condensation occurs. They proposed a model based on the assumption that the major constituents of a high surface burst, such as a high-tower burst, are vaporized iron derived from the bomb components and associated structures, and the air engulfed by the fireball. They also assumed that before condensation occurs, the iron vapor is in the form of free atoms, but that as condensation occurs the iron is oxidized and for a while is in the form of liquid iron oxide. They estimated that for a tower plus bomb weight of 100 tons and a fireball radius of 600 ft, the iron will begin to condense at about 3000°C.

When the tower shot is lower and soil is incorporated into the fireball they conclude that three types of particles are formed:

(1) very small particles of iron oxide formed by condensation and subsequent agglomeration;

(2) much larger iron oxide particles consisting largely of melted tower material;

(3) large particles of liquefied soil materials.

The model apparently does not include the possibility of vaporization of the soil materials.

It is highly informative to compare the nature of fallout particles with the proposed mechanisms of particle formation. These have been described by Adams *et al.*[12] and studies of such particles have been conducted in the author's laboratories over a number of years. Particles formed from surface shots in silicate soils, such as those of the Nevada Test Site, were often but not always spheres. Some were entirely black, others had a greenish color, and many were obviously composites. The black material was more radioactive than the light-colored material, had a higher specific gravity, and was often ferromagnetic.

The study of thin sections of the particles was particularly informative. The method of preparing the sections used by the author is described by Cadle, Wilder, and Schadt.[13] The particles are placed at the bottom of a hollow steel cylinder, powdered methyl methacrylate is added, and the cylinder is heated to about 150°C in a metallographic mounting press. A pressure of about 6000 psi is then applied and the cylinder is allowed to cool to at least 80°C. The transparent cylinder of methyl methacrylate with the particles imbedded in one end is then removed from the press.

The end of the plastic cylinder in which the particles are imbedded is ground and polished, using standard metallurgical techniques, until the particles are flat on one side. The plastic cylinder is then returned to the press, particle side up. A thick layer of powdered methyl methacrylate is placed over the particles, and the heating and pressing are repeated. Most of the plastic is cut away from the unpolished side of the particles which are then ground and polished into thin sections. Most of the remaining plastic is sawed and ground away, leaving the particles mounted in a thin disk of methyl methacrylate. This disk is cemented to a microscope slide to complete the preparation.

Fallout particles sectioned in this manner were examined with a petrographic microscope, using chemical micrurgic techniques,[14] and by preparing autoradiographs. Similar methods were used by Adams et al.[12] Examination of the thin sections showed that the particles were composed largely of transparent glass which ranged from colorless to almost black. Some of the particles contained numerous bubbles. The black material was the most radioactive and was almost certainly magnetite (Fe_3O_4). It was undoubtedly formed from bomb components and in the case of tower shots in part from the iron from the tower. Even the light-colored glass was radioactive, in agreement with the mechanism of formation proposed above.

Tower shots on coral in South Pacific islands yielded somewhat different particles, reflecting the different nature of the soil. The particles were black and spheroidal, weakly magnetic, and often cracked and veined with calcium salts.[12] They contained a core of calcium hydroxide and calcium carbonate which Adams suggests had originally been calcium oxide but had been altered by hydration and carbonation. Around the core was a thick layer of dicalcium ferrite ($2CaO \cdot Fe_2O_3$) which was veined with the calcium hydroxide and carbonate. Radioautographs of thin sections showed that most of the activity was associated with the outer layer.

According to Adams, most of the iron vapor in the fireball must have condensed by the time the temperature dropped to the melting point of calcium oxide (2570°C). Thus, the iron oxide and the calcium oxide reacted while crystallizing to form the dicalcium ferrite, and fission products condensed with the iron to make these regions radioactive.

When very large (megaton) nuclear explosions occurred on or very near the surface, the particles were somewhat different. Adams described two types of particles. One type was angular and consisted almost entirely of calcium hydroxide with a thin outer layer of calcite. Some contained a core of unaltered coral surrounded by calcium hydroxide. The other particles were spherical and were composed largely of partially hydrated calcium oxide. They had an outer coating of calcite.

The hydration process caused as much as 100 per cent increase in volume, often accompanied by a crumbling of the particles.

When bombs in the megaton-yield range were detonated on barges in the Bikini lagoon, little or no material from the bottom of the lagoon reached the fireball. The barges consisted largely of steel and coral sand ballast, both of which presumably were vaporized by the explosion, and condensed and solidified long before the water vapor condensed. The fireball also contained large amounts of sodium chloride. Because of the absence of large amounts of soil, the particles would be expected to be relatively small, but water condensate might be expected to rain out, carrying with it much of the solid material. This was found to be the case. Adams *et al.*[12] collected such particles on films treated with a chloride-sensitive reagent. These particles consisted of drops of a slurry of a saturated aqueous solution of sea salts containing small radioactive spheres and crystals of sodium chloride in suspension. The drops ranged in size from about 50 to 250μ diameter and were composed of about equal parts water and sodium chloride and 4 per cent insoluble solids by weight. The insoluble solids, as might be expected, were small spheres. They ranged in size from about 30μ diameter to at least as small as 0.01μ diameter.

Freiling[15] has also described radionuclide fractionation in particles produced by high-yield bursts on seawater and coral surfaces. The data were correlated using an empirical approach. Perhaps the most interesting finding was that the fractionation was hardly influenced by the nature of the surface or the explosion yield, and apparently was determined almost entirely by the nature of the fission-product series.

Underground bursts

An underground nuclear explosion produces fallout particles by essentially the same processes that produce the particles from surface bursts, except that the amount of soil taken up by the fireball is much greater. Crater formation is much more important than the scouring action of the air drawn in toward the fireball as a mechanism for introducing soil into the fireball in the case of underground explosions.

Some of the soil material is thrown into (or falls back into) the nuclear debris at a later stage in the particle formation process so that molten radioactive particles aggregate with or are impacted on unfused soil particles.

When an underground nuclear explosion occurs in a silicate soil, a much greater variety of shapes and agglomeration arrangements of the particles is observed than when the particles are produced by a surface burst in the same soil. Many of the particles are spheres, but many other shapes are also seen, demonstrating the great turbulence that must exist in the cloud of nuclear debris shortly before the particles solidify. Some are pear shaped, often with drawn-out ends, others are glassy dumbbells, while still others consist of two or more spheres which have almost completely blended with one another. Many of the smaller particles are black and ferromagnetic and as would be expected are particularly radioactive. Even a few threads are pulled out, reminiscent of the "Pele's hair" of certain basaltic volcanic eruptions.

The complexity of many of the particles is demonstrated by a stereopair of photographs of a particle produced by the "Jangle" underground shot at the Nevada Test Site and examined by the author (Figure 4-3). When this particle was initially removed with a probe from a sample of radioactive particles, it was coated with a highly-radioactive black, glossy material. This was broken away to reveal the interior of the particle as shown by the photographs. The black spheres presumably were very radioactive and consisted of fission products, magnetite, and possibly condensed soil. The light-colored, glassy matrix presumably was fused soil which on the Nevada desert is very sandy and contains little humus. The matrix was highly vesicular, presumably because of the release of adsorbed air and water, and water of hydration, during fusion.

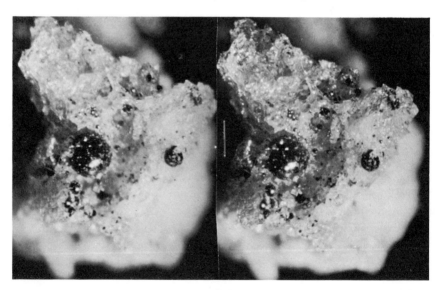

Figure 4-3. Stereo photograph of a particle from the "Jangle" underground shot in Nevada. The largest black sphere was about 220μ in diameter.

Thin sections were prepared of fallout particles from underground shots. These revealed the glassy nature of most of the particles and also demonstrated that a number of the particles contained essentially unchanged soil fragments. Two particles examined contained fragments of metal. The black, highly active material was often only partially mixed with the glassy substrate, producing thin sections having a streaked or mottled appearance and autoradiographs having a similar appearance.

The fallout from surface and underground nuclear explosions has a much greater median particle size that that from air bursts. As a result, much of the fission product activity settles to the ground as "close-in" fallout instead of remaining in the atmosphere for long periods of time to become "worldwide" fallout.

Not much information is available in the unclassified literature concerning the variation of activity with particle size. Sisefsky[16,17] has described the properties of weapon debris particles, collected from the upper troposphere and lower stratosphere, in the size range 0.25 to 5μ diameter. By using autoradiographic and microscopic methods he demonstrated that the activity was proportional to particle volume. Probably these particles were formed by the simultaneous condensation of fission products and relatively nonradioactive material. However, when most of the activity is in a thin coat on the surface of the particle, the activity must be proportional to the particle surface.

Freiling[8] has pointed out that the residual activity for particles of different size from the "Jangle" underground shot is log-normally distributed. The size for median residual activity was about 100μ diameter. However, the size-radioactivity distribution for coral is markedly different from that for silica-rich soil, perhaps indicating that coating is more important in the former case.

A variation of the underground nuclear explosion is one that is so deep that little or no radionuclides escape. A number of such shots have been made and at least some of them have vented to some extent to the open atmosphere. Whether such venting constitutes a health hazard is highly controversial.

Penn and Martell[18] stated that the vented underground Nevada test of September 15, 1961 could be held responsible for most of the iodine 131 fallout in the southeastern and southcentral United States during late September 1961. This was disputed by Reiter[19] and by Machta, List, and Telegadas.[20]

Martell[21] has suggested that iodine 131 associated with fallout reaching the ground in the midwestern United States during May 1962 also originated from the venting of deep underground nuclear explosions.

The mechanics of such venting and the fate of some of the reaction products for such deep underground explosions have been discussed by Goeckermann.[22]

Two other types of nuclear weapons will be mentioned, namely, "clean" weapons and "salted" weapons. The term "clean" in this context refers to the relative amount of radioactivity that is produced. Since fission explosions are used to initiate fusion explosions, no completely clean bomb has been produced, and as Glasstone[1] points out, even a "pure" fusion explosion in air would produce carbon 14 and other neutron-induced activities.

Salted weapons may be considered to be the antithesis of clean weapons. Salting consists of including certain elements in the bomb which are rendered radioactive by the neutrons produced at the time of the explosion. Salting may be used to produce radioactive tracers which are used to follow the course of the debris. Salting has also been suggested as a means for making the fallout more lethal. The so-called cobalt bomb that has received much publicity would be a salted weapon.

Finally, bursts in the very high atmosphere, those above 150,000 ft, should be mentioned. Such shots are of especial interest as a means for introducing large concentrations of ions into regions at various altitudes above the Earth. Little or nothing is known about the particles formed by such shots. In the case of the highest shots where the molecular or atomic mean free paths are extremely large, little or no self-nucleation may occur and radioactive particle formation may largely involve adsorption or condensation on previously existing particles, such as those of extraterrestrial origin.

Crater formation

The weight of fallout formed is to a large extent a function of crater size for surface and underground shots in soil and rock. Also, for a given weapon yield, the fallout particle size distribution is a function of crater size, the mode of the number size distribution tending to increase with increasing size of the crater. These generalities of course do not apply when the explosion occurs so far beneath the surface that the explosion and its products are largely contained.

The "apparent" crater, as contrasted with the "true" crater which includes the region where rupturing without ejection has occurred, scales somewhat differently for surface and for underground explosions. "The Effects of Nuclear Weapons" defines a surface burst, for the purpose of predicting crater dimensions, as one in which the scaled burst depth is

5 ft or less, where scaled depth (or height) is defined as the actual depth (or height) divided by $W^{0.3}$, and W is the explosion yield in kilotons. For a surface burst, the apparent diameter at the original ground level (D_a) and the apparent height (H_a) to this level scale as $W^{1/3}$. The crater volume is given by the expression $\pi D_a^2 H_a/8$. The dimensions of craters produced by underground shots seem to vary with $W^{0.3}$. As would be expected, actual crater dimensions and shapes vary considerably, depending upon the type of soil or rock, upon their stratification, and upon the scaled depth.

Numerous theories of cratering have been developed, many of them in the classified literature. For example, a semiquantitative theory of the mechanics of cratering has been proposed by Nordyke,[23] who emphasizes that the craters produced by high explosives in alluvium are quite comparable with those produced by nuclear explosions. The mechanisms considered include compaction and plastic deformation of the medium immediately surrounding the explosion, spalling of the surface above the explosion by the tensile wave generated at the free surface of the ground, and acceleration of the fractured material above the cavity by the gases trapped in the cavity before and after their escape. When explosions are at or near the surface, plastic deformation and compaction are the most important mechanisms; when they occur at shallow depths, spall is particularly important; at the optimum depth for crater formation, gas acceleration is particularly important; and in the case of very deep explosions subsidence or collapse into the cavity formed by plastic deformation and compaction is the major factor.

Airborne particles from nuclear reactors and separation plants

The main dangers associated with noxious waste products from nuclear reactors and separation plants arise from the possibility of contaminating the soil and water supplies, so that radioactive material is ultimately ingested by human beings. None the less, airborne radioactive particles may also be produced by the operation of reactors and separation plants, and constitute a local potential hazard.

Radioactive gaseous effluents include the air used for cooling reactors and gases liberated from and during the treatment of fission products.[2] The air used to cool some reactors may undergo neutron activation, and the chief source of danger is the gas, argon 41. If the air contains dust particles, as it will unless they are removed by filtration or electrostatic precipitation, they also may be rendered radioactive. Actually, such particles are usually removed after the air has passed through the reactor.

Radioactive gases are given off when the uranium slugs from a nuclear reactor are treated in the production of plutonium. These gases are diluted with air and discharged through tall stacks. Since the radionuclides may be adsorbed by dust particles, the air is usually filtered before it is discharged to the atmosphere.

Accidents

Nuclear reactors are subject to accidents, for example, if the reactors become supercritical. A nuclear explosion involving a nuclear reactor is extremely unlikely, but overheated reactors can emit large quantities of fission products, other highly radioactive material, uranium, and plutonium. Several accidents of various kinds have occurred including that at the Windscale works of the United Kingdom Atomic Energy Authority in October 1957, and that at the Chalk River plant in Canada in May 1958.

Numerous reports are available of the Windscale accident.[3,24-26] Reactor No. 1 overheated and sprang leaks, releasing volatile fission products and particles containing fission products to the stacks. Most of the particles were removed by filters in the stack, but some radionuclides escaped, especially particles rich in iodine 131, and gaseous iodine 131.

Iodine 131 is emitted by irradiated nuclear fuel upon oxidation of the uranium.[24] The total amount of iodine 131 formed by fission is very small, and probably less than a gram was released by the accident. However, probably much of the iodine was adsorbed (chemisorbed?) on particles. Lead and bismuth fumes were present in the pile during the accident, and iodine 131 was found on particles of the oxides in the filters. Also, particles of graphite as large as 15μ in diameter bearing adsorbed activity were found in the vicinity after the accident. Tellurium 132 and cesium 137 were also emitted from the pile during the accident.

Chamberlain[24] believed that most of the active particles were of submicron size.

The possibility that a nuclear weapon will accidentally explode exists, but such an explosion is very unlikely. During about 19 years of handling such weapons, no accidental nuclear explosion has occurred.[1] Nuclear weapons contain a chemical explosive ("high" explosive) for converting the system from a subcritical to a supercritical one, thus triggering the nuclear explosion. This high explosive is much more likely to detonate accidentally than is the fissionable material.

If the high explosive detonates and there is no nuclear reaction, uranium and plutonium may be in part dispersed as an aerosol. The fine particles may rapidly be converted to the oxides. Uranium compounds are chemical poisons. Plutonium is concentrated in the bone, where injury may be caused by the emission of alpha particles.

In the case of a fire in which the high explosive burns instead of detonating, very fine particles of the oxides may be present in the smoke. Studies at the Nevada Test Site indicated that at distances greater than 1500 ft from an accident, the amounts of plutonium that might be received would not exceed accepted Radioactivity Concentration Guide values,[1] and that the maximum permissible concentration of uranium in the body is unlikely to be attained.

It is possible that the detonation of the high explosive in a nuclear weapon will cause the device to go critical and produce fission products and induced activity even in the absence of a nuclear explosion. Even so, the amounts of fission products and induced activity will probably be negligible 1500 ft from the location of the accident.

CLOSE-IN FALLOUT

Base surge

When a cloud of particles is so dilute that the distances between the particles are large relative to the particle diameters, the particles fall independently (except for impaction or agglomeration). As the number concentrations are increased and the particle separation decreased, the falling particles interact with one another as a result of the drag which the particles effect on the medium in which they are suspended. When the concentrations become sufficiently great, the falling particles draw all of the surrounding air along with them and the cloud falls almost as a discrete body. This behavior of airborne particles leads to a phenomenon of underwater and underground explosions known as the base surge.

When a shallow underwater explosion occurs, such as the "Baker" burst at Bikini, a dome of water called the spray dome forms in a few milliseconds. A few milliseconds later the hot gas bubble reaches the surface and a column begins to form, followed by the development of the notorious cauliflower-shaped cloud about the top of the column. When the water droplets begin to fall back to the ocean surface, the phenomenon described above occurs, producing a cloud of droplets surrounding the base of the column which rapidly expands or surges outward, hence the name "base surge."

The base surge produced by underground explosions follows a similar sequence of events. The surge cloud is very rich in fission products as can be seen by comparing isodose rate contours from contamination on the ground following the explosion with photographs showing the progress of the base surge, which is never precisely symmetrical about the explosion location. This relationship was particularly noticeable for the "Jangle" underground shot in Nevada.

Combined effects of meteorology and particle size

The location on the ground of very large radioactive particles following a nuclear explosion is largely a function of the height which these particles reach before they begin to fall and their horizontal movement as a result of the behavior of the fireball and base surge. Furthermore, underground explosions throw out large amounts of material that may follow a trajectory which is largely independent of the subsequent course of the explosion.[27]

The distribution of most of the fallout particles, however, except for those that were brought close to the ground by the base surge, is largely influenced by meteorological conditions such as wind velocity, wind shear, the presence or absence of inversion conditions, and in the case of small particles reaching the stratosphere, worldwide circulation patterns.

It is very useful, from the standpoint of the harmful effects of nuclear weapons, to differentiate between "close-in" and "worldwide" fallout. Close-in, early, or local fallout are designations which refer to fallout near the detonation point or immediately downwind. This fallout is capable of causing acute physiological effects, or even death within a short period of time, as well as chronic effects. It is this type which may justify building "bomb" shelters and which was responsible for acute effects suffered by the natives on Rongelap Atoll in the South Pacific. World-wide or "delayed" fallout causes chronic or long-delayed effects which are particularly insidious. The presence of the fallout is not at all obvious unless elaborate instrumentation is used, and entrance into the body may be highly indirect.

Differentiation between close-in and worldwide fallout is obviously arbitrary. It is useful to define particles that have settled to the Earth within 24 hours as close-in and those that require longer periods of time as worldwide fallout. Small particles are more apt to remain airborne after 24 hours than large ones, but the height at which a particle is produced and meteorological conditions, such as the development of a rainstorm, are very important.

A difference between close-in and worldwide fallout may result from fractionation. Large particles which fall out of the cloud at very early times will contain little of the nuclides (or their daughters) which were gaseous between the times when the large particles formed and when they left the cloud. When the radioactive gases decay to form liquid or solid daughters, they condense onto the remaining, smaller, fallout particles. Thus, the more distant fallout may be relatively richer in those elements in which the close fallout is depleted, although such fractionation is usually limited to fallout from relatively small shots.

Fractionation of fallout from surface bursts over the ocean is usually very small since the fireball must cool to 100°C or less before the evaporated water condenses. The cooling period is sufficiently long so that most of the gaseous precursors such as krypton and xenon have decayed to their solid daughters by the time the water condenses. Furthermore, the droplets are very small and do not settle rapidly from the debris clouds.

By combining considerations of particle size, particle density, meteorological conditions, and the rate of fission-product decay it is possible to predict in a general manner the dose rates and total dosages that might be experienced at various distances from the explosion of a weapon of given yield. Methods for making such predictions are important for civil defense purposes, for safely conducting tests with nuclear weapons, and for predicting the effects of fallout for military purposes.

Obviously, the horizontal travel that a fallout particle experiences on its way to the ground is determined in part by the wind velocity, which has both magnitude and direction. Furthermore, the wind may vary with level (wind shear) and the cumulative effect of all of the wind velocities between the initial height of the particle and the ground must be considered. Factors such as the dimensions of the radioactive cloud, the distribution of radioactivity within the stem and mushroom head, the range of particle sizes, and weapon yield must also be considered.

About 90 per cent of the radioactivity from a surface burst on land is in the mushroom head and the rest is in the stem. The distribution of activity within the head may not be uniform, and seems to vary from explosion to explosion, perhaps because of varying atmospheric conditions.

Prediction of fallout patterns

Before dose rates and total dose can be predicted, it is necessary to consider the rate of decay of dose in fallout. Because of the complexity of the fission-product mixture, which changes markedly in composition with time, the function expressing the change of dose rate produced by the fallout at a given spot with changing time is itself a function of time.

However, for about the first 6 months the dose rate varies approximately directly with $t^{-1.2}$. This is the equivalent of saying that for every seven-fold increase in time after the explosion, the dose rate decreases by a factor of 10. It is convenient to take one hour after the explosion as a reference point, which "The Effects of Nuclear Weapons" refers to as the unit-time reference point.[1] Relative dose rates according to the $t^{-1.2}$ rule are shown in Figure 4-4, in which the relative rate in roentgens per hour is unity at one hour following the explosion. Dose rates estimated from Figure 4-4 are accurate to within about 25 per cent for the first 2 weeks following the explosion and within a factor of 2 up to about 6 months.

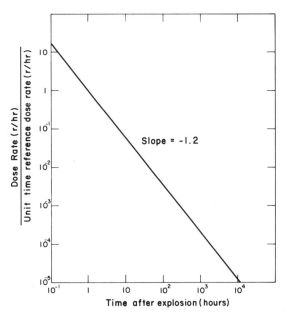

Figure 4-4. Decay of dose rate from close-in fallout.

Fallout patterns are maps consisting of families of isodose rate lines or contours. They can be drawn for various times following the explosion or a single pattern can be drawn as a unit-time reference dose-rate pattern.

Four general methods have been used for predicting fallout patterns.[1,28] The most complex of these is the mathematical fallout model. It is also the method that attempts to provide the most detail. The particles in the initial cloud are traced down to the ground and their combined effect is then computed for a large number of points in the fallout field. In order to undertake such a computation, it is desirable to include in the mathematical model not only the wind velocity at various heights but also the change in these velocities with time and location. Such considerations are particularly important for megaton-range explosions because there may be an interest in "close-in" fallout that reaches the ground 100 or more miles from the explosion point.

Another requirement for use of a mathematical model is a knowledge of the initial distribution of the particles in space, which is closely related to the distribution of activity discussed briefly above. The size distribution of the particles and the variation of radioactivity with size should be known and so should the variation of the size distribution with position. Some of the models attempt to take all of these features into account.

Obviously, the rate of fall for a given particle size at each altitude must be included in the model. And at least one model has attempted to include the spread of trajectories due to turbulent diffusion. The computations have usually been made with digital computers, but special analog computers and even graphical "hand" computations have been used. The results obtained depend both on the details of the mathematical model and assumptions made concerning the above factors. Variations in these assumptions have at times been very large.

The Armed Forces Special Weapons Project (AFSWP and more recently DASA) conducted a symposium on radioactive fallout in 1955. Various groups which had developed mathematical models were invited to apply their techniques to two sets of wind conditions, designated A and B. The results were published in the classified report of the symposium[29] and in reference 28. They are shown in Figures 4-5 and 4-6 and demonstrate the difficulties in making accurate predictions. Many nuclear explosions have occurred since 1955 and both the models and the ability to obtain data to put into the models have undoubtedly improved since that time. Even so, it is very unlikely that good agreement would be obtained if a similar comparison were made today.

The second general method is the analog technique. This is a very common method in weather forecasting. Essentially, it involves sorting through a large number of situations that have occurred in the past, choosing one that seems to match the present or given situation, and assuming that similar situations will lead to similar results. For fallout, the choice is determined by the similarity between the yield and the wind in a given situation and the yield and wind of a pattern in a catalog of patterns. Catalogs of fallout patterns have been produced by The RAND Corporation of Santa Monica, California. The scientist using such a cata-

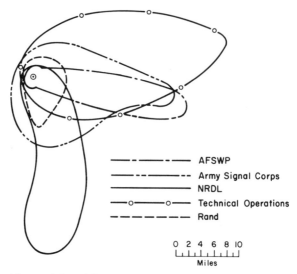

Figure 4-5. AFSWP comparison of fallout computation.[28,29] Cases for "Condition A," 1-megaton yield, showing contours for 1500 r dose accumulated by 48 hours.

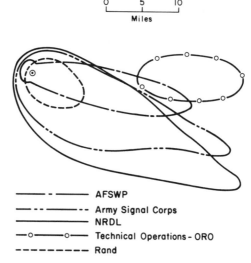

Figure 4-6. AFSWP comparison of fallout computations.[28,29] Cases for "Condition B," 1-megaton yield, showing contours for 1500 r dose accumulated by 48 hours.

log must find a wind field which can be more or less matched to the wind field in question and he then takes advantage of the fact that the fallout pattern has already been computed or determined in considerable detail. Often the yields will be different, in which case certain scaling laws, such as those described later in this section, can be applied. Of course, the same wind field never is exactly repeated, but according to Kellogg[28] the matching can be done quite successfully over a wide range of conditions and yields.

The third method is the development of the danger sector. This requires a minimum of detailed information in order to obtain a general idea of the fallout area and of arrival times. The basic information needed is an observation or prediction of the mean wind speed and direction in a series of 5000-ft thick layers of the atmosphere to the top of the cloud of fallout particles. This information is used to determine the approximate path and arrival times of the fallout at the Earth's surface.

The method is demonstrated with Figure 4-7. Starting at point O, which represents the explosion point, the vector **OA** is drawn which represents the mean velocity of the wind in the lowest 5000-ft layer. Vectors **AB, BC, CD,** etc. are then drawn for successive layers up to the top of the cloud. The dashed lines represent the locus of particles falling from the heights represented by the corresponding letters. Thus, OE is the locus of particles falling from 25,000 ft. The arithmetic mean wind for levels up

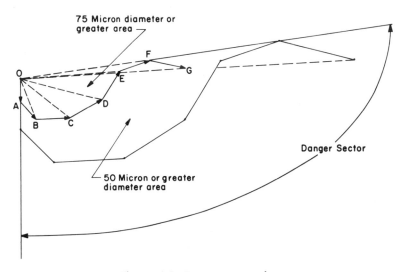

Figure 4-7. Danger sector plot.

to the top of the cloud is the length of the dashed line corresponding to the top of the cloud, in this case OG, divided by the number of 5000-ft levels.

The area enclosed by such a diagram provides a rough indication of directions from the explosion point ("ground zero"). The vectors should be extended by one cloud radius in all directions to account for the physical dimensions of the fallout cloud. Now, if two straight lines are drawn from point O which just enclose the series of vectors, the sector produced is the danger sector, since it is the sector within which the debris will fall if the wind field is constant.

This simple approach can be refined by estimating the times at which the particles starting over ground zero will reach a given point on the ground. If the wind velocity was in miles per hours, line OG is the distance travelled by particles reaching the ground from 35,000 ft in 7 hours. Assuming that the density of the fallout material is 2.5 grams/cm^3, the area enclosed by the vectors and joining lines represents the area on the ground within which nearly all particles of about 75μ diameter or larger will be found (see Figure 4-8). Using the times of fall of particles of various sizes, the lines representing loci can be extended to correspond to particles of any given diameter. Thus, if the lengths of the lines are all doubled, corresponding to doubling the time, the minimum diameter of particles all of which have reached the ground will be about 50μ. Areas can be established in such a sector map representing the extent of deposition of particles of various size.

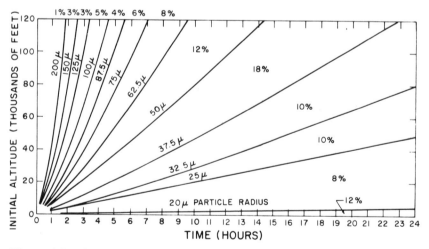

Figure 4-8. Times of fall of particles of different sizes from various altitudes and percentages of total activity carried. Particle density assumed to be 2.5 grams/cm^3 (from "The Effects of Nuclear Weapons"[1]).

Obviously, this method disregards numerous complicating factors. Meteorological factors that are disregarded include vertical air movements, variations in the wind pattern over the area of interest, the possibility of marked wind shear in thin layers, and the effect of any rainfall in the region of interest. The height of the visible cloud may not provide a very accurate indication of the height from which the fallout originates. The fallout particles do not all have the same density.

A modification of this approach is based on data which are reported two to four times daily by U. S. Weather Bureau upper-air observing stations. Upper-air fallout (UF) "winds" are reported which consist of distances and directions from ground zero where particles falling from various heights and requiring three hours to reach the ground will land. These can be plotted in the same manner as the dotted lines in Figure 4-7 and extrapolated to provide arrival times of fallout at any point. This method is designed for civil defense use, since it permits a very rapid evaluation of the regions where hazards from fallout may occur. Danger sectors of course can be drawn from such plots.

The fourth method for computing fallout patterns may be called the "idealized pattern" method. It is based on the early observation that most of the patterns in Nevada had a characteristic cigar shape.[30] Therefore, attempts have been made to characterize fallout patterns in terms of a family of simple elliptical shapes, with a circular section around ground zero. Such patterns present an average fallout field for a given yield and set of wind conditions, and vary markedly from any real situation. Idealized patterns are usually used for planning purposes, for example for estimating the lethal coverage of a country by fallout in case of an attack by nuclear weapons.

The following method is that described in "The Effects of Nuclear Weapons."

In order to prepare an idealized pattern, it is assumed that the actual wind system can be replaced by the mean value of the wind speed and direction from the surface to some representative level in the cloud. This level is usually some place between the base and the middle of the main cloud, where the radioactivity is believed to be concentrated. This assumption produces patterns that are always cigar shaped.

It is important to realize, in constructing such patterns, that at any given point downwind of a nuclear explosion the early fallout does not arrive for some time, usually a matter of hours, after the explosion has occurred, and even when it does arrive it falls at that point for a considerable period of time. Furthermore, the activity associated with any given particle will have decayed to a considerable extent before it reaches that point on the ground. Thus, the dose rate is nearly zero until the fallout arrives, it increases to a maximum value when most of the fallout has been deposited, and then steadily decreases as a result of the decay of radioactivity.

The idealized patterns are based on the concept of unit-time reference dose rates mentioned earlier. Idealized unit-time reference dose rate contours for a surface burst having a 1-megaton fission yield with an "effective" wind speed of 15 mph are shown in Figure 4-9. This figure was based partly on data obtained in connection with various test shots and partly on computations. Note that these patterns do not include the upwind fallout pattern.

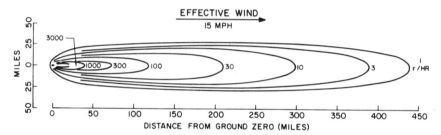

Figure 4-9. Idealized unit-time reference dose-rate pattern for early fallout from a 1-megaton fission yield surface burst (15 mph effective wind speed) (from "The Effects of Nuclear Weapons"[1]).

The idealized pattern is scaled for weapon yield by multiplying the values of the various contour lines by the fission yield in megatons. In the case of a fusion weapon triggered with a fission explosion, only that part of the energy release due to fission should be included. This method apparently gives good results for yields in the range 0.1 to 10 megatons. Actual observations have shown that dose rates in excess of about 10,000 r per hour seldom occur, possibly because the initial volume of the radio-active cloud increases with increasing weapon yield. As a result, the maximum radioactivity on the ground changes very little with changing yield. The scaling law is more reliable at greater distances down-wind, where dose rates are lower, and where the initial cloud volume has little influence on the concentration of fallout on the ground. These same con-siderations apply to the effect of total yield (as contrasted with the fission yield) of a fission-fusion weapon. Increasing total yield for a fixed fission yield might produce a smaller unit-time reference dose rate near ground zero because of the increasing cloud size. Again, at greater distances downwind from ground zero the effect of the total yield would be ex-pected to be rather small.

This method includes a basis for choosing the vertical distances over which wind speeds are to be measured and averaged. For total yields of less than 1MT, 1MT to 5MT, and greater than 5MT these altitudes are 40,000, 60,000, and 80,000 ft, respectively.

In the absence of wind shear, the distance from ground zero at which particles of given size and given initial altitude reach the ground is directly proportional to the wind speed, so for twice the wind speed they spread over roughly twice the area. Even in the absence of wind shear this is not strictly correct, since it ignores widening of the fallout cloud as it moves downstream as a result of turbulent diffusion. Thus, the following scaling laws are proposed to take account of the averaged wind speed, v. The unit-time reference dose rate indicated by each contour of Figure 4-9 is multiplied by $15/v$ since Figure 4-9 is based on a 15-mph wind speed; downwind distances are multiplied by $v/15$. If the equivalent wind speed were 30 mph, the contour values would be halved and the distances doubled.

It is probably apparent from the preceding discussion that the use of idealized patterns based on unit-time reference dose-rate contours tends to exaggerate the downwind extent of the contours. The postulate of no wind shear is usually fairly reasonable for the continental United States. However, if the wind shear exceeds 20° in the mushroom head, "The Effects of Nuclear Weapons" suggests that the wind scaling be modified by leaving the reference dose-rate contours unchanged and multiplying the distances by $(v/15)^{1/3}$. This procedure will considerably widen and shorten the contours. Changes in the average wind direction with distance downwind of ground zero can be taken into consideration by appropriately bending the contour patterns.

A technique for estimating ideal fallout contours in the upwind and crosswind directions has been developed which is based on the results of megaton yield tests at the Eniwetok Proving Grounds. It is assumed that the upwind extent of fallout will depend on three factors: (a) the maximum upwind extent of the cloud, (b) the minimum time needed for particles from the upwind edge of the cloud to reach the ground, and (c) the mean effective wind velocity from the ground to the altitude of the widest part of the cloud.

The data obtained in the South Pacific indicated that the base of the cloud generally is located at the tropopause, which occurs at about 55,000 ft at Eniwetok and at about 40,000 ft in the United States. The average time required for arrival of fallout upwind of ground zero at Eniwetok was found to be 30 minutes; because of the lower tropopause this time would probably be shorter in the continental United States, namely, about 24 minutes (0.4 hour). Particles near the upwind edge of the cloud would be carried back toward ground zero by the wind while they are falling, and the distance carried would equal 0.5 times the effective wind speed at Eniwetok and 0.4 times the effective wind speed in the United States. The assumption is also made that the radius of each contour would be independent of the wind velocity, but that the center of the contour circles would be moved downwind the same distance that the particles are carried downwind from the edge of the cloud.

Radii of contours based on the Eniwetok data for zero wind speed are shown in Figure 4-10 as a function of the total yield of a surface burst having a fission yield of 50 per cent. For other fission yield percentages p, the indicated dose rates are multiplied by $p/50$.

The following method is used for scaling wind velocity. The mean speeds for altitudes up to 40,000 and up to 60,000 ft are considered and the smaller of the two used for scaling. The wind direction used is always

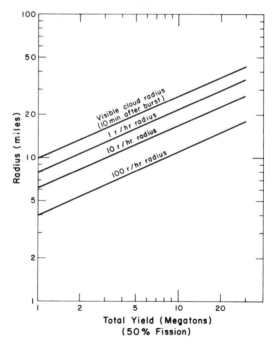

Figure 4-10. Upwind radii for unit-time dose rates from early fallout as a function of total yield for a 50 per cent fission yield for surface bursts.

that at 40,000 ft. The mean wind speed is then multiplied by 0.4 to furnish the displacement downwind from ground zero of the contours in the United States and by 0.5 for shots on the South Pacific islands. Data required for making such calculations for the United States can be obtained from the UF (upper-air fallout) wind data reported by the U. S. Weather Bureau.

The idealized fallout patterns described above were designed primarily for use with explosions in the megaton yield range. However, the same approach can be used for kiloton-range explosions and methods for doing this are described in "The Effects of Nuclear Weapons."

Even very elaborate prediction techniques, such as those involving mathematical models, cannot take account of all possible contingencies. One of the most significant of these contingencies is rainfall. The situation is quite different for the case where a cloud of fallout particles drifts into a region where rain is occurring and that in which the explosion occurs in a rainstorm. Although the tops of some thunderstorms extend into the stratosphere, as many travellers in jet aircraft have observed, the tops of most rainclouds are usually below the 20,000-ft level. The clouds from most nuclear explosions will rise much higher than this, so when such clouds drift over rainclouds the storm can affect only the lowest part of the trajectory of a fallout particle. The main effect may be to produce a rather irregular pattern of activity on the ground.

On the other hand, when a surface explosion occurs in a rainstorm, most of the fallout might condense out and fall within the rainfall layer, in which case all of the particles over a few microns in size would be deposited much closer to ground zero than would otherwise be predicted. Rain is very effective for scavenging large particles, but quite ineffective for particles of submicron size unless the particles themselves serve as condensation or freezing nuclei and take part in the original formation of the rain droplets, or agglomerate with cloud droplets by diffusion. Thus, even in this case the rain might have little effect on the worldwide fallout produced by the explosion. Little is known from direct experience of the effect of rain on early fallout since most tests have been conducted at times chosen to avoid rainfall.

The nature of the terrain also has a considerable effect on fallout patterns, much as the nature of terrain has an important effect on the deposition of snow. Furthermore, all of the patterns discussed above ignore the possible use of shelters and of decontamination. Experience has shown that "hot spots" of unexpectedly high radioactivity may develop. For example, the large radiation doses experienced at Rongelap have been ascribed to such a hot spot.

A comparison of fallout predictions made using various idealized contour patterns (including that described above) with a consideration of wind effects has been made by Ferber and Heffter.[31] They demonstrated, as might be expected, that the various patterns can give very different results, especially if one is interested in the entire fallout pattern produced by a single nuclear burst. When used for estimating casualties, such patterns may provide a good estimate of the numbers of casualties but because of the neglect of certain wind effects, estimates of where the casualties will occur may be very inaccurate.

WORLDWIDE FALLOUT

Close-in fallout is only of practical importance in the immediate vicinity of a test explosion or in case of a nuclear weapon attack involving surface bursts. Worldwide fallout, on the other hand, remains in the air for very long periods of time, slowly settling to the ground where it is ingested by human beings either directly by eating contaminated vegetables and fruits or indirectly by eating products of animals that have eaten contaminated food.

Tropospheric delayed fallout

Worldwide fallout can be divided into two categories: tropospheric fallout and stratospheric fallout. The former is carried rapidly around the earth by the winds, generally by westerly winds, but there is little transport across the equator. The tropospheric fallout reaches the ground over a period of several months. Some of it reaches the ground by direct sedimentation, but apparently scavenging by rain and snow is the main mechanism.

The scavenging action by raindrops has been studied extensively, both experimentally and theoretically. The action of snow is not nearly so well known. However, it has been demonstrated that the amount of delayed fallout reaching the ground in nearby areas is closely related to the amount of precipitation in those areas when the atmosphere contains small fallout particles.

A thorough field study of the effect of precipitation on the deposition of delayed fallout was undertaken by Small[32] at Kjeller, Norway, from September, 1956 to September, 1959. Small stated that it had been thought for some time that particle sizes vary with yield and this could have an important effect upon the general pattern of worldwide deposition. Since it is difficult to determine the particle size distribution of particles in a radioactive cloud, Small investigated what might be deduced from routine measurements of air activity and deposited activity. He found that wet and dry deposition, and surface and air activity, may all be related and, as would be expected, the amounts of fallout material available to be deposited by precipitation may depend on the amounts of material removed from near-surface air layers by processes of dry deposition. Monthly mean values of both wet and dry deposits correlated closely with the air activity. The mean deposition velocity was estimated to be 500 meters/day for dry days and 3000 meters/day for rainy days. This corresponds to an effective particle diameter of 6 or 7μ for the dry fallout material. Small also suggests that a diurnal effect occurs since air fallout radioactivity is reduced during the day by turbulent removal of the particles while during the night continued settling occurs into calmer air. All of this suggests that most of the activity in the lower troposphere is associated with rather large particles.

Although the concentration of fission products varies considerably from one rainstorm to another, values averaged over one or more months are much more uniform, at least for locations having similar meteorological conditions. In such locations the deposition is nearly proportional to the amount of precipitation.

Martell[33] has also discussed the importance of rainfall and pointed out that the low strontium 90 content of soils in low-rainfall areas was the first evidence that rainfall is the controlling factor in fallout deposition. For example, at Antofagasta, Chile, where rain almost never falls, the January, 1956 strontium 90 level in soil was 0.02 millicurie per square mile which is about 0.01 of the level at that time in high-rainfall areas of the southern hemisphere. Similar results have been obtained in the Mediterranean area and in other parts of the world. This is demonstrated in Figure 4-11.

Another interesting observation by Small[32] is that the ratio of radioactivity in rainwater to that in air varies within rather narrow limits. It varied from 0.2×10^{-6} to 2.0×10^{-6} during the period of observation and agreed well with measurements by Blok[34] in Holland (0.4×10^{-6} to 2.5×10^{-6}) between September, 1955 and April, 1957. However, these ratios are somewhat lower than the value of 3×10^{-6} obtained by Hinzpeter[35] in Germany during July to December, 1957.

Small reached the following general conclusions:

(a) Some fallout materials from test explosions have been deposited more rapidly than expected, perhaps because of gravitational settling of relatively large particles.

(b) There may be an especially severe deposition period starting 2 to 3 months after a series of high-yield air bursts and lasting a few months.

(c) It may be possible to forecast both wet and dry deposition rates

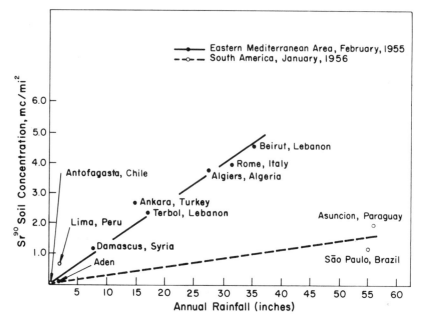

Figure 4-11. Concentration of Sr^{90} in soil versus annual rainfall (*Courtesy of Science*).[33]

from an empirical knowledge of surface air activity over land and ocean regions.

A rather elaborate study of the scavenging of radioactive fallout by rain has been made by Dingle[36] at the University of Michigan. His approach was to automatically collect the rain with a "raindrop sorter" which collected samples according to time during a storm and furnished a record of rainfall intensity vs. time. Samples of rainfall collected in large pans were filtered using a series of graduated membrane filters, and radiochemical analyses were performed. He suggests that the scavenging processes are closely associated with the processes of rain making.

A theoretical study of the scavenging of fallout by rain has been made by Greenfield.[37] Langmuir's theory of collection efficiency was modified to take into account the density of the solid particles, and it was assumed that electrostatic effects can be neglected in the presence of ionizing radiation. He explains the removal of submicron-size particles with a mechanism involving diffusion of the particles to cloud droplets. Relatively large particles in air masses underneath a rain cloud will be removed by direct impaction, but the submicron-size particles will not be removed unless they are mixed with the cloud.

Of course, very small particles of fallout undoubtedly become attached to larger natural particles and hygroscopic particles that can be removed by impaction with rain drops. Given a long enough period of time, even the smallest of fallout particles can be removed by this mechanism.

Dingle and Gatz[38,39] have proposed mechanisms to account for the changes in time of radioactivity concentrations in rainwater from convective rains collected at a fixed point on the Earth. They suggest two categories of parameters that may play important roles in such changes. The first category includes parameters which vary with the life cycle of individual convective cells, including vertical development of cloud tops, rainfall rate, raindrop size spectrum, and the extent and velocity of updraft. The second category includes parameters that vary according to horizontal position of the collection station with respect to the center and boundaries of an individual cell. One of these parameters is the relative amount of entrainment of outside air into various parts of a rain-containing downdraft. Near the leading edge of the downdraft, entrainment of unwashed environmental air into the downdraft probably occurs. Also, the amount of mixing of external air with downdraft air probably decreases toward the center of the downdraft, or contamination is removed from the external air before it reaches the central positions of the downdraft. Thus, the rain near the forward edge of the downdraft should contain a higher concentration of fallout than that further inside the same downdraft, and as the cell proceeds across the station the concentrations of fallout in the rain should decrease with time. The rainfall rate and drop-size distribution are also partially dependent on spatial position.

Field studies of the concentrations of radioactivity in rain from convective systems, according to Dingle and Gatz,[38] strongly suggest that time variations are controlled by processes which vary according to position within individual cells and cell complexes. There is also some evidence that patterns of sharp concentration changes may be repeated if cell complexes are some distance apart. When cells are adjacent, the leading updraft is adjacent only to the leading cell, and concentration changes occur only in the first one or two cells. In this case the concentration reaches and maintains a minimum value during passage of the trailing cells.

Gatz and Dingle[39] analyzed sequential samples of rain, obtained throughout five convective rain-producing weather systems, for radioactivity and for pollen. The concentrations of pollen and radioactive particles followed much the same variation with time during the three storms having the heaviest rainfall. A rapid decrease of concentration with time occurred during the first portions of the rain. This behavior was not observed during the rains of lowest rainfall rate. This similarity of behavior with respect to pollen and radioactivity was taken as evidence that both contaminants were removed from the same air. Since pollens have their source at the Earth's surface, Gatz and Dingle concluded that both pollens and radioactivity entered the convective system from low levels via the convective updraft. They also suggested that the absence of a rapid decrease of concentration in the rains of low intensity might be due to a lack of a persistent, organized updraft in the systems. These conclusions may be correct, but the deductive jump from a positive correlation between two variables to a conclusion based on this correlation concerning their history is dangerous.

The relative amounts of delayed fallout that are injected into the stratosphere and the troposphere depend on the weapon energy yield, the altitude at which the explosion occurs, and the height of the tropopause where the explosion occurs. In the case of a surface or an underground or underwater explosion, a very large percentage of the activity will be associated with large particles and will reach the Earth as early fallout. It is considered that an uncertain fraction between 30 and 80 per cent of the total radioactivity from MT-yield surface water shots contributes to global fallout. Thus, the nature of the soil, as it influences the amount of large fallout particles produced, will play an important role in determining the amount of worldwide fallout injected into the atmosphere by a surface or underground burst. Furthermore, soil or water dispersed in the cloud decreases the maximum altitude achieved by the cloud and thus may increase the proportion of tropospheric delayed fallout.

The altitude to which the cloud rises increases with increasing yield, and the cloud from a low-yield weapon exploded near the Earth's surface may not reach the tropopause. Most of the activity from a high-yield air burst may be associated with stratospheric worldwide fallout, not only because most of the particles reach the stratosphere but also because they are in the submicron size range and settle very slowly.

The latitude at which a shot is fired is important to the distribution of the submicron-size particles between the stratosphere and troposphere since the tropopause is higher in the tropics than in mid-latitudes. As pointed out above, the typical altitude is 55,000 ft in the former case and 40,000 ft in the latter. A nuclear explosion in the United States is apt to produce more delayed fallout in the stratosphere than a similar explosion in the tropics. "The Effects of Nuclear Weapons" provides graphs which show in a semiquantitative way the theoretical percentage of strontium 90 injected into the stratosphere as a function of total yield and burst conditions.

Tropospheric worldwide fallout can actually be considered to originate in at least two ways. One is the direct injection of the fallout particles into the troposphere by the nuclear explosion and the other is the transfer of the stratospheric fallout to the troposphere. As the elapsed time following the explosion increases, the percentage of the tropospheric fallout that originates in the stratosphere must increase. If stratospheric fallout tends to be of smaller particle size than tropospheric fallout at the time of initial injection, this would lead to decreasing particle size with increasing time, but this same effect would result from the settling of the larger particles from a uniformly mixed but polydisperse aerosol.

Several studies have been made of the particle size distribution of the active particles in the tropospheric delayed fallout. Kalkstein et al.[40] determined the beta activity of particles collected 10 meters above the ground, using a two-stage impactor backed up with a membrane filter. The samples were collected in nonurban areas using 1-week collection times and were obtained during the period July 1958 to February 1959. Impactors do not achieve really sharp cuts according to particle size but the results demonstrated a strong trend according to size. About 57 per cent of the activity was associated with particles about 1.8μ in diameter, and about 8 per cent with the particles collected on the filter and thus less than about 0.2μ diameter. As pointed out by Junge,[41] this distribution is similar to the mass distribution of naturally occurring particles which suggests that the ratio of activity to mass does not vary to an appreciable extent over most of the size range of natural aerosols. Quite different results were obtained by Rosinski and Stockham,[42] who found that the beta activity increased with decreasing particle size, 56 per cent of the activity being associated with particles less than 1μ in diameter. They found that 19 per cent was associated with particles larger than 2μ diameter, and 25 per cent with particles 1 to 2μ in diameter. Both sets of results indicate that the tropospheric activity is associated with larger particles than is the stratospheric activity.

Stratospheric delayed fallout

Before proceeding to a discussion of stratospheric delayed fallout it may be helpful to review those aspects of atmospheric structure that have a marked influence on the movement of such fallout about the Earth.

As stated before, the top of the troposphere, the tropopause, varies with latitude. It is often pictured as consisting of three parts, the highest being a band about the equator at about 55,000 ft and extending on either side to mid-latitudes. At the edges of the equatorial tropopause are discontinuities; the northern and southern portions of the tropopause are much lower, sloping downward toward the poles. The tropopause corresponds to the region where the decrease in temperature with increasing altitude stops. Actually, the tropopause is a narrow atmospheric region rather than a definite altitude of atmospheric change, and its altitude and form vary with the seasons. Air above the tropopause, in the stratosphere, is less turbulent than in the troposphere, although turbulence does occur, and exchange of air between the stratosphere and the troposphere is rather slow. The tropopause is most clearly defined in the tropics since the temperature immediately above the tropopause increases with increasing altitude. In mid-latitudes an isothermal region exists immediately above the tropopause which changes to an inversion (increasing temperature) condition in the upper part of the stratosphere. The tropopause may actually disappear during the polar winter night.

Much of the exchange of air between the stratosphere and the troposphere is believed to occur at the discontinuities that occur at mid-latitudes. These gaps are regions of unusual turbulence and are usually associated with polar fronts. The suggestion has also been made that some exchange of air between the stratosphere and troposphere results from a sort of pumping action produced by small variations with time in the altitude of the tropopause at any given place.

As mentioned above, some thunderstorms penetrate the tropopause and it has been suggested that they produce violent, though local, mixing of stratospheric and tropospheric air.

Rather elaborate theories have been developed concerning stratospheric and upper tropospheric circulation which include the exchange of air between the stratosphere and the troposphere. The following is a simplification of theories by Dobson[43] and by Brewer[44] which differed somewhat in detail. Moist tropical air rises to the cold tropopause where it loses most of its moisture by condensation. It then either penetrates the tropopause and spreads toward the polar regions in the stratosphere (Brewer) or, more likely, spreads toward the poles at the tropopause, entering the stratosphere mainly through the gaps mentioned above. The air sinks back into the troposphere near the polar regions, particularly in the late winter or early spring when the air is coldest and heaviest.* This produces a general, sluggish circulation. Months or even years may elapse between the time when an air mass rises near the equator and when it descends in the temperate or polar regions.

The fallout particles in the stratosphere are very small. Drevinsky and Martell[45] undertook particle-size studies, using an impactor having a capacity of 1000 ambient ft^3 per sample. This impactor was carried by a balloon and consisted of 4 separate barrels connected by a manifold to a single pumping system and individually programmed so that a four-point vertical profile was obtained on a single balloon flight. The altitude ranges

---

*Although radioactivity and ozone are obviously carried down, an alternative explanation is that the process is one of vertical eddy-mixing of air, rather than sinking of air.

were 30 to 50, 50 to 70, 70 to 90 and 90 to 100 thousand ft. Each barrel was equipped with a two-stage impactor backed by a polystyrene microfiber filter. The impactors were designed and calibrated so that at the midpoint of the altitude range where they were to be used, the first and second stages had a 50 per-cent collection efficiency for particles of 0.3 and 0.04μ diameter, respectively. A few single level collections were made in the lower stratosphere with an impactor having jets calibrated at 0.36 and 0.018μ diameter, also backed with a fiber filter. These instruments were flown over Minneapolis, Minnesota and over Hyderabad, India. Larger air-filter samples were also collected over Hyderabad, using 10 ft^2 polystyrene microfiber filters.[46]

Most of the beta activity in the lower stratosphere was found to be on the second stage of the impactor, indicating that most of the activity was associated with particles having diameters in the range 0.04 to 0.30μ assuming a particle density of 2 grams/cm^3. There was a marked influence of altitude on the size range of particles with which most of the activity was associated. Some 60 to 80 per cent of the beta activity in the altitude range of 90,000 to 100,000 ft was associated with particles having diameters less than 0.04μ. Similar results were obtained over both India and Minnesota.

Radioactive particles formed by a nuclear explosion and injected into the stratosphere will of course agglomerate with naturally-occurring airborne particles. As was discussed in Chapter 3 in more detail, Junge and his co-workers[41,47-50] have found three types of particles, classed according to particle size, composition, and variation of concentration with height in the stratosphere below about 80,000 ft. The concentrations of particles smaller than 0.2μ diameter decrease with increasing altitude above the tropopause and are probably of tropospheric origin. The particles having diameters between 0.2 and 2.0μ consist largely of sulfates and possibly largely of ammonium sulfate. Junge has stated that these are formed by photochemical reactions in the stratosphere, although Martell[51] has suggested they may be due to coagulation of Aitken nuclei of tropospheric origin. Few particles larger than 2.0μ diameter were found in the stratosphere, and these may have been of extraterrestrial origin. The interaction between radioactive particles and these nonradioactive particles has been discussed by Manson.[52] Calculations were made of coagulation decay constants and half-lives for various sizes of radioactive particles mixed with the natural particles. The calculations were based on the theoretical treatment of Zebel.[53]

Manson concludes that the continuing influx of radioactive material at the altitude for maximum sulfate concentration (about 20 km) results from an influx of finely divided radioactive particles from higher elevations, and suggests that the results of Drevinsky and Martell[45] showing that the upper stratospheric radioactivity is associated with very fine particles substantiate this conclusion. Manson further concludes that at about 20 km a dynamic balance exists between the influx of radioactive particles, the formation of the sulfate aerosol, and the removal of both to the troposphere, and that the radioactive particles may become condensation nuclei for the sulfate particles. In the latter case, agglomeration of several radioactive particles on a larger sulfate particle could not occur.

The above considerations emphasize that the important aspect of the particle size of the delayed fallout particles is that they are small, and probably remain small at least until they enter the troposphere. Settling of the individual particles from the stratosphere is not an important mechanism for transport of such particles to the troposphere. This is demonstrated by Figure 4-12 which shows the fall time to the tropopause in years from various heights for particles of various sizes.

Thus, the particles behave almost as though they are molecules, and they enter the troposphere only as the stratospheric air enters the troposphere. Because of this behavior and because radioactive particles are readily identified as such, delayed fallout serves as an excellent tracer for air masses.

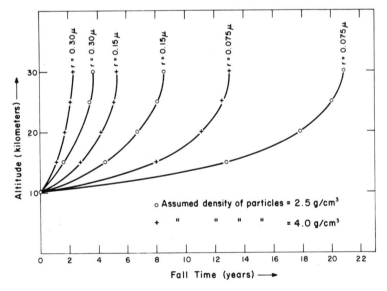

Figure 4-12. Gravitational fall time for spherical particles from indicated altitude to tropopause (Stokes-Cunningham formula), (prepared by E. A. Martell).

From a physiological standpoint, the most important radioisotopes in delayed fallout are probably strontium 90 and cesium 137. They both have long half-lives (27.7 and 30.5 years, respectively), constitute relatively large fractions of the fission products in old debris, and the strontium tends to be concentrated in bone. Thus, these isotopes, and especially strontium 90, are often determined when delayed fallout is studied.

Since stratospheric winds are predominantly easterly or westerly, depending on the time and location, when a radioactive cloud is injected into the atmosphere, it tends to lengthen out parallel to the equator until it eventually girdles the Earth. At the same time it widens and to some extent spreads out in a vertical direction as a result of turbulent diffusion. There will also be a gradual drift toward the polar region.

Several interpretations of strontium 90 fallout measurements have been suggested. The principal features of the measurements which must be explained are the maximum cumulative Sr^{90} deposition which occurs in the middle latitudes of the northern hemisphere and the sharp increase in Sr^{90} deposition rate which was observed for several years in the spring.

Libby[54] has suggested that radioactive fallout injected into the stratosphere becomes uniformly mixed over both hemispheres in one or two years and has an "average storage time" of 10 ± 5 years. He suggests the stratospheric fallout would be uniformly scattered over the Earth's surface except for the result of variations in rainfall. He accounts for both the high mid-latitude deposition and the high rates of fallout in the spring as resulting from tropospheric delayed fallout from relatively low-yield explosions.

Martell,[33] on the other hand, has inferred from considerations including the age of the radioactive debris that the spring peak may involve a substantial contribution from stratospheric fallout introduced into the stratosphere shortly before the fallout reaches the ground. He suggests that the spring peaks have resulted largely from Soviet tests at mid-latitudes in the northern hemisphere. This hypothesis is consistent with the Brewer and Dobson theories of stratospheric circulation which include a more rapid downward mixing in the spring. Such tests would also be responsible for the peak in cumulative Sr^{90} deposition in the middle latitudes of the northern hemisphere.

Miyake et al.[55] have observed this same seasonal variation of radioactive fallout in Japan. They found that the specific radioactivity of rainwater or of air was much higher when there was a "trough" at 18,000 ft or higher and the core of a jet stream was located above or a little south of Tokyo. Since these weather conditions occur frequently in Japan between March and June, Miyake et al. considered them to be the probable cause of the spring maximum.

Machta, List, and Telegadas[56] have concluded that irrespective of the source of the stratospheric fallout, the distribution of fallout on the ground and in the air near the ground is characterized by a peak in temperate zones.

Gustafson, Brar, and Kerrigan[57] describe the results of radiochemical analyses of surface air collected between early 1952 and 1962 at Argonne National Laboratory. They also found the spring maxima but concluded that it was not possible on the basis of their results and other measurements to clearly define the mechanism producing these maxima. They compared the concentrations of cesium 137 in surface air during successive maxima and minima to estimate the mean stratospheric residence times of debris from various sources. These times ranged from 6 to 10 months for Soviet October 1958 debris and from 8 to 15 months for "Hardtack" series debris to several years for Rh^{102}-labeled high-altitude fallout.

One conclusion that can be drawn from these results by different groups is that the concepts of residence time or half-life in connection with both tropospheric and stratospheric fallout have at best only qualitative significance. They would be strictly correct only for steady-state conditions or for non steady-state conditions if the depletion rate in the stratosphere were a first-order process, that is, proportional to the first power of the concentration. It is also worth noting that a seasonal variation of the rate of transfer from the stratosphere will result in a corresponding but lagging seasonal variation in the rate of deposition of fallout on the ground. Even so, approximate limits of "residence times" are useful and the following values were listed by Junge[58] as being the consensus as of autumn 1962:

	Low Stratosphere	High Stratosphere
Low latitudes	1–2 years	about 5 years
High latitudes	0.5–1 year	about 1–2 years

A large variety of nuclear weapon testing was undertaken in 1958, and there were no large-scale injections of fallout into the atmosphere between 1958 and September 1961 when the test moratorium collapsed. Several of the 1958 tests produced special radioactive tracers, some of which could be identified years later. Thus, a particularly favorable situation for studying stratospheric behavior existed and an unusual amount of atmospheric sampling was undertaken both at the surface and up through the atmosphere as far as the stratosphere.

The global history of the 1958 nuclear debris and its meteorological implications have been reviewed by Telegadas and List.[59] They considered two fission products and two neutron activation products: strontium 90, cerium 144, rhodium 102, and tungsten 185. They analyzed the results of aircraft sampling to 21 km over much of the northern hemisphere and balloon sampling to 30 km at latitudes of 45°N and 31°N. Their conclusions agreed in general with the mechanisms suggested above. Thus, they proposed that debris injected at heights above 43 km over equatorial regions descends into the polar stratosphere and subsequently travels downward and toward the equator. North of 35°N and between the altitudes 14 and 20 km, the downward movement in the winter was estimated to be of the order of 1.5 km per month. They suggested that mass air movement rather than vertical turbulent diffusion is the main transport mechanism. Telegadas and List propose that fallout injected into the lower equatorial stratosphere is governed by mixing as far north as about 35°N, but that no simple model explains the distribution north of that latitude.

The behavior of small particles in the stratosphere and troposphere is certainly influenced to some extent by photophoresis and thermophoresis. Orr and Keng[60] have used laboratory measurements of photophoretic effects to determine the possible magnitude of such effects in the stratosphere. Photophoresis consists of the numerous types of motions which particles suspended in a gas undergo when illuminated with a beam of light. The motion may be linear, circular, elliptical, and even consist of figure-eight orbits. By convention, positive photophoretic action is motion away from the light, and negative is motion toward the light. Photophoresis is generally thought to be a radiometer effect, and the motion is almost certainly due to uneven heating of the particles. If this is so, a negative photophoretic action must be due to the focusing of energy in some way through most of the particle to a region near its opposite side.

The experimental technique used by Orr and Keng was essentially that used by Rosen and Orr.[61] Photophoretic force values were obtained for sodium chloride and zinc particles, the former being selected because of meteorological interest and the latter hopefully being somewhat representative of fallout particles, and of meteoric debris. The particle sizes ranged from 0.2 to 4μ diameter; pressures used were 30 and 50 mm Hg for sodium chloride particles, and 4 and 10 mm Hg for zinc particles. A few of the tests were conducted with sunlight but most were made using a high-pressure mercury arc lamp and estimating the behavior in sunlight of intensity 0.108 watts cm^{-2}.

The pressures of 4, 10, 30, and 50 mm Hg correspond approximately to 40, 32, 27, and 22 km altitude, respectively. For each pressure and type of particle the absolute value of the net velocity increased with increasing particle size. For the most part, the velocities were within an order of magnitude of those due to gravity. The greatest velocity reported due to photophoresis was 0.313 cm sec^{-1} for a 4μ diameter sodium chloride particle at a pressure of 50 mm Hg. This is about twice the sedimentation rate at this altitude and corresponds to about 1 km every 8 days, assuming the indicated sunlight intensity exists for 12 hours per day. For particles of submicron diameters the velocities were about an order of magnitude smaller. It seems unlikely that photophoresis contributes to an appreciable extent to the transport earthward of radioactive fallout.

Much the same conclusions can be reached concerning thermal forces.[62] These can only be of importance to particle deposition when the particles are in a very large thermal gradient such as is observed at times in air-surface boundary layers.

Fallout from the high atmosphere

As was pointed out earlier in this chapter, little is known about the nature of radioactive particles in the very high atmosphere. However, they must be largely of submicron size. Two high-altitude nuclear explosions have been initiated which were designed to study the movement of materials from very high altitudes. One was the "Orange" shot of the "Hardtack" nuclear weapons test series on August 11, 1958, and the other was the "Starfish" shot on July 9, 1962. Both shots were above Johnston Island at about 16°N and 170°W, the first occurring at about 43 km altitude and the second at about 400 km. The "Orange" shot produced Rh^{102} as a tracer and the "Starfish" shot produced Cd^{109}.

The first of these shots produced about three megacuries of Rh^{102} and the cloud probably reached an altitude greater than 100 km almost immediately after the explosion. Samples of stratospheric and tropospheric particles were collected by filtration and were analyzed by chemically separating the rhodium fraction and then counting the gamma-rays emitted by the Rh^{102} decay.[63] Actually, two isomers of Rh^{102} were produced, one with a half-life of 210 days and one with a half-life of about 4 years.[64] Both isomers decay by electron capture producing a characteristic 475-keV gamma radiation.

Considerable tungsten 185 was also produced during the "Hardtack" series during the spring and early summer of 1958. The total W^{185} production has been estimated to be about 250 megacuries, an appreciable percentage of which must have entered the stratosphere. Smaller amounts of the isotopes W^{181} and W^{188} were also produced.

The stratospheric filter samples were obtained using U-2 aircraft to an altitude of 21.3 km, and also using balloons. The analytical results demonstrated that there was a sharp increase in Rh^{102} concentrations beginning late in the fall of 1959 and continuing through the early winter. Kalkstein[63] suggests that this time coincides with the time one might expect downward mixing associated with the development of disturbances in the polar region. This agrees with the findings mentioned earlier concerning debris originally injected into the lower stratosphere. The data were consistent with a hypothesis of great downward mixing at high latitudes in winter followed by a horizontal movement in the low stratosphere. There was also an increase in concentration in the stratosphere of the southern hemisphere during the southern hemisphere winter, again indicating a downward mixing at high latitudes in winter.

After the middle of 1960 the Rh^{102} concentrations were quite uniform and equally large at high latitudes in both the northern and southern hemispheres, and much smaller at low latitudes.

The tungsten-181 concentrations observed through 1959 differed less between the hemispheres than the Rh^{102} concentrations. The activity ratios Rh^{102}/W^{181} suggested that the mixing of Rh^{102} with the atmosphere was quite different from that of W^{181}, which would be expected if most of the Rh^{102} was produced at a much higher altitude than the W^{181}.

Kalkstein estimated a residence time for the Rh^{102} injected at high altitudes of 10 years, and estimated an upper limit to the size of the particles. This was accomplished by assuming that above 100 km, horizontal molecular diffusion is rapid and that there is also considerable eddy diffusion. Thus, above 100 km the fallout might be expected to rapidly become uniform by distribution on a worldwide basis. Kalkstein next assumed that particles descend to lower altitudes (80 km) only by molecular diffusion and sedimentation, the latter being the more important. Then on the basis of settling rates and the appearance time of the high-altitude Rh^{102} in the lower stratosphere, an upper limit of about 0.02μ diameter was estimated. Below 80 km, mass transport of air must be controlling.

In the troposphere, concentrations remained quite low throughout 1960, and the first appreciable increase occurred early in 1961. This delay of a year between the increase in the stratosphere at about 20 km and the increase in the troposphere at about 5 km suggests the following:[63] During the delay period and before the spring of 1960 there was insufficient time for good mixing to the stratosphere just above the tropopause. Thus, there was no spring maximum in the troposphere in 1960. The tropospheric results for the next spring suggest vertical gradients similar to those for other stratospheric fallout and ozone.

The "Starfish" explosion at about 400 km above Johnston Island produced about 0.25 megacurie of cadmium 109.[65] Cd^{109} (470 days half-life) decays by electron capture to Ag^{109} (39 seconds) which decays by an

88-keV isomeric transition to the stable Ag^{109} isomer. Also produced was an estimated 0.13 megacurie of the long-lived isomer Cd^{113}. Cd^{109} was first detected in the stratosphere by balloon sampling in December 1962, above 30 km in the southern hemisphere.

Samples collected below 20 km first definitely indicated the presence of Cd^{109} in mid-1963. The first appreciable rise in the Cd^{109} concentrations took place in the early southern hemisphere spring of 1963. The concentrations reached a maximum value at the end of November at high latitudes in the southern hemisphere. Kalkstein et al.[65] pointed out that this is about 3 months later than the corresponding increase in rhodium concentrations in the northern hemisphere during the winter of 1959–60, and is consistent with the difference in the time of appearance of the major winter disturbances in the polar vortex region.[66] Concentrations of Cd^{109} rapidly decreased after November, perhaps because the samples taken in November at 44°S and 48°S represented a hot spot.[65]

The usual disturbances in the polar region were quite mild during the northern hemisphere winter of 1963–64, and the principal disturbances occurred late in the winter. This is consistent with the results of the Cd^{109} measurements, which exhibited a concentration increase which began in December or January and attained high levels in March and April of 1964.[65] Concentrations in the northern hemisphere were consistently lower than those in the southern hemisphere.

The stratospheric concentrations of Cd^{109} were about half those expected on the basis of the rhodium concentrations from the "Orange test." Kalkstein suggests that this could have resulted from a slower than average transport of the cadmium tracer to the low stratosphere, escape of some of the Cd^{109} from the Earth's magnetic and gravitational field, or a lower production of the Cd^{109} than had been estimated.

Fallout from accidents

Fallout produced by accidents will almost always be tropospheric and whether it is early or delayed will be largely a function of particle size. The travel, diffusion, and deposition of the radioactive material emitted during the Windscale accident, described earlier in this chapter, was studied in considerable detail.[24-26] Measurements made during the emission of the activity retained by the filter and of the activity in the air near the ground showed that the release occurred largely during the 24-hour period 1200 GMT on October 10 to 1200 GMT on October 11. During the earlier part of the emission, the wind at the height of the top of the stack was light and mainly from the southwest. A cold front passed over

Windscale between about 0100 and 0200 on 11 October, whereupon the wind veered to the northwest and became stronger.

Fortunately, at the time of the accident the air was being monitored by means of filters in many industrial areas of Great Britain and Europe. Since the filters were changed every 24 hours except on week ends, a rough idea was obtained of the travel and spread of the cloud of radioactive debris. Material collected on the filters was analyzed for iodine 131, cesium 137, and polonium 210.

The results showed that by the end of 24 hours, activity of the order of at least 10^{-12} curie per m^3 had extended in two plumes, one over West Yorkshire and the other over Lancashire, and had travelled a distance of roughly 200 km. During the next 24-hour period the active cloud had spread to Belgium, the extreme west of Germany, and southern Holland. A region of high activity (of the order of hundreds $\times\ 10^{-12}$ curie per m^3 corrected to October 10) extended from South Lancashire to London, with fairly high activities along the south coast of England. The filter at Harrow showed that the cloud first reached the vicinity of London shortly before 1800 on October 11, that the peak activity occurred at 0200 the next day, and that the activity fell to 10 per cent of its peak value by 1200 on October 12. The cloud had moved northeast and had reached the southern Scandinavian countries by October 15–16.

Deposited activity was studied in two ways. One involved laboratory analyses of samples of grass, or grass and soil, from known locations. The other involved field surveys of the gamma dose rate from the deposited activity, using a gamma radiation monitor. The results were corrected for natural background radiation and for radiation from fallout produced by distant nuclear bomb tests. They were also corrected for radioactive decay between the times of emission and of measurement.

The highest activities, in the range 20–$30\mu c\ m^{-2}$, were found in the vicinity of the accident, as might be expected. The highest concentration of deposited I^{131} was found about 6 km downwind of Windscale, and the highest concentration of Cs^{137} was found about 1 km downwind. The isodose rate contours differed markedly from the idealized contours of Figure 4-9, meandering considerably and exhibiting several hot spots. One megacurie per square mile of 1-MeV energy gamma radiation at 3 ft above the ground produces a dose rate of about 7 r/hr. Thus, the highest dose rates corrected to the time of emission were of the order of a few roentgens per hour. This is much too low a dose rate to produce acute effects, but is obviously undesirable in terms of the philosophy that any radiation in excess of that occurring naturally should be avoided except under overriding circumstances.

Chamberlain[24] estimated a velocity of deposition of 0.3 to 0.4 cm sec^{-1}. This could be accounted for by sedimentation of graphite particles of about 8μ diameter or of uranium oxide particles of about 4μ diameter. However, judging from radioautographs of collected particles, little of the activity was associated with particles this large. Chamberlain suggested that a more likely mechanism was diffusion of vapor and particles to the ground. This might have been largely eddy diffusion, contact with surfaces being effected by molecular diffusion, coulomb attraction, or possibly even thermal forces. Impaction could not be an important mechanism for such small particles.

Chamberlain made theoretical estimates of the deposition of iodine, assuming that it was diffusion-controlled and that the adsorption or absorption at the ground was sufficiently rapid that the vapor pressure of iodine at the surface was zero. From the meteorological conditions over Lancashire and Yorkshire at the time of passage of the radioactive cloud, a deposition velocity of 0.8 cm sec^{-1} was calculated. This is not bad agreement with the estimated 0.3–0.4 cm sec^{-1} mentioned above, considering the assumptions and estimates that were required.

It is rather interesting, from the standpoint of using the Windscale experience to predict the possible result of other similar accidents, that washout by rain may have contributed to the deposition in some localities. Rainfall which Chamberlain described as "patchy" occurred in northwest England during the 24-hour period 0900 on October 10 to 0900 on October 11. Such rain might be expected to have scrubbed out the iodine vapor but not the very small radioactive particles unless they attained higher altitudes than seems likely and became mixed with the rain clouds, or the rain clouds were unusually low. It was not possible to establish a correlation between the occurrence of rain and the concentration of deposited activity, which may indicate that the rain under these conditions was not an especially effective scrubbing agent.

THE FATE OF DEPOSITED FALLOUT

Once fallout has been deposited, its fate depends on many factors, and very important among these factors is particle size. If the particles are quite small, less than a few microns in diameter, they are apt to cling tenaciously to the surface on which they were deposited, whereas large particles may be relatively easily removed. However, once small particles have been re-entrained in air or in water, they may remain in suspension and be carried for long distances before they are redeposited. The degree of fractionation may vary with particle size, in which case the rate of decay of radioactivity will also vary with particle size. Extraction of radioisotopes from particles by rainwater will be more rapid for smaller particles because of the greater surface to mass ratio, and for the same reason small radioactive particles will dissolve more rapidly than larger particles of the same composition.

The other factors that might affect the history of deposited fallout are innumerable, but important ones include the nature of the surface on which the particles are deposited, the degree of exposure of the deposited particles to wind and rain, the chemical nature of the particles (for example, whether or not they are chemically attacked by carbonic acid in rainwater), the physical nature of the particles (for example, solubility and porosity), whether they are deposited on foodstuffs, and whether they are recognized by man as being undesirable and are subject to decontamination procedures.

REFERENCES

1. Glasstone, S., "The Effects of Nuclear Weapons," revised Ed., U. S. Atomic Energy Commission, April, 1962.
2. Glasstone, S., "Sourcebook on Atomic Energy," New York, Van Nostrand, 1950.
3. Fowler, J. M., Ed., "Fallout," New York, Basic Books, 1960.
4. Hunter, H. F., and Ballou, N. E., *Nucleonics,* 9, No. 5, C2 (1951).
5. Moteff, J., *Nucleonics,* 13, No. 5, 28 (1955).
6. Nelms, A., and Cooper, J. W., *Health Phys.,* 1, 427 (1959).
7. Björnerstedt, R., *Arkiv Fysik,* 16, 293 (1959).
8. Freiling, E. C., in "Radioactive Fallout from Nuclear Weapons Tests," TID-7632, U. S. Atomic Energy Commission, 1962.
9. Magee, J. L., "Mechanism of Fractionation," U. S. Atomic Energy Report M-7140, 1953.
10. Stewart, K., *Trans. Faraday Soc.,* 52, 161 (1956).
11. Björnerstedt, R., and Edvarson, K., *Ann. Rev. Nuclear Science,* 13, 505 (1963).
12. Adams, C. E., Farlow, N. H., and Schell, W. R., *Geochim. et Cosmochim. Acta,* 18, 42 (1960).
13. Cadle, R. D., Wilder, A. G., and Schadt, C. F., *Science,* 118, 490 (1953).
14. Cadle, R. D., *Anal. Chem.,* 23, 196 (1951).
15. Freiling, E. C., *Science,* 133, 1991 (1961).
16. Sisefsky, J., *Brit. J. Appl. Phys.,* 10, 526 (1959).
17. Sisefsky, J., *Science,* 133, 735 (1961).
18. Penn, S., and Martell, E. A., *J. Geophys. Res.,* 68, 4195 (1963).
19. Reiter, E. R., *J. Geophys. Res.,* 69, 786 (1964).
20. Machta, L., List, R. J., and Telegadas, K., *J. Geophys. Res.,* 69, 791 (1964).
21. Martell, E. A., *Science,* 143, 126 (1964).
22. Goeckermann, R. H., in "Proceedings of the Second Plowshare Symposium," Univ. of Calif. Report UCRL-5675, 1959.
23. Nordyke, M. D., *J. Geophys. Res.,* 66, 3439 (1961).
24. Chamberlain, A. C., *Quart. J. Roy. Meteor. Soc.,* 85, 350 (1959).
25. Crabtree, J., *Quart. J. Roy. Meteor. Soc.,* 85, 362 (1959).

26. Penney, Sir William, "Report of Committee on Investigation; Accident at Windscale," H. M. S. O. Cmnd. 302, 1957.
27. Hess, W. N., and Nordyke, M. D., *J. Geophys. Res.,* **66**, 3405 (1961).
28. Kellogg, W. W., in "The Nature of Radioactive Fallout and Its Effects on Man," Hearings before the Special Subcommittee on Radiation, Congress of the United States, U. S. Government Printing Office, 1957.
29. Fallout Symposium, Armed Forces Special Weapons Project Report 895, January, 1955 (Secret, R. D.).
30. Training Manual for Computing and Coding Civil Defense Fallout Winds, U. S. Weather Bureau, Washington, D. C., April, 1955.
31. Ferber, G. J., and Heffter, J. L., in "Radioactive Fallout from Nuclear Weapons Tests," Proceedings of a conference held in Germantown, Md., November, 1961, Office of Technical Services, Washington, D. C., 1962.
32. Small, S. H., *Tellus,* **12**, 308 (1960).
33. Martell, E. A., *Science,* **129**, 1197 (1959).
34. Blok, J., "Radioaktieve Besmetting van die Biodfeer in Nederland," Academisch Proefschrift, Vrije Universiteit te Amsterdam, 1957.
35. Hinzpeter, M., in "United Nations—Peaceful Uses of Atomic Energy," Proceedings of the Second International Conference, Vol. 18, p. 285, Geneva, 1958.
36. Dingle, A. N., in "Radioactive Fallout from Nuclear Weapons Tests," Proceedings of a conference held in Germantown, Md., November, 1961, Office of Technical Services, Washington, D. C., 1962.
37. Greenfield, S. M., *J. Meteor.,* **14**, 115 (1957).
38. Dingle, A. N., and Gatz, D. F., "Rain Scavenging of Particulate Matter from the Atmosphere," Contract No. AT(11-1)-739, The University of Michigan, College of Engineering, September, 1963.
39. Gatz, D. F., and Dingle, A. N., "Air Cleansing by Convective Storms," Presented at the Second Conference held in Germantown, Md., on Radioactive Fallout from Nuclear Weapons Tests, in November, 1964.
40. Kalkstein, M. I., Drevinsky, P. J., Martell, E. A., Chagnon, C. W., Manson, J. E., and Junge, C. E., "Natural Aerosols and Nuclear Debris Studies," Progress Report II, GRD Research Notes, No. 24, 1959.
41. Junge, C. E., "Air Chemistry and Radioactivity," New York, Academic Press, 1963.
42. Rosinski, J., and Stockham, J., "Preliminary Studies of Scavenging Systems Related to Radioactive Fallout," Summary Report ARF 3127-12, Armour Research Foundation, Contract No. AT(11-1)-626 (1960).
43. Dobson, G. M. B., *Proc. Roy. Soc.,* **A236**, 187 (1956).
44. Brewer, A. W., *Quart. J. Roy. Meteorol. Soc.,* **75**, 351 (1949).
45. Drevinsky, P. J., and Martell, E. A., in "Radioactive Fallout from Nuclear Weapons Tests," Proceedings of a conference held in Germantown, Md., November, 1961, Office of Technical Services, Washington, D. C., 1962.
46. Cadle, R. D., and Thuman, W. C., *Ind. Eng. Chem.,* **52**, 315 (1960).
47. Junge, C. E., Chagnon, C. W., and Manson, J. E., *J. Meteorol.,* **18**, 81 (1961).
48. Junge, C. E., *J. Meteorol.,* **18**, 501 (1961).
49. Chagnon, C. W., and Junge, C. E., *J. Meteorol.,* **18**, 746 (1961).
50. Manson, J. E., Junge, C. E., and Chagnon, C. W., in "Proceedings of the International Symposium on Chemical Reactions in the Lower and Upper Atmosphere," April 18–20, 1961, New York, Interscience, 1961.

51. Martell, E. A., Paper presented at CACR Symposium on Atmospheric Chemistry, Circulation, and Aerosols, Visby, Sweden, August 18–25, 1965.
52. Manson, J. E., in "Radioactive Fallout from Nuclear Weapons Tests," Proceedings of a conference held in Germantown, Md., November, 1961, Office of Technical Services, Washington, D. C., 1962.
53. Zebel, G., *Kolloid-Z.*, **196**, 102 (1958).
54. Libby, W. F., *Proc. U. S. Nat. Acad. Sci.,* **42**, 365, 945 (1956).
55. Miyake, Y., Saruhashi, K., Katsuragi, Y., and Kanazawa, T., *J. Geophys. Res.,* **67**, 189 (1962).
56. Machta, L., List, R. J., and Telegadas, K., in "Radioactive Fallout from Nuclear Weapons Tests," Proceedings of a conference held in Germantown, Md., November, 1961, Office of Technical Services, Washington, D. C., 1962.
57. Gustafson, P. F., Brar, S. S., and Kerrigan, M. A., *J. Geophys. Res.*, **67**, 4641 (1962).
58. Junge, C. E., *J. Geophys. Res.*, **68**, 3849 (1963).
59. Telegadas, K., and List, R. J., *J. Geophys. Res.*, **69**, 4741 (1964).
60. Orr, Jr., C., and Keng, E. Y. H., *J. Atmos. Sci.*, **21**, 475 (1964).
61. Rosen, M., and Orr, Jr., C., *J. Colloid. Sci.*, **19**, 50 (1964).
62. Schadt, C. F., and Cadle, R. D., *J. Phys. Chem.*, **65**, 1689 (1961).
63. Kalkstein, M. I., *J. Geophys. Res.*, **68**, 3835 (1963).
64. Kalkstein, M. I., *Science*, **137**, 645 (1962).
65. Kalkstein, M. I., Thomasian, A., and Nikula, J. V., "Cd[109] Results up to 20 Kilometers," Presented at the Second Conference held in Germantown, Md., on Radioactive Fallout from Nuclear Weapons Tests, in November, 1964.
66. Wexler, H., *Quart. J. Roy. Meteor. Soc.*, **85**, 196 (1959).

Chapter 5 Interplanetary Dust

THE ZODIACAL LIGHT

The zodiacal light, as a subjective experience, is a phenomenon which is especially pronounced in the tropics. It is usually seen for a few hours starting about an hour after sunset and consists of a faint glow in the western sky. It is usually described as pyramid-shaped, the base of the pyramid resting on the horizon. It is about as bright as the Milky Way, and is brightest at the base, fading away toward the zenith (Figure 5-1). With the passage of a few hours after its first appearance, the tip of the pyramid sinks below the horizon. The term "zodiacal light" arises from the fact that the light extends along the zodiac which is the imaginary belt or direction in the sky along which the Sun, Moon, and major planets appear to travel.

A few hours before sunrise the zodiacal light reappears in the eastern sky. The faint tip appears first and the entire pyramid is evident about an hour before sunrise. With the continued passage of time the display might become brighter and more spectacular if it were not lost in the scattered light from the rising Sun. The evening exhibit is best seen in the spring when the zodiac is most nearly perpendicular to the horizon, while the early morning exhibit is best seen in the autumn.

The light has sometimes been seen to extend about 45° north of the Sun and presumably it also extended about 45° south. On very clear nights in the tropics the tips of the evening and morning pyramids overlap, forming the zodiacal band. A bright region, called the gegenschein; can then be seen just opposite the sun. Photometric measurements indicate that the zodiacal light may constitute as much as 30 per cent of the light of the sky on a clear, moonless night.

Two major schools of thought have developed concerning the origin of the zodiacal light. One holds that the zodiacal light originates in the Earth's atmosphere. However, nearly 300 years ago, Cassini observed that the position of the light was the same when it was seen from different locations, and concluded that it must be caused by the scattering of sunlight by extraterrestrial particles. The other school, which includes most

Figure 5-1. Photograph of the zodiacal light taken by Dr. D. E.
Blackwell. (*Courtesy of the Royal Astronomical Society*)

modern observers, holds that it is produced by the scattering of sunlight
by extraterrestrial particles, that these particles are part of the Sun's
atmosphere, which extends to the Earth and beyond, and that the zodiacal
light is part of the solar corona.

There is considerable evidence in support of the latter hypothesis. The
solar corona has been photographed during an eclipse from a high-flying
(30,000 ft) aircraft, and the corona was observed to extend 13.5° from the
Sun.[1] The zodiacal light has not been seen closer than 18° from the Sun.
Thus, there is a gap, though not a large one, based on actual observations.
However, as Blackwell[1] points out, the sky during an eclipse is much
brighter than on a moonlit night, and moonlight obliterates the zodiacal
light. When brightness of the zodiacal light and of the solar corona are
plotted against the angular distance from the Sun, the gap, of course,
occurs, but the lines on either side of the gap appear to be portions of the
same curve.

Probably also highly significant is the fact that the zodiacal light is more
nearly symmetrical about the plane of the orbit of Jupiter than about the
ecliptic (the apparent path of the Sun through the sky). Jupiter's orbit

lies at an angle of 1.3° to the ecliptic. Since Jupiter is the most massive planet, if the zodiacal light results from a cloud of extraterrestrial particles, the plane of symmetry of this cloud might be expected to correspond to the Jovian orbit. Thus, the evidence is strongly in favor of an extraterrestrial source rather than an atmospheric source for the zodiacal light.

At least two types of particles have been postulated as being the light scatterers. One of these is dust particles and the other is solar electrons. A very strong argument in favor of the electron theory states that the corona close to the sun does not exhibit the Fraunhofer lines of the solar spectrum. The absence of these lines can be explained as resulting from Doppler broadening produced by the rapid motions of electrons at very high temperatures. The temperatures would have to be of the order of a million degrees (C or F) which is sufficiently high to produce the required ionization. However, Fraunhofer lines appear at a relatively short distance from the solar disk and these lines are generally attributed to scattering by dust particles.

A question remains, however, as to whether both electrons and solid particles contribute to the zodiacal light. One of the strongest arguments for the existence of a component in the zodiacal light due to scattering by free electrons is the degree of polarization of the light.[2] When the airglow is eliminated and only the polarization of the zodiacal light is measured, the degree of polarization is about 19 percent at 60° from the Sun, and is about twice that which might be expected for light scattered by dust. This suggests that at least one half of the zodiacal light at this angular distance from the Sun is caused by electron scattering. The concentration of electrons necessary to produce this degree of polarization is in good agreement with concentrations estimated from the behavior of "whistlers." These are radio signals produced by lightning in the hemisphere opposite that in which the signals are received.

Ingham and Blackwell[1] reasoned that if the zodiacal light is caused by dust scattering alone, its spectrum would be identical with that of the solar disk, but if a large part of it is caused by electron scattering, Fraunhofer lines would not appear in the spectrum. Accordingly, they photographed the spectrum of the zodiacal light from the cosmic ray station at Chacaltoya in the Bolivian Andes, at 17,000 ft. Since Fraunhofer lines were found, they concluded that electron scattering can make only a small contribution.

A theoretical difficulty arises when we ascribe the zodiacal light to scattering of sunlight by dust. When a body revolves around a star such as the Sun, receives heat from it and radiates this heat into space, its distance from the star slowly decreases until the two collide. This is known as the Poynting-Robertson effect. The time in years required for such a body to fall into the Sun is given by the expression $7 \times 10^6 \, r\rho R^2$ where R is its initial distance in astronomical units, and r and ρ are the radius of the body in cm and the density in g/cm^3, respectively. A sphere of rock having a radius of 1 cm and initially orbiting the Sun at the distance of the Earth would fall into the Sun after about 20 million years. Thus, during the lifetime of the Earth, the region of the zodiacal light would have been swept free of small particles unless some mechanism exists to replenish them, some force counters that of the Poynting-Robertson effect, or both. Several investigators[3-5] have suggested that comets or asteroids disintegrate with sufficient rapidity to maintain the concentration of particles in the zodiacal cloud.

This problem has been investigated by Harwit.[6] His analysis indicated that comets cannot supply the required quantity of dust to the cloud since radiation pressure prevents most of the comet debris and its secondary collision products from entering closed orbits about the Sun. However, he emphasized that more observations on the emission rates of very short-period comets are needed before this conclusion can be considered to be established. Harwit's calculations showed that collisions among asteroids could provide sufficient particles, but that the injection rate must be extremely variable since most of the debris is produced by very rare collisions between very large asteroids.

Information concerning the sizes of the particles in the zodiacal cloud is almost vanishingly small. According to van de Hulst,[7] the size distribution must be large since diffraction rings are not observed, but it is possible to explain the observed brightness distribution with a fairly wide variety of assumptions about size distribution and particle albedo. Opik[8] has suggested that the particles cannot be smaller than a few tenths of a micron or they would be swept from the solar system by radiation pressure, and that the upper size limit must be of the order of 300μ radius, based on dynamical considerations. Largely on the basis of calculations by van de Hulst,[9] he suggests that the size distribution is represented by the equation

$$dN/dr = Cr^{-p} \tag{5.1}$$

where C and p are constants having values of about 10^{-20} and 2.8, respectively, dimensions being in cm. Opik also concludes that zodiacal dust is the most important source of extraterrestrial dust in the atmosphere, and that the mass influx from this source is more than 100 times greater than the total influx from meteorites. If this is so, most of the particles larger than 1μ radius collected by Junge and his co-workers in the stratosphere must have come from the zodiacal dust cloud. Opik sugʒests that the total annual influx of such particles over the entire Earth is about 250,000 tons. This can be compared with Pettersson's[10,11] estimate of 1.4×10^7 tons, and the Fiocco and Colombo[12] estimate of 2×10^7 tons.

Beard,[13] on the basis of light scattered by particles in the solar corona a few solar diameters from the Sun's disk, concluded that the smallest particles were a few microns in radius and that p in equation 5.1 is 2.5 or a little larger.

The size distribution of zodiacal particles has been investigated theoretically by Southworth.[14] He considered the problem from the standpoint of the Poynting-Robertson effect, assuming a steady-state zodiacal cloud for which a source of particles exists to replace the losses caused by the Poynting-Robertson effect. The distribution of the orbits of the injected particles determines the density distribution in the cloud. Southworth calculated the size distribution of particles in 5 of the 7 tails of the comet Arend-Roland, obtained by rough photographic photometry, assuming an albedo of 0.03. He used this value to estimate the amount contributed by all comets, assuming that ejection was uniformly distributed over the entire sunward hemisphere of the cometary nucleus. He arrived at a total contribution of 0.18 ton/sec and compared this with an estimate by Whipple[3] of 1 ton/sec required to maintain the zodiacal cloud. Southworth considers this satisfactory agreement. This conclusion disagrees with that reached by Harwit,[6] mentioned above.

Southworth also concluded that the distribution of sizes among the particles observed in the zodiacal cloud must be quite different from the distribution among the meteors, which are larger particles in the same volume of space. He states that whereas the total mass of small meteors exceeds that of large meteors, the mass associated with the larger zodiacal particles much exceeds that associated with the smaller ones. He estimates a mean diameter, d_{32}, of 30μ. He found that the size distribution of the dust particles ejected from comets into the zodiacal cloud agrees with results for the cloud itself.

Even now there is no unanimity among scientists concerning the source of the zodiacal light. Thus, Dauvillier[15] states that he considers the light to be the trace in space of the emission of electrons from the Sun on which cometary activity in part depends.

METEOROIDS AND METEORITES

A meteoroid may be defined as a small solid body in the solar system which becomes a meteor on entering the Earth's atmosphere. Thus, the particles responsible for the zodiacal light may be considered to be meteoroids, but the inverse is not necessarily true. The term "meteor" refers to all extraterrestrial bodies entering the atmosphere, and very small meteors (radii less than about 300μ) are often called micrometeorites. At times the latter term has been used to refer to all small meteoroids in space, but here the term "micrometeoroid" will be used to refer to such particles. The term "meteorite" is used to designate particles which reach the Earth's surface.

Until the development of rockets that could reach the Earth's upper atmosphere and beyond, meteoroid investigations were confined to terrestrial observations. Investigations from the Earth's surface have been of two types: optical (photographic) and radar. Both methods provide information concerning visual magnitude (from which the mass of individual meteors or micrometeoroids can be derived) and the meteor flux. With the advent of both unmanned and manned space vehicles, more complete knowledge of the meteoroids likely to be encountered by such vehicles has become of practical importance. Thus, various devices have been developed to be carried by rockets and to indicate the meteoroid flux and mass distribution. The microphone detector has been used extensively for this purpose. It is essentially a microphone consisting of a diaphragm, a piezoelectric crystal, and electronic amplification and storage equipment. A meteoroid striking the diaphragm produces an impulse the magnitude of which is related to the mass of the particle, the velocity of impact, and the position of the impact on the diaphragm surface. A second sensor is the wire grid detector, which consists of arrays of wires of known electrical resistance connected in parallel and monitored during flight for electrical conductivity. A meteoroid is detected if it severs a wire. The individual arrays may consist of thin enameled wire wound on flat bobbins. No information concerning mass is obtained using this technique. A third sensor is the membrane detector, which takes several forms. One consists of an aluminized "Mylar" film, a spherical glass light collection system, and a cadmium sulfide photoconductive element. When the film is punctured by a meteoroid, sunlight is focused on the photoconductive element. The magnitude of the resulting signal is a function of the size of the hole and the solar angle. Another variation is the pressure can. A membrane is stretched over the open side of a chamber (the "can"). The pressure in the can at launch time is 1 atm, so that it is pressurized with respect to the vacuum of "space." When the membrane is punctured, the rate of pressure drop or gas flow is determined to provide a measure of the size of the hole. Such detectors have been calibrated using stainless steel particles travelling at high velocity. The size of the hole seems to be quite close to the size of the particle, usually within a factor of 2.[16] A fourth sensor, the impact flash detector, is based on the small explosion, accompanied by a burst of light, which may occur when a meteoroid or micrometeoroid hits a solid surface. One form consists of an aluminized "Lucite" cone, the narrow end of which is connected to the window of a photomultiplier tube. Micrometeoroids striking the exposed aluminized surface penetrate the surface and the flash of light produces a pulse from the photo tube.

The results of studies using these techniques undertaken up to January, 1963 have been surveyed by Schmidt,[17] and results up to 1960 have been summarized and compared by Goettelman *et al.*[16] The former report lists 31 separate estimates of the annual mass influx of extraterrestrial particles to the Earth's surface.

Masses of meteorites can be estimated from photographic and radar measurements using the concept of visual magnitude (M_v), defined by the equation

$$M_v = 24.6 - 2.5 \log_{10} I \qquad (5.2)$$

where I is the visual intensity (ergs/sec). Methods are available for converting both photographic and radar data to estimates of the visual magnitude.[16] Theoretical and empirical considerations indicate that the mass of a meteor decreases by a factor of 100 per 5 magnitude steps. Then, using a value of 30 grams as corresponding to a visual magnitude of zero,[18] masses can be calculated from the values of M_v. Meteor flux data from three independent studies, arranged according to increasing order of visual magnitude, are shown in Table 5-1 taken from reference 16. The data shown in column three of the table were obtained by extrapolating the results of observations of large meteors.

Meteor flux data, such as those of Table 5-1, can be represented by a relationship of the form

$$N = Km^{-\alpha} \qquad (5.3)$$

where N is the number of particles per unit area per unit time, K and α are constants, and m is the particle mass. Numerous estimates of the value

TABLE 5-1. METEOR FLUX OBSERVATIONS[16]

Visual Magnitude (M_v)	Mass (gms)	Meteor Flux (meteors/meter sq/sec)		
		Photographic[20]	Radar[19]	Radar[21]
0	30	—	1.6×10^{-14}	2.8×10^{-15}
5	0.3	9×10^{-12}	1.6×10^{-12}	2.8×10^{-13}
10	3×10^{-3}	1.08×10^{-9}	1.6×10^{-10}	2.8×10^{-11}
15	3×10^{-5}	1.08×10^{-7}	1.6×10^{-8}	—

of α have been made and a value of one or very close to one is very common. Therefore, equation 5.3 can be expressed in the form

$$N = K/m \qquad (5.4)$$

The results shown in Table 5-1 demonstrate that the values of K vary markedly (by one or two orders of magnitude in the table), depending on the method of determining meteor flux and visual magnitude as well as on the relationship used to calculate meteor mass from visual magnitude.

Data relating to particles smaller than the meteors investigated by radar and photographic techniques have been obtained with the rocket-borne sensors described above. Most of this information was obtained using the microphone-type detector. The response of this type of detector is roughly a linear function of the momentum of the impacting micrometeoroid. The threshold momentum required before a response is indicated is determined experimentally prior to the rocket flight. The results obtained with a given microphone are reported as impacts by particles having a momentum greater than the threshold value. In order that the threshold mass be calculated from the threshold momentum, it is necessary to assume an impact velocity. The velocities of meteors as measured by photographic and radar techniques vary from about 10 to 75 km/sec and it is obvious that selection of a single value is a great oversimplification. However, such a simplification seems to be necessary and a value of 30 km/sec is often used. Histograms for cases observed vs. velocity are commonly bimodal, the highest of the modes being between 15 and 40 km/sec, so the selection of 30 km/sec seems reasonable.

Since microphones having various minimum response values were flown, data obtained with microphones can be used to determine the variation of flux with meteoroid mass. The analyses by Goettelman et al.[16] indicated a value for α in equation 5.3 of 0.63 for all of the flights studied and of unity for the Explorer I and Vanguard III flights, the latter two being selected on the basis of record performance and completeness of preflight calibration. These results cover a range of mass of 10^{-8} to 10^{-11} grams.

Hawkins[22] has also reviewed the subject of interplanetary debris near the Earth's surface, and included data for very large meteorites in his analysis. He has shown that stone and iron meteorites differ in their mass distribution.[23] The number of stone meteorites that fall on 1 km^2 of the Earth's surface during 1 year with mass greater than or equal to m was given by the equation

$$\log_{10} N = -0.73 - \log_{10} m \qquad (5.5)$$

The flux for iron meteorites is given by the equation

$$\log_{10} N = -3.51 - 0.7 \log_{10} m \tag{5.6}$$

Thus, the cumulative number of stoney meteorites varies with m^{-1} while the number of iron meteorites varies with $m^{-0.7}$. A summary of cumulative impacts for a very wide range of object mass is shown in Figure 5-2.

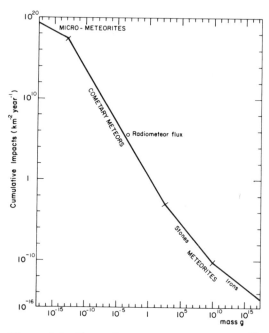

Figure 5-2. Flux of extraterrestrial objects.[22]
(*Courtesy of Annual Reviews, Inc.*)

Hawkins suggests that the difference between equations 5.5 and 5.6 yields information concerning the origin of the meteorites. Equation 5.5 is similar to that representing powders formed by crushing and grinding for long periods of time, while 5.6 is similar to that representing powders formed by more moderate crushing. If meteorites are fragments of asteroids formed by collisions in space, the more friable nature of the stones would subject them to a greater amount of crushing.

Particle sizes can only be deduced from the particle masses if the densities are known. The average density of the irons* is 7.8 gram cm^{-3}

---

*Actually the "iron" meteorites contain 3 to 15 per cent nickel.

and of the stones is 3.4 gram cm^{-3}. However, most of the extraterrestrial material consisting of objects with masses less than 100 grams seems to consist of particles ejected from comets. At least 50 per cent of these meteors are sporadic, are not associated with meteor streams (showers), and the flux can be represented by the equation:[24]

$$\log_{10} N = +0.41 - 1.34 \log_{10} m \qquad (5.7)$$

Cometary meteors appear to be very fragile and to have a very low density. Whipple[25] has estimated that the density of such objects having masses between about 1 and 100 grams is about 0.4 gram cm^{-3}. For these reasons many observers believe that cometary meteors are loose aggregates of small particles.

Micrometeoroids, the smallest of the extraterrestrial particles studied, have been collected by Hemenway and Soberman.[26] Their rocket, fired in June 1961, reached an altitude of 168 km. Particles were collected on various types of surfaces, and elaborate precautions were taken to avoid contamination and to recognize extraterrestrial particles. Three types of particles were collected. Some were loose aggregates and apparently were cometary meteoroids of the type mentioned above. Others were more compact and showed no signs of having been melted. The third type consisted of small spherules. Thus there was a wide range in density. Correcting for the vertical motion of the rocket and assuming a mean density of 3.0 gram cm^{-3}, the cumulative mass flux N could be represented by the expression[22, 26]

$$\log_{10} N = 12.43 - 0.39 \log_{10} m \qquad (5.8)$$

This equation held for particles with diameters as large as 2.5μ, corresponding to a mass of 10^{-13} gram, which suggests that the regime of cometary meteoroids extends to masses as small as 10^{-13} gram.

The particles were analyzed by neutron activation and the electron-probe technique. These showed the presence of Al, Si, Fe, Ni, Ti, Ca, Mg, and Cu, but relative abundance could not be assigned. Electron diffraction techniques failed to reveal crystal patterns for the majority of the meteoroids, so they were probably of a microcrystalline nature. When such particles were vaporized with the electron beam and recondensed, they produced a diffraction pattern which corresponded to three possible crystal structures: austenite, copper, and taenite. The latter is a constituent of large meteorites.

Goettelman *et al.*[16] have proposed that it is useful, from the standpoint of evaluating the hazards to space vehicles from meteoroids, to classify the flux of meteoroids into three types or models. The first is a continuous particle field with no time variation of flux, except, of course, for very short times representing minor fluctuations in the particle field. This type represents the long-period loading conditions for a space vehicle. The second type consists of meteor "streams" or "showers" which can be represented in model form as idealized discrete clouds. The third is an altitude-dependent modification of the continuous-particle-field model in the form of a meteoroid belt surrounding the Earth to an altitude of about 4000 km. The existence of such a belt has also been postulated by Whipple.[27]

The problem of applying data such as those described above has been reviewed by Hawkins[22] and by Whipple.[25] A fair estimate of the hazards from meteoroids which might be encountered in space travel can be made by combining the above data with quantitative expressions representing our current knowledge of cratering and penetration. Thus, Hawkins[22] referred to work by Herrmann and Jones[28] which showed that the depth x of a crater formed in a semi-infinite surface by a projectile of mass m is given by the semiempirical equation

$$x = 1.70m^{1/3}\rho^{1/3}\rho_t^{2/3}\log_{10}(1 + 0.25\rho^{2/3}\rho_t^{1/3}v^2H^{-1}) \tag{5.9}$$

where ρ is the density of the projectile, ρ_t is the density of the target, v is the impact velocity, H is the Brunell hardness, and the units are in the cgs system. According to Whipple,[25] a plate will not be punctured if the plate thickness exceeds $1.5\,x$. The uncertainty in estimating hazards to space vehicles from meteoroids is emphasized by Whipple's statement to the effect that the calculated perforation rate for a 0.1-cm thick plate of aluminum in the vicinity of the Earth was reduced by a factor of 3000 between 1957 and 1963. This change is in part the result of the accumulation of additional data concerning meteoroids and in part the result of improvements in the impact formula. Whipple's best estimate of the flux of meteoroids moving randomly in space and able to perforate a thin aluminum skin of thickness P is given by the equation

$$\log_{10} N = -4.02 \log_{10} P - 13.33 \tag{5.10}$$

The dimensions of N are $m^{-2} sec^{-1}$ and the dimension of P is cm. This equation should obviously not be taken very seriously, and to emphasize this Whipple has suggested a pessimistic equation:

$$\log_{10} N = -4.02 \log_{10} P - 12.12 \tag{5.11}$$

and an optimistic equation:

$$\log_{10} N = -3 \log_{10} P - 12.94 \tag{5.12}$$

The artificial satellite Explorer XVI was designed to assess the magnitude of the meteoroid hazard to present and future spacecraft, especially when operating near the Earth. One of the experiments aboard this satellite involved exposing stainless-steel surfaces to determine whether such surfaces are penetrated by micrometeoroids.[29]   Stainless steel, AISA 304, was selected for exposure because of the general interest in austenitic stainless steel for space vehicles. Three thicknesses were selected, namely, 0.001, 0.003, and 0.006 in., and the corresponding areas covered were 1.50, 2.00, and 0.25 ft^2.

The areas were selected on the following basis. The thinnest section had an area which provided a high probability of recording at least one penetration in about two weeks. The 2 ft^2 area was selected to give a high probability of at least one penetration if the experiment lasted 6 months. Penetration of the thickest surface was considered unlikely unless a meteoroid shower of great magnitude was encountered.

A very fine gold grid which had electrical continuity was used to detect penetration of the stainless steel. The grid was bonded to a dielectric material which in turn was bonded to the unexposed surface of the stainless steel. A micrometeoroid penetrating the metal surface over the grid broke the grid and destroyed its electrical continuity. Such an event was telemetered to stations on the ground. The three surfaces were divided into smaller segments each of which was monitored by a sensor.

Explorer XVI was launched from Wallops Island, Virginia on December 16, 1962. Perigee was about 750 km and apogee was 1180 km. Up to May 29, 1963, 6 penetrations of the thinnest surface, 1 penetration of the next thickest surface, and no penetrations of the thickest surface were recorded. The results were found to be consistent with mass flux distributions proposed by Watson[30] and penetration criteria of Summers.[31]

Another experiment on the same satellite involved 160 semicylindrical cans that were stacked in rows around the last stage.[32-34] The cans were filled with helium, and a change in pressure following puncture by a micrometeoroid actuated a microswitch. The number of switches open was telemetered to ground stations. The cans were made of a copper-beryllium alloy with thicknesses of 0.001, 0.002, and 0.005 in. Usable data were obtained for only the first two thicknesses. The data were used to estimate the flux of particles R able to produce punctures. The relationship between R and the rate of puncturing, dn/dt is

$$dn/dt = R(A_0 - nA) \qquad (5.13)$$

where A_0 is the initial exposed area of all cans and A is the area of one can.

Upon integration this becomes

$$n = \frac{A_0}{A}(1 - e^{-ARt}) \tag{5.14}$$

By means of these equations it was shown that a flux of 1.18×10^8 km^{-2} yr^{-1} corresponded to the 0.001-in. thickness and a flux of 6.68×10^7 km^{-2} yr^{-1} to the 0.002-in. thickness. Too few penetrations of the 0.005-in. thick cans occurred to permit a reliable estimate of flux for this thickness.

A schematic drawing of Explorer XVI is shown in Figure 5-3.

Hawkins[22] has compared these results with the Herrmann and Jones[28] equation (5.9) as follows. Hastings[32] states that a beryllium-copper sheet of 0.001-in. thickness is equivalent to aluminum of twice this thickness.

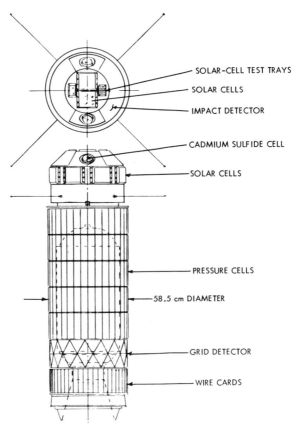

Figure 5-3. Schematic drawing of Explorer XVI (1962 Beta Chi I) Satellite. (*Courtesy NASA*)

On this basis equation 5.9 predicts that penetration of the 0.001-in. beryllium-copper should be effected by particles of mass $\geq 10^{-8}$ gram. By equating the above values for flux with the meteoroid rates of Figure 5-2, the masses of the meteoroids responsible for the puncturing can be estimated. These are 1.91×10^{-6} gram or greater and 2.93×10^{-6} gram or greater for the 0.001 and 0.002-in. thick metal, respectively. Therefore, the Herrmann and Jones[28] equation greatly overestimates the penetrating capabilities of such micrometeoroids. This is not surprising if the particles are of low density and rather fluffy, as is generally believed. Such particles would tend to splatter over the metal surface. A similar discrepancy is seen by comparing the Explorer XVI results with equation 5.10 which is based on 5.9.

The pressurized-can experiment also provided information concerning the effects of meteor streams. The experiment started during the final phases of the Geminid stream and lasted throughout the Quadrantid stream on January 3. The puncturing rate did not increase noticeably during these periods, which indicates that the effects of major meteor streams is very small. This agrees with radio records which suggest that the flux of small meteors is affected by the presence of meteor streams to a much smaller extent than the flux of large meteors.

Rates of penetration calculated from results of the beryllium can experiment were consistent with those calculated from the results of the stainless-steel experiment.[29,34]

The periscope lenses of the Project Mercury vehicles have provided an opportunity for the direct examination of cosmic dust impact sites. Numerous craters were found which may have been the sites of micrometeoroid impact.[35]

Information concerning small particles in interplanetary space was obtained with Mariner II and Mariner IV. The Mariner IV measurements indicated an increasing flux as the heliocentric distance from the Sun increased and Mars was approached. Near Earth and Mars, the flux varied as a function of $m^{-0.55}$ while between the planets it varied as $m^{-0.9}$. No statistically significant evidence of dust-particle streams was found with Mariner IV, and there was no measurable enhancement of the flux in the vicinity of Mars.

The Mariner IV detectors counted particles for which the momentum exceeded 1.96×10^{-3} dyne sec. At heliocentric distances between 1 and 1.25 astronomical units (AU), the cumulative flux was 7.3×10^{-5} particle $m^{-2} sec^{-1} (\pi \, steradian)^{-1}$. The flux reached a peak of 3.3×10^{-4} particle $m^{-2} sec^{-1} (\pi \, steradian)^{-1}$ between 1.36 and 1.43 AU and decreased to 1.8×10^{-4} particle $m^{-2} sec^{-1} (\pi \, steradian)^{-1}$ in the vicinity of Mars. The maximum flux was at a heliocentric distance approximately equal to the perihelion distance of Mars (1.38 AU).

Only two impacts were recorded by Mariner II, between 0.72 and 1.25 AU. The Mariner IV results indicated that 3 ± 2 impacts could have been expected from the Mariner II measurement, so the results were consistent.

Part of our knowledge concerning meteoroids has been obtained by examination of material collected at or beneath the Earth's surface. Collections have been made from soil, ocean sediments, snow, and glacial ice. The technique usually involves collecting samples, as of sediments, of known age or location, separating magnetic spherules found in the samples, and investigating the nature and concentration of the spherules. It is generally assumed that such spheres are of extraterrestrial origin. One such study, undertaken by the Lamont Geological Institute of Columbia University, has been described by Cassidy.[36] The spherules were obtained from ocean sediments "well below the modern ocean floor" and thus could be assumed to be free of modern technological contamination. A photomicrograph of a few of the spherules is shown in Figure 5-4. The spherules were analyzed by nondestructive neutron-activation analysis and the results compared with similar analyses of particles of three other types: (a) spherules collected in plankton nets, (b) spherules from soot and smoke, presumably "fly ash," and (c) welding beads. The primary purpose of this study was to establish criteria for distinguishing between natural and artificial spherules. A second purpose was to determine whether useful data concerning composition could be obtained by nondestructive neutron activation of the natural spherules. The results indicated that the method can be used to differentiate natural spherules from some types of man-made spherules but not from iron spherules of artificial origin.

Even when the natural origin of collected spherules has been established the possibility that they are of volcanic rather than of extraterrestrial origin must be considered. This possibility has been discussed in a series of papers by Wright and Hodge.[37-40] They found that magnetic spheres in the size range 10 to 100μ are produced by various types of volcanoes. However, the composition of such spherules from both ancient and very recent eruptions usually differed markedly from that of spheres found in polar-ice sediments and presumed to be of extraterrestrial origin. Furthermore, they found that the numerical ratio of spherules to irregular particles for the volcanic dust differed greatly from that for the ice sediments.

Information concerning the nature and origin of spherules of extraterrestrial origin has been obtained from scattered meteoritic matter in the vicinity of the fall of a large meteorite. An example is the Sikhote-Alin

Figure 5-4. Natural magnetic spherules recovered
from ocean-bottom core.   Diameter of largest
spherule was 150μ. (*Courtesy New York Academy
of Sciences*)

iron meteorite which was studied by Krinov,[41] and was actually a shower
of meteorites which fell in the coastal region of Sikhote-Alin, USSR, on
February 12, 1947. The shower of meteorites was caused by disruption of
the single original meteoroid as it passed through the atmosphere. Most
of the small particles were highly angular and irregular in shape. A small
fraction consisted of spheres of nearly spherical particles. A very few
magnetic particles had a complete fusion crust. However, most of the
spherules had smooth surfaces. Their diameters varied from 4μ to
0.7 mm. Some of the spherules were hollow or porous and many were
grooved. Some particles were described as having shapes like droplets,
that is, they were roughly oval and had a pointed tail, while others were
described as being like flasks in that they were hollow with spheroidal
shapes and had grooved necks leading outside.

Another meteorite fall, that of the Tunguska meteorite, has been described by Kirova.[42] It fell on Siberia on June 30, 1908, exploding while passing through the Earth's atmosphere. In 1958, soil samples were collected throughout an area where the forest had been destroyed by the explosion. The samples were separated into magnetic and nonmagnetic fractions, and particles which apparently were of meteoritic origin were found in each fraction. The magnetic material contained magnetite, hematite, leucoxine, and, rarely, magnetite spherules. Silicate spherules and other forms that appeared to consist of fused silicates were separated from the nonmagnetic fractions. Transition forms between the magnetic and nonmagnetic spherules were observed, including dark silicate spherules with magnetite inclusions. Kirova concluded that the siliceous and magnetic spherules were formed from a heterogeneous meteoroid and stated that it had been established that the Tunguska meteorite represented the nucleus of a small comet.[43] He concluded that the nucleus contained particles of both magnetic and nonmagnetic material. However, Kirova does not seem to have eliminated the possibility that some or all of the nonmagnetic particles were formed from soil in much the manner that silicate spherules are formed by a surface or underground nuclear explosion.

Fechtig and Utech[44] state that there is evidence that spherules of extraterrestrial origin have been deposited on the Earth throughout all geological ages. However, spherules in Tertiary and older sediments contain little or no nickel, and the presence of nickel has been used as a criterion of extraterrestrial origin. They concluded that the ancient spherules once contained a nickel-iron core and that it had slowly been dissolved. They studied polished thin sections of spherules from deep-sea sediments of Quaternary age and found a brown zone surrounding the nickel-iron nucleus which they believe represents the first stage of core dissolution. They also point out that modern cosmic spherules do not necessarily contain a nickel-iron nucleus.

The origin of the spheroids is generally believed to be the melting of meteorites entering the atmosphere and the sweeping off the surface of droplets which harden to form the spheroids.

A few particles of extraterrestrial origin have been obtained with recoverable sounding rockets, particularly using the collection device known as the Venus Fly Trap (Figure 5-5). The particles were almost all of submicron size. Most were irregular in shape and only a small proportion were fluffy or spherical.[26]

The origin of meteoroids has been reviewed by Dauvillier.[15] He concludes that the meteorites are of recent origin and that there are no fossil meteorites, although this is certainly a controversial opinion. It cannot be

Figure 5-5. Venus Fly Trap nose cone. (*Courtesy of AFCRL*)

correct if spheroids have the origin indicated above and have been deposited on the Earth's surface during much of its lifetime. Nonetheless, it is commonly believed that meteorites are remnants of the planet or planets that broke up to form the asteroids. The large fragments become asteroids while the oribits of the smaller ones have been perturbed and fall to the surface of the Earth. Micrometeoroids may have quite a different origin. It is likely that they are the remnants of comets and first existed as the dusty tails of comets. Perhaps the most convincing evidence of this is that comets have been known to break up, following which meteor showers have occurred when the Earth intercepted the cometary orbit. For example, in 1872 the "lost" double comet Biela was expected to pass near the Earth. Instead, a shower of meteors occurred. Dauvillier[15] has suggested that comets are asteroids whose orbits have been perturbed by Jupiter. If this is so, the origin of micrometeoroids and meteorites may not be much different after all.

TEKTITES

Tektites are glassy objects that may be of extraterrestrial origin. Some are in the size range considered in this book while others are larger, and may be as much as 10 cm in diameter. They generally have rounded rather than angular shapes and their appearance suggests that they were molten while suspended in space or in the air. They are found in only a few regions on the Earth's surface, such as Australia and the region surrounding the South China Sea.[45]

The tektites are silicates and contain between 68 and 80 per cent silicon calculated as SiO_2. They also contain aluminum and smaller amounts of iron, calcium, sodium, and other metals. The composition is similar to, but not identical to, many continental rocks. Perhaps the most striking difference between tektites and common rock is the large difference in water content, that of the tektites being remarkably low. Except for water adsorbed on the surfaces, the content is usually less than 0.05 per cent and averages about 0.005 per cent. Friedman[46] states that the small percentage of water makes it very likely that tektites were melted either in an environment in which the partial pressure of water vapor was very low, or the tektites were heated to above about 2000°C.

The concentrations of minor constituents of tektites have been studied extensively. The concentrations of vanadium, titanium, chromium, zirconium, manganese, and strontium are similar for tektites and continental rocks while those of nickel, copper, tin, and lead are lower in tektites. This subject has been reviewed by Mason.[47]

Most tektites are black and nearly opaque, although thin flakes are transparent or translucent. A type of tektite known as a moldavite is green by transmitted light, and a few tektites are yellow. The densities are remarkably uniform, between 2.3 and 2.5. The electrical resistivity and viscosity of tektite glass has been investigated by Hoyte, Senftle, and Wirtz.[48] The viscosities of a number of tektites varied by about 2 orders of magnitude.

Several attempts have been made to determine the length of time tektites may have spent in space. This information would be useful in establishing whether they are of extraterrestrial origin and the distance from which they have come. Reynolds[49] concluded from a study of rare gases in two samples that the upper limits of exposure time were 28,000 years and 40,000 years. Viste and Anders[50] suggested an upper limit of 90,000 years for the average cosmic ray exposure age of more than 70 tektites. Fleischer et al.[51] made use of the fact that damage regions created along the paths of fission fragments in tektites may be made visible by chemical attack. They concluded that tektites exposed to primary cosmic radiation will contain induced-fission tracks, a large fraction of which will survive the heating that occurs as the tektites pass through the Earth's atmosphere (assuming an extraterrestrial origin). No such tracks were found although tektites from several groups were examined, indicating a probable cosmic ray exposure age of less than 300 years.

A similar technique has been used to determine tektite ages.[52, 53] The tracks are those produced by the spontaneous fission of uranium 238. The times since the tektites were last molten were about 34 million years for North American tektites, 14 million years for Czechoslovakian tektites, and 700,000 years for Eastern tektites. Rubidium-strontium isotope ratios indicate that a few hundred million years have elapsed since the tektite material was separated from its source.

The ratios of certain isotopes in tektites are remarkably constant.[45] For instance, there is little variation in the ratios of oxygen 18 to oxygen 16 and of strontium 87 to strontium 86 in tektites from different regions.

The origin of tektites remains a mystery. As implied above, it is by no means certain that their origin is extraterrestrial. Numerous suggestions have been made concerning their origin. When lightning strikes the ground, it may fuse the soil, often producing dendritic forms, and this has been a suggested origin. However, the fused material only superficially resembles tektites. Volcanic activity has been suggested but can be dismissed if for no reason other than that volcanoes have never been known to produce tektites.

Some Philippine tektites contain small metallic spheres consisting of iron and a few per cent of nickel. This alloy is found in iron meteorites but not in other natural material found on Earth. This strongly suggests a meteoritic origin for tektites and this possibility has often been analyzed. One theory is that very large meteorites struck the Earth, fusing the soil and throwing out molten material which hardened as it flew through the air to form tektites.[54-56] This explains the occurrence of tektites in strewn fields, but material known to have been thrown out by meteorites differs markedly in many respects from tektites. Urey[57] suggested that they are formed when a comet intercepts the Earth's atmosphere. This would produce a shock wave which would melt and scatter large amounts of rock when it reached the Earth's surface. A major difficulty is that this mechanism would produce tektites that varied markedly in composition, depending upon the composition of the rocks from which they were formed.[47]

A number of hypotheses of extraterrestrial origin have been proposed. An extraterrestrial origin is attractive for a number of reasons, but particularly because the glass of the tektites seems to have been melted twice, once completely and again partially as the tektites passed through the Earth's atmosphere. It seems unlikely that they are meteorites or ablation products of meteorites, judging from their composition. Other suggestions are that they came from a disrupted planet-like body with a glassy surface layer, from comets, and from the Moon. For example, Chapman and Larson[58] estimated atmospheric entry trajectories from the amount of ablation, the distortion of striae, and the spacing between ring waves on australites. They concluded that the Moon is the only known celestial body which could have been the source of objects having these trajectories.

The meteorite impact theory probably remains the one most generally accepted. Arguments in favor of it have been reviewed and strengthened by Hawkins.[59]

REFERENCES

1. Blackwell, D. E., *Sci. Amer.*, **203**, No. 1, 54 (July, 1960).
2. van de Hulst, H. C., in "Vistas in Astronomy," A. Beer, Ed., London, Pergamon, 1956.
3. Whipple, F. L., *Astrophys. J.*, **121**, 750 (1955).
4. Piotrowski, S., *Acta Astron.*, A, **5**, 115 (1953).
5. Fesenkov, V. G., *Russian A. J.*, **24**, 39 (1947).
6. Harwit, M., *J. Geophys. Res.*, **68**, 2171 (1963).
7. van de Hulst, H. C., "Light Scattering by Small Particles," New York, Wiley, 1957.
8. Öpik, E. J., *Irish Astron. J.*, **4**, 84 (1957).
9. van de Hulst, H. C., *Astrophys. J.*, **105**, 471 (1947).
10. Pettersson, H., *Nature*, **181**, 330 (1958).
11. Pettersson, H., *Scientific American*, p. 123, February, 1960.
12. Fiocco, G., and Colombo, G., *J. Geophys. Res.*, **69**, 1795 (1964).
13. Beard, D. B., *Astrophys. J.*, **129**, 496 (1959).
14. Southworth, R. B., in "Cosmic Dust," H. E. Whipple, Ed., New York, New York Academy of Sciences, 1964.
15. Dauvillier, A., "Cosmic Dust," New York, Philosophical Library, 1964.
16. Goettelman, R. C., Softky, S. D., Arnold, J. S., and Farrand, W. B., "The Meteoroid and Cosmic-Ray Environment of Space Vehicles and Techniques for Measuring Parameters Affecting Them," Wright Air Development Division Technical Report TR 60-846, Wright-Patterson Air Force Base, Ohio, December, 1960.
17. Schmidt, R. A., "A Survey of Data on Microscopic Extraterrestrial Particles," Research Report Series 63-2, Geophysical and Polar Research Center, The University of Wisconsin, January, 1963.

18. Hawkins, G. S., *Astrophys. J.*, **128**, 727 (1958).
19. Manning, L. A., and Eshleman, V. R., Proceedings of the I. R. E., **47**, No. 2, (February 1959).
20. Whipple, F. L., in "Vistas in Astronomy," A. Beer, Ed., London, Pergamon, 1956.
21. Davis, J. G., *Nature*, **179**, 123 (January 19, 1957).
22. Hawkins, G. S., in "Annual Review of Astronomy and Astrophysics," L. Goldberg, Ed., Vol. 2, Palo Alto, Calif., Annual Reviews, Inc., 1964.
23. Hawkins, G. S., *Nature*, **197**, 781 (1963).
24. Hawkins, G. S., and Upton, E. K. L., *Astrophys. J.*, **128**, 727 (1958).
25. Whipple, F. L., *J. Geophys. Res.*, **68**, 4929 (1963).
26. Hemenway, C. L., and Soberman, R. K., *Astron. J.*, **67**, 256 (1962).
27. Whipple, F. L., *Nature*, **189**, 127 (1961).
28. Herrmann, H., and Jones, A. H., "Proc. Symp. Hypervelocity Impact Tri-service Committee, 5th," **1**, 389 (1962).
29. Davison, E. H., and Winslow, P. C., Jr., "Micrometeoroid Satellite (Explorer XVI) Stainless-Steel Penetration Rate Experiment," NASA TN D-2445, 1964.
30. Watson, F. G., "Between the Planets," Cambridge, Harvard Univ. Press, 1956.
31. Summers, J. L., "Investigations of High-Speed Impact: Regions of Impact and Impact at Oblique Angles," NASA TN D-94, 1959.
32. Hastings, E. C., Jr., "The Explorer XVI Micrometeoroid Satellite—Description and Preliminary Results for the Period December 16, 1962 through January 13, 1963," NASA TM X-810, 1963.
33. Hastings, E. C., Jr., "The Explorer XVI Micrometeoroid Satellite—Supplement I, Preliminary Results for the Period January 14, 1963 through March 2, 1963," NASA TM X-824, 1963.
34. Hastings, E. C., Jr., "The Explorer XVI Micrometeoroid Satellite—Supplement II—Preliminary Results for the Period March 3, 1963 through May 26, 1963," NASA TM X-899, 1963.
35. Hemenway, C. L., Linscott, I., Secretan, L., and Dubin, M., in "Cosmic Dust," H. E. Whipple, Ed., New York, New York Academy of Sciences, 1964.
36. Cassidy, W. A., in "Cosmic Dust," H. E. Whipple, Ed., New York, New York Academy of Sciences, 1964.
37. Wright, F. E., and Hodge, P. W., *J. Geophys. Res.*, **68**, 5575 (1963).
38. Hodge, P. W., and Wright, F. E., *J. Geophys. Res.*, **69**, 2449 (1964).
39. Hodge, P. W., and Wright, F. E., *J. Geophys. Res.*, **69**, 2919 (1964).
40. Wright, F. E., and Hodge, P. W., *J. Geophys. Res.*, **70**, 3889 (1965).
41. Krinov, E. L., in "Cosmic Dust," H. E. Whipple, Ed., New York, New York Academy of Sciences, 1964.
42. Kirova, O. A., in "Cosmic Dust," H. E. Whipple, Ed., New York, New York Academy of Sciences, 1964.
43. Fesenkov, V. G., *Meteoritika*, **20**, 27 (1961).
44. Fechtig, H., and Utech, K., in "Cosmic Dust," H. E. Whipple, Ed., New York, New York Academy of Sciences, 1964.
45. Glasstone, S., "Sourcebook on the Space Sciences," New York, Van Nostrand, 1965.
46. Friedman, I., *Geochim. et Cosmochim. Acta*, **14**, 316 (1958).
47. Mason, B., "Meteorites," New York, Wiley, 1962.
48. Hoyte, A., Senftle, F., and Wirtz, P., *J. Geophys. Res.*, **70**, 1985 (1965).

49. Reynolds, J. H., *Geochim. et Cosmochim. Acta*, **20**, 101 (1960).
50. Viste, E., and Anders, E., *J. Geophys. Res.*, **67**, 2913 (1962).
51. Fleischer, R. L., Naeser, C. W., Price, P. B., Walker, R. M., and Maurette, M., *J. Geophys. Res.*, **70**, 1491 (1965).
52. Fleischer, R. L., Price, P. B., and Walker, R. M., *Geochim. et Cosmochim. Acta*, **29**, 161 (1965).
53. Price, P. B., and Walker, R. M., *Phys. Rev. Letters*, **8**, 217 (1962).
54. Spencer, L. J., *Mineral Mag.*, **23**, 387 (1933).
55. Krinov, E. L., "Principles of Meteoritics," New York, Pergamon, 1960.
56. Barnes, V. E., *Scientific American*, **205**, No. 5, 58 (1961).
57. Urey, H. C., *Nature*, **179**, 556 (1957).
58. Chapman, D. R., and Larson, H. K., *J. Geophys. Res.*, **68**, 4305 (1963).
59. Hawkins, G. S., *J. Geophys. Res.*, **68**, 895 (1963).

Chapter 6 # The Moon

The Moon is our nearest celestial neighbor, the mean distance between the center of the Earth and that of the Moon being 238,857 miles. The Moon is unique as a planetary satellite in that the ratio of its mass to that of the Earth is greater than that of any other satellite to that of its primary planet. The center of mass of the Earth and Moon lies within the Earth, about 2900 miles from its center. The Moon's diameter is a little more than one-fourth that of the Earth. The Moon's albedo is low; only about 7 per cent of the light falling on its surface is reflected, the rest being absorbed. Since the Moon makes one revolution on its axis in the same time required for one revolution around the Earth, there is little variation with time in the portion of the Moon that can be observed from the Earth. However, since there are certain apparent rocking movements or librations, about 59 per cent of the Moon can be seen from the Earth. One type of libration results from the inclination of the Earth's equator to the plane of its orbit. Another results from the lack of uniformity in the rate of the Moon's revolution.

The lunar surface is covered with plains and highlands (Figure 6-1). The former are large dark regions that were once thought to be oceans and are called maria, but since there is little or no water on the Moon, these maria must be great plains. Many, but by no means all, of the mountains surround craters. Others seem to have a random orientation while still others appear to be set in a row.

The craters are much more common in the highlands than in the maria, and probably most of the craters were formed prior to the present surfaces of the maria. Some of the craters in the maria appear to be almost submerged, only the faint outlines being visible. Other craters in the maria give no indication of having been buried, and are probably of more recent origin than the maria. Some of the craters, particularly the larger ones, contain one or more peaks. The largest crater on the visible side of the Moon is Clavius, which has a diameter of 227 km. Many of the craters are little more than walled plains, since their diameters are large relative to the height of the crater walls. For such craters, the heights of the walls

Figure 6-1. Northern region of the Moon, Caucasus Mountains, including Alpine Valley. Age 8 days. (*Photo: Mount Wilson and Palomar Observatories*)

may be only 2 or 3 per cent of the distance across the interior plain. Photographs taken from the Ranger spacecrafts (such as Figures 6-2a and 6-2b) revealed the presence of craters as small as 50 cm in diameter. The number of craters of a given size has been found to increase with decrease in crater size.

ORIGIN OF THE MOON

Two aspects of particles on the Moon are of special scientific interest. One is the possibility that visible clouds, presumably consisting of gases and particles, have been observed to rise from mountains in craters (or at least from one mountain in one crater). This would suggest a volcanic origin for at least some of the mountains and craters. The other is the possibility that a layer of dust covers much of the Moon's surface. This would not only be an interesting phenomenon in itself, but might have an important influence on any "soft" landing of a space vehicle on the Moon, since the vehicle might be expected to sink into the dust. As will be explained later, such sinking is unlikely.

In order to formulate intelligent theories concerning the nature of the surface of the Moon and of the possibility that volcanoes exist or have existed, it is helpful to consider possible origins of the Moon. A possibility that has received much support is that the Moon consists of matter that was torn loose from the surface of the Earth early in its history. This theory seems reasonable since the density of the Moon is about that of the Earth's mantle rather than that of the Earth as a whole. While the origin of this theory is lost, George Darwin, the son of the famous Charles Darwin, is generally credited with first suggesting a reasonable mechanism for such a separation. He proposed that resonance occurs between the natural period of oscillation of the Earth and the period of the tides produced in the material of the Earth by the Sun.[1,2] This type of coupling has caused many disasters, such as that of the Tacoma Narrows bridge in which resonance between the natural period of oscillation of the bridge and wind gusts produced its collapse. According to this theory, the separation of the Moon from the Earth must have occurred after the Earth's mantle had separated from the core. Specifically, Darwin pointed out that if the Moon and Earth were combined, the angular momentum would require a 4-hour rotation period. The period of the solar tides would then be 2 hours, which is about the period of free oscillation of the Earth.

There are several difficulties with this theory. For instance, if the Earth had been solid, the resonance energy would have been rapidly dissipated into heat, and if the Earth had been liquid, it is questionable[2] whether it could have secured and maintained a high temperature. Nölke[3] found that a newly separated Moon would produce a tide that would cause the Moon to recombine with the Earth. Accordingly, Urey[2] concludes that the Moon could not have been formed by separation from the Earth.

An interesting variation of the fission theory has been proposed by Wise.[4] He assumed that just prior to the separation of the Moon, the Earth had a nearly homogeneous composition and was spinning so rapidly that a small increase in the centrifugal force resulting from an increased spin rate would produce separation of material in the equatorial region. On the basis of early work by Jeans, this should have occurred when the Earth had a period of rotation of about 2.65 hours. According to Wise' hypothesis, gravitational settling, coalescence, compaction, or collapse of the interior, forming the Earth's core, reduced the moment of inertia. In order that angular momentum be conserved, the rotational speed of the Earth had to increase by one-half hour, and this led to disruption and separation of the Moon from the Earth.

The shapes that the Earth would assume during the period of instability are an important part of this theory. The shape for low spin rates is an

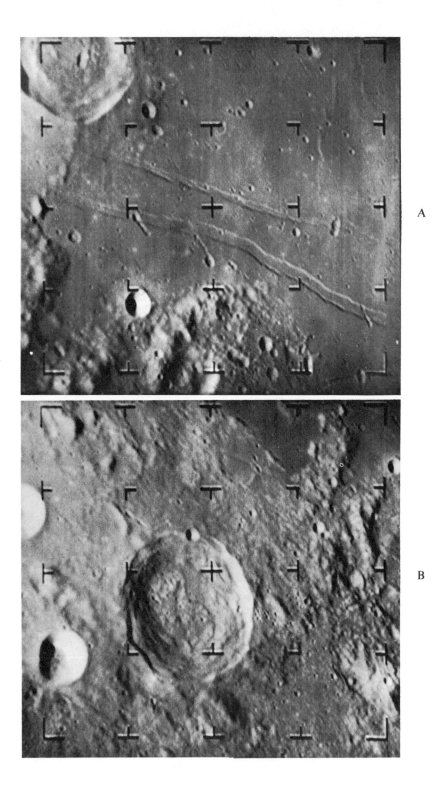

A

B

oblate spheroid, much like the present shape. As the spin increases, the spheroid flattens until rotation becomes unstable, whereupon a cigar shape (triaxial ellipsoid) is attained. The Earth then spins on its short axis and one end forms a neck to produce a dumbbell-shaped object, a Poincare figure. Eventually the neck pinches off to release the Moon. The Earth would then return to a stable form, presumably an oblate spheroid. Pinching off the Moon would also produce a number of fragments that eventually would fall into the Moon or the Earth.

Wise' theory does not require a molten Earth, merely a plastic Earth, and there is much evidence which demonstrates that the material comprising the Earth does flow when subjected to very large forces for very long periods of time. Wise states that the strongest argument against Darwin's proposal and Wise' modification is that at present there is too little kinetic energy and angular momentum in the Earth-Moon system. He presents evidence which suggests that this criticism is itself on rather weak ground.

Another theory or class of theories has been called the double-planet origin. One form assumes that the Earth and Moon first existed as a gaseous mass called a protoplanet that was formed from material that originally was part of the solar nebula. As the hot protoplanet cooled, iron would condense first, accounting for the formation of the Earth's core. The Earth and Moon are assumed to have formed separately from the protoplanet. The major difficulty with this theory is to account for the difference in density of the Earth and the Moon. If the latter formed after the iron had condensed and agglomerated to form the Earth's core, it is difficult to explain why the gases of higher molecular and atomic weight than helium are so scarce in the Earth and its atmosphere.[2,5]

Another variation of this hypothesis is that the Earth and Moon were formed from the same swarm of solid material. This does not account for the density difference.

A third theory is that the Moon was formed in the solar system separately from the Earth and later was captured. Urey[2] subscribes to this theory and suggests that the Moon is a more primitive object than the terrestrial planets. He also suggests that the composition of the Moon is similar to that of the Sun and to that of the original solids in the primitive

Figure 6-2. Television pictures taken by Ranger VIII on February 20, 1965. Figure 6-2A taken 4 minutes before impact. North is at the top when the shadows are at the left of the craters. The Sabine crater is in the northwest corner. The two parallel rills may be similar to terrestrial grabens. Dimensions are about 58 by 43 miles. Figure 6-2B taken about 7 minutes before impact. Delambra, 32 miles in diameter, is near the center of the photograph.

dust cloud. An interesting modification of this idea is that the Moon once came very close to the Earth. A portion was torn loose, falling to the Earth and eventually forming the continents.[6] The Moon then gradually receded to its present distance.

None of these suggestions is particularly satisfactory, and during the last few years there has been increasing speculation that Darwin's tidal theory is essentially correct after all.

THE LUNAR SURFACE FEATURES

The most distinctive lunar surface features are the craters. There are numerous theories as to their origin, but two have received the most attention. These are that the craters have resulted from collisions of meteoroids with the Moon's surface and that the craters resulted from volcanic activity.

The large lunar craters bear a superficial resemblance to volcanic craters of the caldera type. Such calderas have generally been formed at the summit of a volcanic edifice by collapse following withdrawal of magma from a chamber or chambers beneath the edifice. The resulting caldera is often much wider than deep, as are the craters of the Moon. Calderas often contain central cones produced by eruptions subsequent to the formation of the caldera. The large cinder cone in the Crater Lake caldera in Oregon is a familiar example. Peaks which may have summit depressions are common in lunar craters and Green[7] has pointed out the marked resemblance between a prominent cone in Mokuaweoweo caldera in Hawaii and the central peak in the lunar crater Alphonsus. The Hawaiian calderas with their lava-flooded floors do look much like the large craters of the Moon. There are several difficulties with this theory. The floors of almost all calderas are above the land surface beyond the volcanic structure although there may be an exception in Iceland. Furthermore, the large lunar craters are much larger than calderas. On the other hand, lunar craters are almost certainly very much older than any volcanic forms that can now be observed on Earth, since the former have not been subjected to the intense forces of erosion that exist on Earth. Possibly early in the Earth's history volcanoes produced craters similar to the large ones on the Moon.

Many lunar craters resemble the terrestrial volcanic craters known as maars. These are craters that appear to have been formed by a single explosive eruption that has torn away the ambient rock. The crater lip is usually relatively low and the crater is partially filled in with material which has collapsed from the walls, producing a relatively level crater floor (Figure 6-3). Maars tend to occur in chains over fractures or rifts

Figure 6-3. Ubehebe Crater, a maar-type crater in
Death Valley, California.

in the Earth's crust. Chains of craters on the Moon are common and at
least some of these may be similar to the maars in origin. Shoemaker[8] has
pointed out that there are several types of crater chains on the Moon and
has described them in considerable detail.

Other features of the Moon resemble shield volcanoes. Shoemaker[8]
states that all the lunar features that resemble terrestrial shield and strato-
volcanoes have dimensions comparable to their terrestrial counterparts,
and that volcanic processes have operated on about the same linear scale
on the Moon as on the Earth.

There are a number of indications that volcanic activity still occurs
on the Moon and presumably at least some dust is produced by such
activity. Dinsmore Alter observed that in photographs taken on October

26, 1956, fissures in Alphonsus crater appeared to be more blurred than fissures in the neighboring Arzachel crater when the photographs were taken with blue light instead of infrared. Alter suggested that an emission of gas in the western part of Alphonsus may have been responsible for the blurring. Kozyrev[9] has pointed out that such a haze could not have been produced on the Moon by Rayleigh scattering but might have been produced by fluorescence of the gas by solar radiation.

Kozyrev[9] took a spectrogram of the central peak of Alphonsus on November 3, 1958 which showed the fluorescence of gases issuing from this peak. During the period of exposure, the peak appeared brighter and whiter than usual. When the appearance returned to normal another spectrogram was taken, and this one did not exhibit the fluorescence. The gas emission lasted between $\frac{1}{2}$ and $2\frac{1}{2}$ hours. Kozyrev[9] suggests that the new spectral bands were from the Swan resonance series of diatomic carbon (C_2). On October 23, 1959, another unusual spectrum of Alphonsus was obtained. A red detail of this spectrum was interpreted as having been produced by a lava flow at a temperature of about 1200°K. Kozyrev,[9] incidentally, believes that the large craters are volcanic calderas and that the larger diameter of the lunar craters can be accounted for by the fact that the Moon's gravity is one-sixth that of the Earth.

Other observations of red glows on the Moon have been described by Glasstone.[1] There is little doubt that such glows actually occur, and they are quite possibly of volcanic origin.

A large number of terrestrial craters almost certainly resulted from meteorite impact and most of these craters closely resemble in form the larger craters of the moon. The best-known example of a terrestrial impact crater is Meteor Crater in Arizona, which closely resembles a maar. It is about 200 m deep, a little over one km in diameter, and the crater rim is about 30 to 60 m above the surrounding surface.[8] Meteoritic iron has been found in the material beneath the crater floor, establishing the nature of its origin. Another example is the Ries Basin near Stuttgart, Germany. Originally it was about 50 km in diameter and thus is closer in size to the larger lunar craters than are most terrestrial craters.

Long, light-colored rays extend outward from some of the larger lunar craters (Figure 6-4). According to the impact theory of crater formation the rays are composed of crushed material ejected upon impact. According to the volcanic theory these are rift zones or dikes. The rays contain large numbers of small craters that, according to the impact theory, are secondary or tertiary craters formed by impaction of material ejected from the primary or secondary craters. The large lunar craters are almost all circular, while many of the supposedly secondary craters are elongated. Craters formed by high-velocity collisions probably are circular in form,

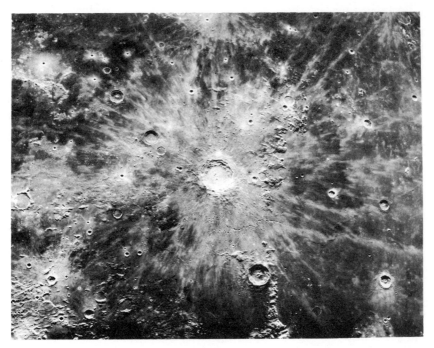

Figure 6-4.   Copernicus Crater.   (*Photo: Mount Wilson and Palomar Observatories*)

regardless of the angle the approach trajectory makes with the surface. Similarly, ejected material would be thrown out in a symmetrical pattern. Secondary and tertiary craters would not necessarily be circular since the impact velocity would be lower.   Gault *et al.*[10,11] have undertaken laboratory investigations of hypervelocity impacts with materials having a wide range of porosity.   Records of the impact phenomena were obtained with a high-speed framing camera.   The porosities were as high as 87 per cent and in all cases fragmented material was ejected from the craters formed by the impact.   Their results confirmed the proposition that, except for "jetting," impact at oblique angles produces spray patterns that are essentially symmetrical about an axis normal to the target face.   This jetting, occurring on the Moon, probably emits some particles into cislunar and interplanetary space; it may have some significance with regard to tektite formation, mentioned in the preceding chapter.

Gault *et al.*[11] found that the craters formed in the bonded particulate material were usually bowl-shaped with poorly defined edges.   Finely crushed rock was observed in the bottom of such craters.   Craters formed in pumice were bottle-shaped, the subsurface diameter being somewhat larger than that at the surface. The interior of the "bottle" and especially the lower half was covered with powder and some fused material. The differences from the craters in particulate substrates were attributed to increased porosity, greater strength, and the cellular structure of the pumice.

The total mass ejected from the particulate targets was about 10^3 times the màss of the projectiles and was about three times the mass thrown out from basalt craters under comparable conditions. However, the mass ejected from the pumice craters was only about 40 times the mass of the projectile.

Gault et al.[10] suggested that the continuous impaction of meteoroids on the lunar surface will produce a "steady-state" swarm of ejected material which is continually flying above the lunar surface. The cloud was estimated to have a concentration from 10^5 to 10^7 that for the meteoroids in interplanetary space. The authors describe this as presenting a "hostile environment" for space vehicles but emphasize that since these are secondary particles, the particle velocities and therefore the likelihood of serious punctures is low.

The lunar maria are also very distinctive surface features. The relationship of the dark, relatively smooth maria to the uplands has produced the familiar "man-in-the-Moon" appearance. Most of the lunar craters appear to have been formed prior to the formation of the maria. There is some evidence which suggests that the maria are about the same age as that of the Earth. If so, the pre-mare craters must have been formed during about 100,000 years. This in turn suggests that the rapid crater formation must have occurred during the last stages of the accumulation of the solid objects which formed the Moon and the Earth. This explanation is not universally accepted. Some scientists believe that the maria are relatively recent, geologically, and that the rate of formation was about the same for pre-mare and post-mare craters.

The most generally accepted theory for maria formation is that they were formed from massive lava flows.* In this regard they might be similar to the tremendous lava plateaus of Washington and Idaho, the last stages of which formed the "Craters of the Moon." The origin of the lava may also have been similar, in that it issued from great rifts in the Earth's surface. A variation of this theory is that the lava was formed as the result of the tremendous release of energy when large meteoroids struck the Moon's surface. Urey[2] differentiates between maria that are nearly circular in outline and those of more irregular shape. He suggests that

---

*Early in February, 1966, the Soviet Union's spacecraft Luna 9 achieved a "soft" landing on the surface of the Moon and televised photographs of the surface to the Earth. The surface in the vicinity of the space craft was very rough, closely resembling basaltic, highly vesicular, lava.

the former, such as Mare Imbrium, were formed directly by collision, and that previously existing features were destroyed by the resulting shock wave. According to this theory, the other maria were formed by flooding by secondary processes such as lava flowing from the circular maria. Urey also suggests that if the lunar surface or the colliding object contained volatile materials, a huge cloud of finely divided and possibly melted solids would have been produced. The most convincing aspect of Urey's suggestion is that the Mare Imbrium is surrounded by ridges and furrows extending outward from the "shores." These give the appearance of having been produced by material thrown out by the impact. On the other hand, the furrows may be faults produced in other ways.

There are a number of arguments against the proposition that if there were lava floods, the lava was produced by impact. Numerous laboratory studies have demonstrated that high-velocity impacts on silicates produce shattering but not melting. However, the surface-to-volume ratio is vastly different for these experiments than for lunar impacts and such results, while suggestive, are not conclusive.

Another theory concerning the nature of the surface of the maria is that it is composed of a special type of lava called ignimbrite. The vast lava flows of the Columbia Plateau in Washington, mentioned above, were produced by floods of liquid lava. Basalt floods produced in this way are readily recognized by the ropy, twisted nature of the hardened surface such as the flow shown in Figure 2-8, or by an extremely rough surface. Lava plateaus can be formed in another way. If the magmas are unusually viscous, which may result from a high silica content, and are highly charged with gas, the lava may be emitted as tremendous clouds of incandescent particles.[12] Such clouds probably consist of fluidized particles which are kept suspended by the gases evolved from the particles. The clouds are very heavy and flow like a liquid. In this regard they may be similar to the base surges formed by nuclear explosions, described in Chapter 4. Consolidation of the particles after the gas phase is spent produces relatively solid rock. Much of the Yellowstone Plateau in the United States was probably produced in this way and so was the "Valley of Ten Thousand Smokes" in Alaska. Such flows tend to assume somewhat the configuration of the surface beneath and this has been proposed as the explanation of the "ghost" craters in some maria.

Another suggested origin is impact by the nuclei of comets. If such nuclei consist of particles held together by some sort of "ice," as discussed in Chapter 7, the results of an impact might be localized and the resulting craters relatively much more shallow than if a meteor had struck the surface.

Photographs of the far side of the Moon obtained from a Russian spacecraft indicate that few maria exist on the far side compared with that visible from the Earth. Glasstone[1] states that this difference suggests that the maria were largely formed by impact of bodies orbiting between the Earth and the Moon after the Moon had assumed an orbit with one side always toward the Earth. Wise' hypothesis[4] concerning the separation of the Earth and Moon, described above, provides an explanation both for the fact that one side of the Moon always faces the Earth and for the hypothetical objects between the Earth and the Moon.

Another feature of the Moon's topography is the mountains. Many of these are along the circular maria. According to the impact theory of maria formation they consist of material pushed or thrown from the Moon's surface by the impact.

THE LUNAR ATMOSPHERE

The most important aspect of the lunar atmosphere is that there is so little of it. A comparison of the escape velocity for the Moon with lunar surface temperatures, and their significance with respect to the velocities of individual atoms and molecules, demonstrates that no more than trace amounts of oxygen, nitrogen and lighter gases can exist in the lunar atmosphere. There are several ways of setting an upper limit to the lunar atmospheric pressure. A lunar atmosphere would polarize light under certain conditions, but no such effect has been observed, indicating that if a lunar atmosphere exists, it must have a density less than 10^{-8} that of the atmosphere at the Earth's surface.

Another technique for determining the density of the lunar atmosphere involves measuring the electron density in its ionosphere. An ionized medium can refract radio waves, and the extent of refraction is a function of the electron density. The refraction of radio waves from the Crab Nebula passing close to the Moon indicated an electron density for the lunar ionosphere of 10^3 to 10^4 electrons per cm^3. This corresponds to a total particle density of less than 10^{-13} of that at the surface of the Earth.

Such a small atmosphere implies that particles near the lunar surface will fall to the surface essentially unhindered by the air. Particles ejected in some manner from the surface would follow essentially ballistic trajectories rather than being carried by the atmosphere as part of a dust cloud.

EVIDENCE OF DUST ON THE LUNAR SURFACE

The possibility that the surface of the Moon is covered with a layer of dust has intrigued scientists for many years. It is a matter of practical importance with the advent of "soft" landings on the lunar surface, that is, landings that do not destroy the space vehicle or its contents. A space vehicle might sink in a deep layer of yielding dust if such a layer exists.

There are many types of evidence indicating that all or part of the lunar surface is covered with dust or at least highly vesicular, dendritic, or fibrous material. One of these is the nature of the polarization of moonlight, which has been reviewed by Dollfus.[13] Light waves can be considered to be electromagnetic vibrations. If the vibrations are of equal amplitude in all directions normal to the direction of travel of the light, it is said to be unpolarized. If the amplitudes vary with the direction, the light is at least partially polarized. The degree of polarization can be expressed quantitatively by the expression

$$P = \frac{I_1 - I_2}{I_1 + I_2} \qquad (6.1)$$

where I_1 is the radiation intensity in the vibrational direction of maximum intensity, and I_2 is the intensity at right angles to this direction.

When a beam of unpolarized light is reflected from a surface it is generally polarized to some extent, and the degree of polarization depends on the angle the beam makes with the surface, the angle of observation, and the nature of the surface.

The degree of polarization of moonlight has often been measured using a high-precision polarimeter. Lyot[14,15] as quoted by Dollfus,[13] found a maximum polarization of 0.066 when the Moon waxes and of 0.088 when it wanes, the difference resulting from the difference in the number of maria on the various parts of the visible Moon. From the first quarter to the full Moon the polarization decreases. The polarization of light from various parts of the Moon has also been determined. According to Dollfus, the polarization is greatest for Oceanus Procellarum and Mare Serenitatis, and weakest for Hipparchus. Additional results for specific regions of the Moon were obtained by Wright, by Öhman, and by Dollfus.

To interpret these results in terms of the nature of the lunar surface, obviously it is necessary to know the manner in which light is polarized by various types of surfaces. When light is reflected by a surface, part of it, I_r, is reflected and is polarized to the extent P_r. The remaining light I_p passes through the surface whereupon it is absorbed, scattered, or refracted. The refracted light is polarized to the extent P_p at right angles to the polarization resulting from the reflection. The over-all polarization is given by the equation

$$P = \frac{P_r I_r + P_p K I_p}{I_r + K I_p} \qquad (6.2)$$

where K is the fraction of the remaining light which is refracted. Dollfus points out that if the material is a glass, the P's and I's are determined by Fresnel's laws of reflection and refraction, and if the material is not transparent, the polarization is produced almost entirely by reflection at the surface. When the surface is a plane, I_r is largely in the direction dictated by the usual equality law for the angle of incidence and reflection, and the strongest polarization is from this direction. When the surface is rough, light is reflected in many directions and the polarization maximum is less pronounced. Thus, the polarization behavior of light reflected and scattered by a surface is markedly influenced by the physical nature of the surface (rough, smooth, wavy, etc.) and the physical and chemical nature of the material forming the surface.

Numerous investigations have been made of the polarization of light reflected by various materials. Dollfus concluded that only surfaces consisting of opaque powders having zero values of P_p produce polarization curves (P vs. scattering angle) similar to those produced by the lunar surface. He also concluded that the natural terrestrial material exhibiting polarization behavior closest to that of the Moon's surface is volcanic ash.

Dollfus also measured the polarization of the "ashen" light, which is reflected earthlight rather than sunlight from the Moon. The situation differs for the two types of illumination of the Moon since sunlight is unpolarized whereas light from the Earth, like moonlight, is partially polarized. Again, the results were consistent with the theory of a lunar surface covered with opaque dust.

While there are small differences in the polarization produced by various parts of the Moon, in all places examined, even the steepest slopes, the surface behaves as though covered with a layer of dust. Polarization data, however, yield essentially no information concerning the thickness of such a dust layer.

A closely related method for obtaining information concerning the nature of the lunar surface involves making photometric measurements. Essentially, it consists of determining the variation of intensity of reflected sunlight as a function of the angle of incidence and observation. The method has been reviewed by Fesenkov,[16] Hapke and van Horn,[17] and Hapke.[18]

An unusual property of the Moon's surface is that it reflects and scatters light in such a manner that the brightness of almost all regions of the Moon rises to a maximum value when the Moon is full. At that time the Sun is immediately behind the observer. Most rough terrestrial substances, on the other hand, reflect light in such a manner that the brightness is largely independent of the direction of observation. Another peculiar property is that when the Moon is full, the center of the lunar disk has almost the same brightness as the edges, although usually a sphere having a rough surface and illuminated with a distant light source, and observed with a phase angle near zero, has a center which is brighter than the edges. Fesenkov[16] states that this property of the Moon was first pointed out by Galileo. The shape of the photometric curve is similar for all of the lunar formations studied, and for a given type of formation the maximum at zero phase angle is independent of position on the lunar disk, in agreement with Galileo's observation.[18] The shape of the curve is independent of latitude but does vary with longitude.

Fesenkov concludes that, since the lunar surface "has nothing in common with ordinary diffusing surfaces," the Moon cannot be covered by a uniform layer of dust. He suggests that it is covered with a layer of extremely porous material which contains separate grains. These must be capable of reflecting light in a backward direction and of casting shadows.

Hapke and van Horn[17] conducted a series of photometric studies of complex surfaces in an attempt to obtain an understanding of the factors affecting the scattering characteristics of such surfaces and particularly to understand the reason for the unusual way in which the Moon's surface scatters and reflects light. They point out that the large backscatter could be produced by corner reflectors or by transparent spheres having the proper refractive index, but believe that such structures would not persist on the Moon's surface because of the micrometeoroid bombardment. They agree with Fesenkov that the most reasonable explanation is that the photometric behavior results from the effects of shadows produced by an intricately structured material. These structures would have to be much larger than the wavelength of visible light in order to produce the required backscatter.

More than 200 materials were studied. The photometer consisted essentially of a modulated light source and an AC detector, permitting operation in a lighted room. The only surfaces which reproduced the lunar scattering behavior were those having the structure described above. They included lichens, grass, silver whiskers, a cellulose sponge, and various powders which were forced to pile up gently by sifting them. The latter included carbon, silver chloride, nickel sulfide, and cupric oxide. The sifting produced what Hapke has called a fairy-castle structure. This is a very open packing which cannot be produced merely by pouring a powder from a container onto a flat surface. Powders having the fairy-castle structure have bulk densities between 10 and 20 per cent of the density of the material comprising the particles. Hapke and van Horn believe that such structures result from the charges on the particles, long-range coulombic forces acting between the particles during deposition. Once the structures have been formed they are maintained by van der Waals polar forces. Fairy-castles built up of terrestrial rocks are too transparent to produce lunar photometric behavior, but lunar powders may have been subjected to a number of processes, such as bombardment by hydrogen ions in the solar wind, which have caused darkening.

Several laboratory investigations have been made to determine whether such darkening occurs.[19-21] Numerous powdered materials were subjected to a low-pressure hydrogen plasma which was produced with high-frequency fields. Ion bombardment was achieved by applying a high-frequency voltage to a metal electrode beneath the material being studied. Two seconds of bombardment corresponded to about a year of solar wind bombardment on the Moon.

Numerous powdered minerals and oxides were studied. Powdered basalt, largely in the size range 2 to 10μ diameter, developed albedo and reflection characteristics most like those of the lunar surface.[21] The albedo was rapidly reduced to a low level but the specular reflection characteristic required the equivalent of about 10^5 years of bombardment of the lunar surface to be converted to the lunar value.

Surface alteration was less pronounced when helium bombardment was substituted for hydrogen bombardment, suggesting that chemical effects of the hydrogen are important. The surfaces of the bombarded copper and iron oxides contained metallic copper and iron.

The bombarded surfaces were covered with very small needles and spires of nearly opaque material, and this probably accounts for the reduction of the specular reflection and for the strong backscatter.

Hapke[18] has developed a theoretical photometric function for the lunar surface. The function is based on a model surface of the fairy-castle type, that is, a highly porous layer for which the interstices are interconnected.

A third general method for studying the structure of the Moon's surface involves measuring the electromagnetic radiation which it emits. All bodies having temperatures above absolute zero emit radiation, the intensity of which is a function of temperature and of the emissivity as indicated by Planck's radiation formula. The intensity vs. wavelength curve passes through a maximum value for the intensity, and the wavelength corresponding to the maximum intensity increases with decreasing temperature. For example, the "radiation temperature" of the Sun is about $6000°K$, corresponding to a wavelength for maximum intensity of about 0.45μ, but since the Earth's surface temperature is about $300°K$, it radiates largely in the infrared wavelength region.

Measurements of the Moon's radiation have been made in the infrared, the millimeter, and the microwave regions. Both the wavelength dependence of intensity and the rate at which the radiation curves change as the Moon cools, as during an eclipse, furnish clues as to the nature of the Moon's surface.

The theory of the lunar surface temperature was developed by Epstein,[22] Jaeger,[23] and Wesselink,[24] and reviewed by Sinton.[25] The temperature T at any distance χ below the surface of a homogeneous body extending infinitely far in all directions beneath the plane surface is given by the equation

$$\frac{\partial T}{\partial t} = \frac{k}{\rho c} \frac{\partial^2 T}{\partial \chi^2} \tag{6.3}$$

where t is time, k is the thermal conductivity, ρ is the density, and c is the specific heat. The heat flux, F, is given by the equation

$$F = k \frac{\partial T}{\partial \chi} \tag{6.4}$$

If heat is received from the Sun at the rate I_s, at the surface,

$$\sigma T_s^4 = I_s + F_s \tag{6.5}$$

where the subscript s refers to surface conditions and σ is the Stefan-Boltzmann constant. When the Sun shines on the lunar surface,

$$I_s = \frac{G}{D^2}(1 - A)\cos 2\pi(t/P) \tag{6.6}$$

where G is the solar constant, D is the distance of the surface from the Sun in astronomical units, A is the albedo of the surface and P is the period of rotation of the Moon. Otherwise, $I_s = 0$.

These equations can be solved for the Moon only in terms of the thermal-inertia parameter, $(k\rho c)^{\frac{1}{2}}$. It is convenient to plot theoretical curves of the surface temperature of the Moon against the phase difference from the full Moon for different values of the thermal inertia and compare the results with lunar temperatures. The latter are calculated from the radiation measurements, assuming an emissivity of unity, a questionable assumption. Good agreement between the theoretical curve and temperatures calculated from measurements of infrared radiation has been obtained when the thermal-inertia parameter of the Moon was assumed to be 0.0023.*

Temperatures have been determined from the infrared radiation during an eclipse. The temperature changes much more rapidly than in the case of phase changes and I_s drops from its maximum value to zero in about 1 hour. Values obtained for the inertia are somewhat less than that mentioned above, and are about 0.001.

*Units are calories, centigrade degrees, and cgs.

These values for $(k\rho c)^{\frac{1}{2}}$ are so low that the surface of the Moon cannot be covered with rock. Sinton[25] points out that most rocks have values near 0.05, and the lowest value for natural terrestrial materials, that for pumice, is 0.004 which is still much too high. Even dusts have too high a value, almost certainly because k is too large. However, it is possible that the thermal conductivity of dust on the lunar surface is much less than it is on the earth. This possibility has been discussed in detail by Salisbury and Glaser.[26] The thermal conductivity of powders on the Moon might be altered as a result of the very low atmospheric pressure; x-ray, ultraviolet, and particulate radiation; and the packing characteristics of the material. The first of these, namely, the high vacuum, is most apt to be responsible for low thermal conductivities.

Heat may be transferred from one particle to another at regions of direct contact and also through the gas between the particles. Since the thermal conductivity of gases is usually low and the area of contact for powders is small, the thermal conductivities of powders are relatively low. When a gas fills the voids, most of the heat is conducted through the gas. When most of the gas is removed and the powder is in a vacuum, most of the heat transfer occurs at the contact points. Therefore, the conductivity of such a powder is markedly influenced by the packing arrangement and the contact pressure.

Radiative heat transfer also occurs in a powder, and at low pressures, when gas conductivity is not important, it may contribute a significant part of the over-all thermal conductivity.

Numerous investigations, including the pioneering work of Smoluchowski,[27] have demonstrated that for sufficiently low gas pressures the value of $(k\rho c)^{\frac{1}{2}}$ for a number of powders is about that required for the lunar surface.

It is not necessary that the surface be a dust in the conventional sense. Needles would also satisfy the radiometry requirements, and Hibbs[28] has proposed that the surface of the Moon is covered with needle crystals. He suggests that such crystals were the primary form of solid material in the solar system. Also, it has been demonstrated in the laboratory that many substances condense from a vapor to a solid which is in the form of needles or "whiskers." Thus, Hibbs theorizes that any lunar material which has not been melted, and any which has undergone vaporization and redeposition as a result of meteoroid impacts, should exist on the lunar surface as needles. It is of interest in this connection that solar wind bombardment can also produce needles,[21] as mentioned above.

Lunar radiation in the millimeter wavelength region has been measured by Coates[25,29] at $\lambda = 4.3$ mm, Sinton[25,30] at $\lambda = 1.5$ mm, and Gibson[31,32] at λ = 8.6 mm. A number of measurements have also been made in the microwave region, such as those by Dicke and Beringer[33] and by Piddington and Minnett.[34] Again, the measurements have been made for various phase angles or during an eclipse.

Gibson[32] has concluded on the basis of his measurements at 8.6 mm and some measurements at other wavelengths that a typical lunar surface is stratified into at least two and possibly three layers. The topmost layer is about 5 mm thick and must be in finely divided form (Gibson says it resembles ordinary sand). The intermediate layer may be a number of centimeters deep and has a high electrical conductivity, while the lowest layer is of indeterminate depth and may be merely rock.

Radar reflections also provide information concerning the solar surface. The reflection coefficient for waves of radar frequency depends on the dielectric constant, and this is a function of composition, surface roughness, and density.

Giraud[35] undertook a theoretical analysis of radio-wave emission from the Moon, taking into account the results of lunar radar reflection studies. He concluded that the Moon is covered with a layer of degenerate material, possibly damaged by radiation, with a low density and loose structure. Like so many others, he suggested a surface covered with dust, having a particle size distribution largely between 10 and 300μ diameter. He stated that the dielectric constant of the surface material is probably between 1 and 1.5, the thermal conductivity between 5×10^{-6} and 10^{-5} cal sec^{-1} cm^{-1} deg^{-1}, and a volumetric specific heat of about 0.1 or 0.2 cal deg^{-1} cm^{-3}.

Hapke[36] undertook a laboratory investigation of the packing properties of fine particles in an attempt to answer certain questions raised by studies of the radar reflectivity of the lunar surface. The very low dielectric constant indicates not only that the density of the surface material is very low but that it is rather thick, of the order of a meter or more, over much of the Moon's surface. The low density can be explained by assuming that most of the lunar surface consists of rock foam or similar material, covered with a thin layer of dust, or by assuming that the dust layer is a meter or more in thickness.

The powder studied was dunite, ground to an average particle diameter of less than 10μ, and baked in an argon atmosphere to remove grease and water. The powder was sifted and the change in density as a function of pressure was determined. The resulting function was inserted into the equation for hydrostatic equilibrium

$$dp = \rho g dx \qquad (6.7)$$

where p and ρ are the pressure and bulk density, respectively, g is the gravity field at the surface of the Moon, and x is the depth below the surface.

The resulting expression was integrated numerically to furnish the density profile of a hypothetical lunar soil, in which the material at any given depth has been compacted only by the weight of the material above. At the surface of a dunite-like deposit, the bulk density would be about $0.3 \text{ gram}/\text{cm}^3$ and at a depth of 30 cm it would be about $0.5 \text{ gram}/\text{cm}^3$. At about 30 meters depth, the density would be about $1.0 \text{ gram}/\text{cm}^3$. Cementing the grains would permit the powder to support a greater pressure and lower the bulk density at a given depth, but impaction by micrometeoroids might tend to increase the density.

Hapke[36] concluded that extensive deep dust deposits on the surface of the Moon are not incompatible with radio-frequency, infrared, and optical observations of the Moon.

Gehrels[37] has developed a model of the lunar surface based on all of the above types of evidence which differs markedly from the usual suggestions. He proposes that the top layer is a cloud of particles containing about 0.5 per cent by volume solid material. The particle radius is about 0.8μ and the particle separation is about 8μ. According to Gehrels, the thickness of this cloud or layer may be about 0.06 mm. The particles are assumed to be charged by about 10^{-8} esu and these charges keep them suspended. They may have reached the Moon from interplanetary space, that is, they may be micrometeoroids. The layer below this cloud consists of rubble or "frothy rock."

One additional bit of evidence should be mentioned, namely, the photographs obtained by Rangers VII, VIII, and IX such as Figure 6-2. Details as small as 50 cm across could be observed in the closest photographs. Of particular interest was the absence of boulders and rubble in the maria and the crater Alphonsus. The outer edges of most of the small craters were rounded rather than sharp, and this has been interpreted as indicating a dusty surface. However, this conclusion is highly controversial.

A very interesting demonstration of the importance of combining information concerning the surface obtained by different techniques is supplied by the crater Tycho. This crater appears to be one of the youngest features on the lunar surface since the rays extending from the crater are not overlapped by other features. Furthermore, the crater rim is very rugged compared with that of most other craters. The optical properties of the interior of Tycho are similar to those of the rest of the Moon, but it reflects radar very strongly and the thermal properties, unlike those of most of the Moon's surface layer, are close to those of ordinary rocks.

These results suggest that in this relatively recent crater only a very thin layer of dust has accumulated.

SOURCE OF DUST ON THE LUNAR SURFACE

Many suggestions have been made concerning the sources of dust on the lunar surface; a number of mechanisms must be responsible for its production and distribution. Since the nature of the dust must be related to these mechanisms, it is important to establish which ones are the main sources.

Meteoroids of tremendous size range have hit the Moon and have contributed to dust formation in at least two ways: (a) the impact by meteoroids produced fine particles by several mechanisms, and (b) micrometeoroids themselves ended up as particles of lunar dust as mentioned at the conclusion of the last section.

As has been pointed out by Kopal,[38] when a planet is surrounded by an atmosphere, the only meteoroids which can come into contact with the solid surface are those which can withstand the deceleration produced by the braking action of the atmosphere. If the meteoroids are large, little deceleration occurs and they may reach the surface, although they may be altered by ablation. If they are very small, they may be decelerated in the thin upper atmosphere of the planet without evaporating. Meteoroids of intermediate size are destroyed. On Earth, according to Kopal, the intermediate size (weight) range is 10^{-7} to 10^3 grams. The Moon, however, is not protected in this manner and its surface is subjected to bombardment with meteoroids of tremendous size range. This is consistent with the photographs taken with the Ranger space vehicles which show a monotonically increasing number of craters with decreasing size down to at least 50 cm diameter. As a result, the dust- and crater-forming bombardment of the Moon is much more intense than the corresponding bombardment of the Earth.

Fragments, including dust, formed by hypervelocity impacts have been investigated extensively, particularly by Gault and his co-workers.[10,11,39] Some of their results have been described above.

Kopal[38] has suggested that minute pits formed by impacts might be responsible for the unusual light-scattering properties of the Moon, and he objects to Hapke's "fairy-castle" structure on the grounds that micrometeoroids rain down on the Moon's surface with much too great a velocity to produce such structures. However, fairy-castle structures could be built up from dust ejected from the surface by meteoroid impact. Of course, even if microcraters were responsible for the light-scattering properties of the lunar surface, they could not be responsible for the radar-reflecting properties which require a very low density to depths of the order of a meter or more.

It is rather unlikely that micrometeoroids themselves constitute a large fraction of the lunar dust. One reason is that even micrometeoroids probably eject much more than their weight of fragments. It can be argued that the fragments are micrometeoroids that arrived earlier, but even so the degree of compaction would be greatly modified by the secondary infall.

Repeated heating and cooling has often been suggested as a possible mechanism of dust formation on the Moon. This possibility has been treated both theoretically and experimentally by Ryan.[40] He determined the tensile stresses produced in spheres of various sizes under the temperature conditions existing on the surface of the Moon, and compared them with stresses calculated from experimental studies. The results indicated that although theoretical calculations showed that thermal fracture can occur, the experimental results showed that it is not likely. These results suggest that the temperature changes on the lunar surface are not an important source of lunar dust.

Temperature changes on the Earth's surface produce thermal fracture largely because water is present. The water undergoes a large change in volume at $0°C$. It is highly unlikely that such a mechanism operates on the Moon, because of the apparent absence of water, and Salisbury and Smalley[41] suggest that this mechanism has probably not been operative on the Moon for at least 10^9 years.

Radiation of the lunar surface by ultraviolet light, x-rays, and particles such as protons has been suggested as being responsible for much of the lunar dust. However, there is little evidence to support this mechanism. In fact, the few experimental and theoretical investigations which are pertinent to this hypothesis indicate that such radiation is not an important dust-forming mechanism. Fisher,[42] for example, investigated the rate of erosion of an iron meteor in space. The calculation was based on data on the rare gas content of the Grant meteorite, using a procedure developed by Whipple and Fireman.[43] Fisher obtained a maximum value for the erosion rate of about 1.1×10^{-8} cm/yr.

Radiation bombardment may charge particles that have already been produced by some mechanism, and the charging may lead to transport of the particles. This hypothesis was originally proposed by Gold[44] and has since been developed by Grannis,[45] Walker,[46] and Coffman.[47]

There are several ways by which solar radiation can produce charging of dust particles on the Moon's surface. The flux of solar protons statistically equals that of solar electrons, but they may produce a charge when hitting a grain because of local variations in flux. Furthermore, both protons and electrons can bring about the emission of secondary electrons, which will produce a charge unless the number of returning electrons is just equal to those emitted. Grannis developed a general expression based on these mechanisms for the charge probability. Next he considered the fact that charging of lunar dust particles may cause neighboring particles to have the same sign of charge. Coulombic repulsion may then cause the particles to jump apart and one may fly up above the surface. If the surface is level, such "hopping" will cause no net transfer of dust, but on a slope there will be a net transfer downhill. This action is essentially the same as that proposed by Gehrels[37] as being responsible for a hypothetical very thin cloud of dust above the lunar surface. Grannis calculated that the time required to move a 1-km depth of lunar dust of density 1 gm/cm^3 a distance of 10 km would be about 4×10^{11} years, which is about 100 times the supposed age of the Earth-Moon system. Thus it is concluded that hopping alone cannot produce appreciable transport.

Possibly the charges result in a levitation of the dust grains in which the electronic space charge keeps the positively-charged particles above the surface. This would permit such particles to glide down a slope as a result of gravitational action. Since the gliding action may be interrupted by irregularities in the surface and in the space charge, the lodging of particles at irregularities will tend to smooth the surface and increase the lengths of the glides. The particles may be lifted initially by hopping or by impact of a micrometeoroid. Grannis' theoretical considerations indicated that electrostatic levitation and gliding may be an important mechanism for particle transport on the Moon. Such transport would deplete the highlands of dust, concentrating it on the crater floors and other depressions.

Walker,[46] and Singer and Walker,[48] again on the basis of theoretical calculations, concluded that electrostatic forces are too small to tear loose small particles or even to raise them. Their calculations also indicated that although impacts by meteoroids could raise particles from the surface, electrostatic effects on these particles could produce only a minor degree of fluidity.

Coffman[47] disagreed with Walker on theoretical grounds, and Salisbury and Smalley[41] because of the results of experiments they conducted. Coffman concluded that a particle of sand of 5μ radius could attain a maximum charge of 7.6×10^3 charges. The latter authors produced a negative charge on particles in a powder by sifting, and showed that individual highly charged particles carried at least 10^4 elementary charges. Ninety per cent of these particles were stated to have been "less than 17 microns," presumably in diameter. The powder was allowed to sift in an ultrahigh vacuum onto 3 rods supported on a glass tube frame. One rod was copper, and was grounded; a second was copper, and insulated; and a third was quartz. Much more powder collected on the grounded copper rod than on the others, indicating that the charge buildup on the 2 insulated rods repelled a large percentage of the falling powder sufficiently to prevent its collection on those rods. Salisbury and Smalley conclude that if similar charge intensities arise on the Moon as a result of radiation, significant transport of particles must occur.

Obviously, electrostatic levitation as a process for the transport of powders on the lunar surface remains highly controversial.

Another mechanism which has been proposed for powder formation on the lunar surface is volcanic action. As mentioned earlier in this chapter, there is considerable evidence that volcanism is still active on the Moon. If lunar volcanic eruptions are similar to many that occur on Earth, tremendous explosions making aerosols of the magma and of the materials forming the crater walls, such eruptions would be an important source of lunar dust. It is also possible that certain types of ignimbrite and the related "glowing cloud" eruptions could be important sources and the same is true of great rift eruptions, pouring out tremendous amounts of fume as well as of lava. There is no evidence for violent or extensive volcanism in recent times, but during the geological history of the Moon volcanic eruptions may have been very important sources of dust.

Seismic shock has also been suggested as a dust-producing mechanism.[49] This would undoubtedly produce some dust, particularly in the immediate vicinity of faults. Also, extensive "moon-quakes" could shake loose boulders and trigger land slides where considerable weakening had already occurred or soil had been deposited by other processes. This could only very slowly affect a major portion of the Moon's surface, but over a period of billions of years might have been effective. This mechanism cannot be evaluated without a greater knowledge than we now possess of present and past seismic activity on the Moon.

Naughton, Barnes, and Hammond[50] have pointed out that when rocks melt in a vacuum, the alkali metals they contain volatilize. They found that when such metals are deposited in a vacuum on pieces of broken rock or on polished sections of rock, the containers sealed to exclude air, and the temperature maintained at 100°C for about 2 weeks, the rock begins to disintegrate to a powder. When the exposure is at 350°C, erosion is evident within an hour and complete disintegration of the rock results from an exposure of 12 hours. The powder is formed in a porous loosely packed condition. Naughton *et al.* conclude that if impact by meteors or lunar volcanic action has produced vaporization or molten lava, alkali metal erosion may have produced dust in adjacent areas.

PROPERTIES OF PROBABLE LUNAR SURFACE MATERIALS

A number of characteristics of materials and types of materials which may exist on the lunar surface have already been discussed in connection with the probable nature of that surface. However, there are other properties of such materials that are important, especially in connection with the successful soft landing of a space vehicle. One of the important questions to be answered when designing such a vehicle is what precautions, if any, must be taken to prevent its sinking in dust on the lunar surface. And even after a few soft landings have been made, questions will remain concerning surface characteristics that will require laboratory investigations of properties of materials in an ultrahigh vacuum.

An important property of powders which has a major bearing on its ability to support an object is the cohesion or adhesion among the particles. The term "cohesion" refers to particles of the same composition while "adhesion" refers to particles of different composition.

Cohesion or adhesion between two particles results from the appearance of attractive forces when the particles are brought sufficiently close together. Such forces between individual pairs of particles have been investigated theoretically and experimentally by Derjaguin and his associates.[51] As two particles in a gas or vacuum are brought closer together, van der Waals attraction increases with decreasing distance, and Born repulsion forces occur on direct contact. Thus, a maximum attractive force occurs as the particles are brought together, and the height of the maximum F for cohesion is given by the equation

$$F = 2\pi r \sigma \tag{6.8}$$

where r is the radius of the particles and σ is the surface tension of the particles.

When the particles are in humid air, they are separated by a liquid film. When they are in direct contact, except for this film, the molecular attraction N is

$$N = 2\pi r \sigma_{1,2} \tag{6.9}$$

where $\sigma_{1,2}$ is the surface tension at the interface between the particle and the liquid.

If we consider only molecular and ionoelectrostatic forces, the force barrier P is

$$P = (1/r)(\beta/\delta - 2\sigma) \qquad (6.10)$$

where $\beta = aD(kTZe)^2 V_m$, a is a numerical coefficient which depends on the ratio between the valences of two ions, D is the dielectric permeability, e is the charge of the electron, Z is the electro-valence of the counterion, δ is the intermolecular distance, V_m is the molar volume, and k is the Boltzmann constant. According to this equation, the tensile strength of a powder is inversely proportional to the particle radii.

Frictional forces can be just as important as the forces of cohesion and adhesion in determining the flow properties of a powder unless the particles are actually cemented together in some manner. The magnitudes of such forces are difficult to predict on theoretical grounds, and recourse to experiment is usually necessary.

The influence of air on the flow of a powder can be demonstrated qualitatively by a simple laboratory experiment. Powdered rock or similar material is placed in the lower few centimeters of each of two test tubes and a steel ball, such as a bearing, is added to each tube. The tubes are then sealed, one while still containing air at atmospheric pressure and the other after evacuating the air. The tubes are now held in a vertical position and the steel balls raised to the tops of the tubes with a magnet. When the ball in the tube containing air is released it sinks through the powder but the ball in the other tube barely deforms the surface of the powder. Such experiments suggest that a space vehicle might sink into a certain type of dust on the Earth's surface, but might not sink into the same type of dust on the surface on the Moon. On the other hand, it is dangerous to extrapolate the conditions of the test tube to the conditions of the Moon.

An attempt to obtain quantitative information concerning the effect of air on the flow of powder was undertaken by Salisbury et al.[26,52] Samples of powdered silicate rocks were sifted in a vacuum chamber at pressures of 10^{-10}, 10^{-9}, and 750 mm Hg. The rocks were selected for the probability of their occurrence on the lunar surface, and included chondrite, tektite, obsidian, basalt, andesite, dunite, and pyroxenite. Only samples with fresh surfaces were used and these were ground until 80 per cent of the particles were less than 3μ, 90 per cent were less than 17μ, and 99 per cent were less than 70μ in diameter.

The vacuum chamber was constructed of stainless steel. The sieving mechanism was operated with a bellows attachment. A sample holder on which the falling particles were collected could be placed in the chamber.

Its temperature could be varied between -150 and $+600°C$, using internal electrical heaters and a liquid nitrogen cooling coil.

Angle of repose studies were made by placing powdered samples in a sieve above the sample holder and tapping the sieve mechanism so that less than a monolayer of particles per tap was deposited on the sample holder below the sieve. The angle of repose in air was generally low, but when the pressure was decreased to 9×10^{-10} mm Hg, angles of repose of 90° were attained, and some powder clung to the underside of wires strung across the holder.

Semiquantitative information was obtained concerning the strengths of the cohesive bonds and of the adhesive bonds between the grains and the surfaces upon which they rested by vibrating the sample holder. An accelerometer was mounted at the top of the sample holder column. At the damage threshold for basalt powder sieved at 10^{-10} mm Hg, the peak acceleration was about 10^5 cm/sec^2 in the direction of impact and between 5.0 and 7.5×10^4 cm/sec^2 in the other directions. This corresponded to a maximum shear force between the particles and the substrate of 1.4×10^{-4} dyne. The actual shear stresses were much more difficult to evaluate. If the attractive forces are assumed to have acted only at the point of contact, and the particles are assumed to have been elastic spheres, the contact stress was about 2×10^8 dynes/cm^2. If, however, the bonding was electrostatic, the particles must have behaved with respect to the substrate almost as though they were in contact over the entire interface. In this case the shear stress was about 350 dynes/cm^2. Similar results were obtained when the strengths of the bonds were studied by determining the depth of a layer of powder which would cling to the under side of glass, metal, or rock.

A number of experiments were undertaken to determine whether the increased cohesion in a vacuum resulted from electrostatic forces. The results all indicated that it did not. Probably van der Waals forces and covalent and ionic bonds are responsible for the cohesion in a high vacuum.

When magma is emitted from the ground, the process may be explosive, it may form glowing clouds, or it may produce lava fountains. The nature of the process depends on the rate of pressure release above the magma, on its gas content, and on its viscosity. The products produced might be expected to be different if the magma is emitted into the atmosphere at the Earth's surface rather than into the near vacuum at the lunar surface.

Dobar et al.[53] have investigated the physical nature of "lava" produced by the upwelling and solidification of a simulated magma in a vacuum. All of the experiments were conducted with silica sand or flint glass tubing as the liquid (as contrasted with the gaseous) phase of the magma. The silica was melted in an electric furnace at 1500°C and maintained in the molten state for 1 hour to allow equilibrium between the melt and the air to be attained. The sample was then placed under a bell jar and a quick-opening valve was actuated to produce rapid decompression to a pressure of 400 microns. During decompression the sample expanded to a foam and solidified.

The internal structure of the material formed from sand resembled that of a sponge. Small spines or whiskers covered the web area. The internal structure formed from the flint glass was essentially identical to that from the sand. The exterior of the former, unlike that of the latter, was covered with glass strands resembling the "Pele's hair" formed by lava fountains.

Samples of the expanded material were subjected to 4.47×10^6 roentgens of gamma radiation, which produced marked discoloration. The irradiated material possessed a photometric reflection curve similar to that of the lunar surface.

The chief importance of these results with silica is that they emphasize the need for caution in extrapolating results obtained with terrestrial materials to conditions on the Moon. These experiments can be criticized on the grounds that a natural magma contains a large amount of gas dissolved under high pressure. It is possible that such a magma could expand under atmospheric pressure to produce a product similar to that obtained by Dobar *et al.*[53] with a "magma" containing much less gas and expanding into a vacuum.

REFERENCES

1. Glasstone, S., "Sourcebook on the Space Sciences," New York, Van Nostrand, 1965.
2. Urey, H. C., in "Physics and Astronomy of the Moon," Z. Kopal, Ed., New York, Academic Press, 1962.
3. Nölke, F., *Gerlands Beitr. Geophys.*, Bd. 41, Heftl. (1934).
4. Wise, D. U., *J. Geophys. Res.*, **68**, 1547 (1963).
5. Urey, H. C., *Geochim. et Cosmoch. Acta*, **1**, 207,255 (1951).
6. Alfvén, H., *Icarus*, **1**, 357 (1963).
7. Green, J., in "Proceedings of the Lunar and Planetary Exploration Colloquium, Volume III, No. 3," North American Aviation, November, 1963.
8. Shoemaker, E. M., in "Physics and Astronomy of the Moon," Z. Kopal, Ed., New York, Academic Press, 1962.
9. Kozyrev, N. A., in "Physics and Astronomy of the Moon," Z. Kopal, Ed., New York, Academic Press, 1962.
10. Gault, D. E., Shoemaker, E. M., and Moore, H. J., "Spray Ejected from the Lunar Surface by Meteoroid Impact," NASA TN D-1767, 1963.
11. Gault, D. E., Heitowit, E. D., and Moore, H. J., in "The Lunar Surface

Layer," J. W. Salisbury and P. E. Glaser, Eds., New York, Academic Press, 1964.

12. Rittmann, A., "Volcanoes and Their Activity," New York, Interscience, 1962.
13. Dollfus, A., in "Physics and Astronomy of the Moon," Z. Kopal, Ed., New York, Academic Press, 1962.
14. Lyot, B., *C. R. Acad. Sci., Paris*, **179**, 1796 (1924).
15. Lyot, B., *Ann. Obs. Paris*, **8**, Fasc. 1 (1929).
16. Fesenkov, V. G., in "Physics and Astronomy of the Moon," Z. Kopal, Ed., New York, Academic Press, 1962.
17. Hapke, B., and van Horn, H., *J. Geophys. Res.*, **68**, 4545 (1963).
18. Hapke, B., *J. Geophys. Res.*, **68**, 4571 (1963).
19. Anderson, G. S., Mayer, W. N., and Wehner, G. K., *J. Appl. Phys.*, **33**, 2991 (1962).
20. Wehner, G. K., Kenknight, C. E., and Rosenberg, D. L., *Planetary Space Sci.*, **11**, 885, 1457 (1963).
21. Rosenberg, D. L., and Wehner, G. K., *J. Geophys. Res.*, **69**, 3307 (1964).
22. Epstein, P. S., *Phys. Rev.*, **33**, 269 (1929).
23. Jaeger, J. C., *Proc. Camb. Phil. Soc.*, **49**, 355 (1953).
24. Wesselink, A. J., *Bull. Astr. Inst. Netherlands*, **10**, 356 (1948).
25. Sinton, W. M., in "Physics and Astronomy of the Moon," Z. Kopal, Ed., New York, Academic Press, 1962.
26. Salisbury, J. W., and Glaser, P. E., Eds., "Studies of the Characteristics of Probable Lunar Surface Materials," Air Force Cambridge Research Laboratories, Bedford, Mass., AFCRL-64-970, January, 1964.
27. Smoluchowski, M., *Bull. Acad. Sci. Cracovie*, **A**, 129(1910); **A**, 548 (1911).
28. Hibbs, A. R., *Icarus*, **2**, 181 (1963).
29. Coates, R. J., *Astrophys. J.*, **64**, 326 (1959).
30. Sinton, W. M., *Astrophys. J.*, **123**, 325 (1956).
31. Gibson, J. E., *Proc. Inst. Radio Engrs.*, **46**, 280 (1958).
32. Gibson, J. E., *Astrophys. J.*, **135**, 175 (1962).
33. Dicke, R. H., and Beringer, R., *Astrophys. J.*, **103**, 275 (1946).
34. Piddington, J. H., and Minnett, H. C., *Aust. J. Sci. Res.*, **A2**, 63 (1949).
35. Giraud, A., *Astrophys. J.*, **135**, 175 (1962).
36. Hapke, B., *J. Geophys. Res.*, **69**, 1147 (1964).
37. Gehrels, T., *Icarus*, **3**, 491 (1964).
38. Kopal, Z., in "The Lunar Surface Layer," J. W. Salisbury and P. E. Glaser, Eds., New York, Academic Press, 1964.
39. Gault, D. E., and Heitowit, E. D., in "Proc. of the 6th Hypervelocity Impact Symposium," Cleveland, Ohio, April 30, May 1–2, 1963.
40. Ryan, J. A., *J. Geophys. Res.*, **67**, 2549 (1962).
41. Salisbury, J. W., and Smalley, V. G., in "The Lunar Surface Layer," J. W. Salisbury and P. E. Glaser, Eds., New York, Academic Press, 1964.
42. Fisher, D. E., *J. Geophys. Res.*, **66**, 1509 (1961).
43. Whipple, F. L., and Fireman, E. L., *Nature*, **183**, 1315 (1959).
44. Gold, T., *Monthly Notices Roy. Astron. Soc.*, **115**, 585 (1955).
45. Grannis, P. D., *J. Geophys. Res.*, **66**, 4293 (1961).
46. Walker, E. H., *J. Geophys. Res.*, **67**, 2586 (1962); **69**, 566 (1964).
47. Coffman, M. L., *J. Geophys. Res.*, **68**, 1565 (1963).
48. Singer, S. F., and Walker, E. H., *Icarus*, **1**, 112 (1962).

49. Gilvarry, J. J., *Nature*, **180**, 911 (1957).
50. Naughton, J. J., Barnes, I. L., and Hammond, D. A., *Science*, **149**, 630 (1965).
51. Derjaguin, B. V., in "Powders in Industry," Society of Chemical Industry Monograph No. 14, London, 1961; Nerpin, S. V., and Derjaguin, B. V., *Ibid*; Darjaguin, B. V., and Abrikassova, I. I., *Quart. Rev.*, **10**, 295 (1956); *Disc. Faraday Soc.*, **18**, 24 (1954); Derjaguin, B. V., *Scientific American*, July, 1960.
52. Salisbury, J. W., Glaser, P. E., Stein, B. A., and Vonnegut, B., *J. Geophys. Res.*, **69**, 235 (1964).
53. Dobar, W. I., Tiffany, O. L., and Gnaedinger, J. P., *Icarus*, **3**, 323 (1964).

Chapter 7

Planets, Comets, and Galactic Dust

MARS

Mars has probably been of more interest, or at least popular interest, than any other planet in the solar system except Earth itself. There are several reasons for this, including its proximity, the fact that its solid surface can be observed from the Earth, and the possibility that life of some sort occurs on Mars.

The orbit of Mars lies outside that of the Earth. As a result, most or all of the surface turned toward the Earth is always illuminated with sunlight. Mars exhibits only two phases to the Earth: full phases at opposition and conjunction, and gibbous phases near quadrature.

Relative to the orbits of other planets, that of Mars is very eccentric. Its arithmetic mean distance from the sun is 227,700,000 km, and its closest approach to Earth is about 56,000,000 km. The Martian solar day is 24 hours and 39.5 minutes, much like that of Earth. The inclination of the Martian equator to the orbital plane is about 25°, which is similar to the 23.5° for Earth. Because of this inclination, Mars has seasons similar to those on Earth. However, since its sidereal year is 687 terrestrial days, the Martian seasons are longer than ours. Also, because of the eccentricity of the orbit, the Martian seasons are of unequal length. Spring and summer are shorter and hotter in the southern than in the northern hemisphere, and autumn and winter are longer and colder.[1]

The temperature of the surface of Mars has been determined from its infrared radiation. The average maximum surface temperature at the equator is about 22°C, and the average minimum surface temperature at the equator is about −70°C. Thus, the diurnal temperature range is very large compared with ours. There is, of course, also a large variation of temperature with latitude.

The main features of the surface of Mars are the polar caps, the bright areas, the dark areas, and the canals (Figure 7-1). It is generally believed

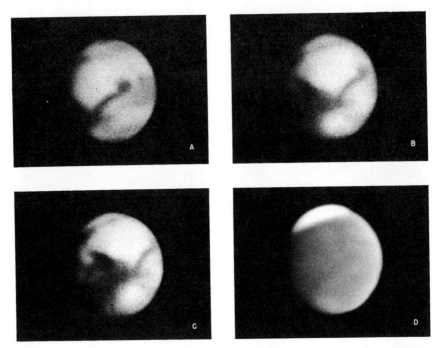

Figure 7-1. Mars: views (a), (b), and (c) taken in red light, showing rotation; (d) taken in blue light. (*Photo: Mount Wilson and Palomar Observatories*)

that the polar caps consist of small ice crystals, like hoar frost, and thus constitute fields of Martian particles. The caps are largest during the local Martian winter, gradually decreasing in size during the spring and summer. The temperatures at the polar regions are probably always less than 32°C, and the ice crystals probably form and evaporate by sublimation, that is, without an intermediate phase. In the spring, the outer edges of the caps evaporate first, and about the middle of spring a black border, which turns dark blue in the northern hemisphere,[1] forms around the edge. This border disappears as the summer advances. It may be ground that was sufficiently warm for water to accumulate.

The bright areas are probably deserts. They are reddish in color, cover almost three-fourths of the surface of Mars, and are responsible for the reddish color of the planet as observed with the unaided eye. Two suggestions which have been made concerning the nature of the reddish material are (1) that it is limonite ($2Fe_2O_3 \cdot 3H_2O$) and (2) that it is rhyolite, which is a lava rich in silica.

The dark areas, like those on the Moon, have been called maria although they contain no water. They are concentrated in the equatorial regions and undergo seasonal changes in depth of color. During the winter they are rather uniformly grey, but during the spring they darken near the pole and the darkening spreads toward the equator. One theory of this darkening is that it is caused by plants, presumably similar to lichen. Such plants are dormant in dry weather but revive and grow when the moisture content of the air increases. According to this theory, evaporation of the polar cap ice crystals supplies the water causing the renewed growth.

The polarization of the dark areas also changes with the seasons. A characteristic phase-angle vs. polarization curve is obtained for a given Martian season. With changing season, the general shape of the curve is retained, but the magnitude of the polarization changes. This can be explained by assuming that the dark areas are covered with small, opaque particles about 100μ in diameter which change in size or absorptivity with the season. These might be living organisms or small nonliving particles which change in size or darkness with changing moisture content of the air.

The so-called canals are elusive features which are best observed visually, rather than photographically, with a high-powered telescope, when the viewing conditions are exceptionally good. Long, dark features do seem to exist on the Martian surface, but they are too wide to be similar to any canals on Earth. There is some indication that they are discontinuous, the apparent continuity resulting from insufficient resolution. Photographs of the Martian surface taken with Mariner IV included regions through which canals have been sketched (Figures 7-2 and 7-3). No trace of such features was discernible. However, the canals seem to be variable with time.

The main features that could be seen on the Mariner IV photographs were craters (Figure 7-3). Leighton et al.[2] have interpreted the similarity in appearance of the surface of the Moon and that of Mars as demonstrating that the surface of Mars is very old, perhaps 2 to 5 billions of years. If the surface is this ancient, the absence of the visible remnants of rivers and oceans, and the small amount of erosion that seems to have occurred, indicate that Mars has not had a dense atmosphere or sufficient water to form oceans or rivers since its surface was first formed. Several investigators have suggested that the surface of Mars must be much younger than Leighton concluded and is probably between 300 and 800 million years old.[3-5] This conclusion is based on the concept that the rate of crater formation has been much higher on Mars than on the Moon and that the crater density on Mars is much too low for the surface of Mars to be "primitive." If this is true, no conclusions can at present be drawn from the Mariner IV photographs concerning early conditions on Mars.

Figure 7-2. Model of the Mariner IV Mars spacecraft. (*Courtesy NASA*)

The Martian atmosphere is much less dense than that of Earth. Prior to the flight of spacecraft Mariner IV, the pressure at the Martian surface was believed to be between 10 and 20 millibars, as contrasted with about 1000 millibars at the Earth's surface. However, data obtained by Mariner IV indicate that the Martian atmospheric pressure must be between 4 and 7 millibars.[6]

The only substances which have been positively identified in the Martian atmosphere are carbon dioxide[7,8] and water vapor.[9] Spectroscopic measurements show that little oxygen is present (less than 250 cm-atm). The amount of water vapor is probably between 5 and 40μ,[9-11] and very low upper limits have been established for O_3, N_2O, CH_4, C_2H_4,

Figure 7-3. Photographic representation of data radioed from
Mars by the Mariner IV spacecraft. Slant range = 7800 miles.
Viewed with data block at left, north is at the top. Area covered:
east-west, 170 miles, north-south, 150 miles. Description:
Atlantis, between Mare Sirenum and Mare Cimmerium.
(*Courtesy NASA*)

C_2H_6, NH_3, NO_2, and N_2O_4. If the atmospheric pressure at the Martian
surface is as small as the Mariner IV results suggest, the Martian atmosphere may be almost entirely composed of carbon dioxide. Nitrogen and
argon are also expected to be present, based on theoretical considerations.

Estimates of the height of the Martian tropopause place it from 10 to 40
km above the surface of the planet. Thus, most of the particles in the
Martian atmosphere must be below such altitudes, much as they are in the
Earth's atmosphere.

Fine particles in the atmosphere of Mars make up clouds which are
recognized by the fact that they obscure surface details on the planet.
They have been studied by visual, photographic, and polarimetric means
which indicate the existence of several distinct types. They are usually

designated according to the color of the filter through which they are most apparent. Thus there are white clouds, blue clouds, yellow "veils," and violet "hazes."

The white clouds, which scatter light of all wavelengths, include very dense clouds which may be so high and deep that they extend from the terminator like solar prominences and very thin fogs that can hardly be observed.[12] The polarization of light is similar from all such clouds, and they seem to be of the same nature, differing only in their optical density. Plots of the degree of polarization against scattering angle in the equatorial and mid-latitude regions produced a curve shape that is markedly different from that for a cloud of water droplets but is consistent with the curve for a cloud of ice crystals. Therefore, Dollfus[12] concludes that the white clouds on Mars consist of ice crystals as do the cirrus clouds in Earth's atmosphere. There is sufficient water to produce the visible ice (frost?) caps and cloudiness, but insufficient to produce the extensive ice fields that occur on Earth. If the clouds are similar to those on Earth the particles are in the size range 1 to 60μ diameter, and this is consistent with the polarization results.

Several types of white clouds have been observed.[13] The clouds sometimes occur in large formations that may extend for 2000 km and exist for several weeks. They may move with the wind and Dollfus reports wind velocities up to 35 km/hr. The clouds may also be small and isolated and remain in about the same place. These may be formed by processes similar to those responsible for cloud caps on mountains or rain clouds over high tropical islands. Other clouds are observed near the limbs of Mars at opposition, and may consist of ice crystals, formed by radiation cooling.

The possibility that the white clouds sometimes or always consist of carbon dioxide cannot be ruled out. Carbon dioxide sublimes at about $195°K$ at 760 mm Hg and whether it condenses in the Martian atmosphere depends on the variation of both pressure and temperature with height in that atmosphere. These are not at all well known, particularly the latter.

The white clouds seem to form in atmospheric regions where the temperatures are particularly low, and are often seen near the sunrise and sunset limbs, the former disappearing as the atmosphere warms. Glasstone[1] states that clouds observed near the sunset limb tend to be larger and brighter than the sunrise clouds and they may reappear on successive days over the same surface areas, particularly desert regions. Such clouds also appear above the polar caps, especially in the autumn and winter. White clouds sometimes form in less than 24 hours and last more than 2 weeks.[7]

The blue clouds are observed through dark blue filters and are always present in the Martian morning and evening but disappear later in the day. Sometimes they are associated with white clouds. These clouds appear to be higher than the white clouds and may be similar to the mother-of-pearl clouds in the terrestrial polar atmosphere. The particle diameters are probably less than a few microns and may be of the order of 0.1 to 1 μ. The clouds seen at the shorter wavelengths, near 4500A, are often called the blue or violet haze or layer (Figure 7-1). The opacity rises sharply as the wavelength decreases from 6000 to 4500A. The suggestion has been made that the haze is produced by solar protons. Sagan[14] states that to produce sufficient molecular ionization to produce the observed obscuration, the proton flux would have to exceed 10^{11} cm^{-2} sec^{-1} at Mars and that the interplanetary magnetic field strength would have to be less than 10^{-8} gauss. It seems unlikely that these requirements are met. Dollfus suggests that the blue veils are similar to the terrestrial noctilucent clouds, but more dense and more frequent. Other suggestions have been that they consist of dry ice (solid carbon dioxide) or carbon.

The blue haze sometimes dissipates and surface details can be seen. The clearing is usually observed at favorable oppositions but this is not always the case.[15] Local clearings also occur.[7]

Palm and Basu[16] have explained the blue clearings on the assumption that the blue haze is caused by an accumulation of micrometeoroids in the Martian atmosphere. This assumption is based on a suggestion by Link[17] that the Earth, Mars and Venus are likely to possess a micrometeoroid layer in their upper atmospheres, an idea which is reinforced by data obtained by Bouska and Svestka[18] during a number of lunar eclipses and showing that the dimensions of Earth's shadow exceed the theoretical values by about 2 per cent. Palm and Basu investigated the extent of the blue clearings as a function of the number of the meteor showers intersecting the orbit of Mars at 10° intervals of heliocentric longitude. A small but statistically significant negative correlation was demonstrated between the extent of blue clearing and meteor shower activity. According to their theory, neither local nor planet-wide clearings will follow a precise time sequence since meteor showers undergo changes in flux in time and space, and particles formed from asteroids may also contribute to the blue haze.

Evans[19] has described ultraviolet spectrograms of Mars in the wavelength region 2400 to 3500A, obtained with an objective grating spectrograph on an Aerobee rocket. He developed a model to represent the data on the basis of which the appearance of the planet through filters of different colors can be explained without postulating atmospheric absorbers in the blue and ultraviolet. Instead, the photographic appearance of the planet through blue filters is interpreted as resulting from a loss of surface contrast and reflectivity. Evans suggests that the blue clearing is indeed due to the disappearance of a cloud or haze, but that it must be very tenuous since the total reflectivity of Mars in the 3000 to 4000A region of the spectrum is only about 0.04.

Hess[20] has calculated that if the blue clearing results from particle settling, the particles must be at least 10μ in diameter. If the blue haze is due to forward scattering alone, the particles cannot be this large. However, if it results from a combination of absorption and scattering, the particles might have this size.

If the blue haze is composed of crystals of ice or carbon dioxide, an atmospheric change might cause evaporation of the crystals and thus blue clearing. Such crystals might form on nuclei such as carbon particles. A decrease in the ambient temperature might cause crystal growth to such a size that the particles would settle out and clearing would result.

Another characteristic of the blue image of Mars is that it becomes increasingly bright with distance from the center toward the limb. A homogeneous thin absorbing layer would produce limb darkening instead of limb brightening. However, the haze may not be homogeneous, and its obscuring action may include both scattering and light absorption.

The yellow clouds are low-level clouds that almost certainly consist of fine desert dust blown about by the winds. Such desert storms are rather rare and usually occur in the southern spring. For any given wind velocity, the particles that are airborne are probably smaller than those in the terrestrial atmosphere, and after the winds have diminished, the particles of a given size and density settle out faster in the Martian atmosphere. Under the Martian conditions of atmospheric pressure and gravity, a given spherical particle has been estimated[13] to fall 3.8 times as fast as it would in the Earth's atmosphere, and this was based on a denser atmosphere than is now believed to exist. Thus, the particles in Martian atmospheric dust are probably smaller than the dust particles in our atmosphere.

At times the yellow clouds seem to leave a yellow deposit on the dark areas, but after a short time the dark color is again attained. One explanation is that the dark material is vegetation which is covered by yellow dust carried by the dust storm. Growth of the vegetation up through the dust reestablishes the dark color.

VENUS

Venus is the closest planet to the Earth and in size and distance from the Sun is almost a twin of the Earth. Its surface is probably always obscured by dense clouds, so our knowledge of the nature of Venus is much less than that of our next nearest neighbor, Mars. Because of these clouds the albedo of Venus is particularly great, amounting to about 59 per cent reflection of the light falling on its surface. In contrast, the albedo of the Moon is only about 7 per cent. Because of its high albedo and proximity it is the brightest natural object in the sky after our Moon and Sun. It is sufficiently bright that it will occasionally cast a shadow and at times can be seen in daylight.

The atmosphere of Venus probably contains about 100 times the amount of nitrogen in the Earth's atmosphere and very little water vapor. Cameron[21] suggests that the atmospheres of the two planets have quite different origins and that most of the Venus atmosphere is a remnant of the primitive solar nebula. The atmosphere also contains large amounts of carbon dioxide, but very little oxygen. Kuiper[22] determined the near infrared spectrum of Venus from 1 to 2.5μ and found nearly 40 absorption bands, all due to carbon dioxide. The results suggest an abundance of carbon dioxide in the Venus atmosphere of about 2 km-atm, but that it varies from region to region on the planet. His results also showed that the amount of carbon monoxide is not more than 3 cm-atm.

The observation of Venus is somewhat complicated by the fact that its orbit is inside that of Earth, so that when it is closest to Earth most of the sunlit region is obscured by the planet itself and it appears as a crescent. There are observable irregularities on the cloud surface of Venus but they are difficult to see because of the low contrast and because of the brightness gradient between the limb and the terminator.[13] The markings are of two kinds: (a) slightly darker regions and (b) shadings along the bright limb which Dollfus states are physiological effects due to the projection of the bright crescent on a dark background. Dollfus interprets the observations as follows: A lower layer is seen, which may be the planet surface or a cloud layer associated in some way with the surface. Above this layer are large discrete clouds which are temporary or moving.

The clouds have a yellowish color, and this, together with the low water content of the atmosphere, has led to the widely accepted hypothesis that they are dust clouds, raised by violent winds acting on a parched surface. However, numerous other suggestions have been made as to the composition. These include water droplets, crystalline ammonia, polymers of formaldehyde, and sodium chloride. The water hypothesis was first suggested by Lyot[23] who compared a plot of degree of polarization of the light reflected by Venus vs. scattering angle with similar plots for water droplets. He suggested that the diameters are about 2.5μ. Kuiper proposed the dust hypothesis and suggested that the particles must be at least 20μ in diameter since the clouds at times are seen to settle very rapidly.

Menzel and Whipple[24] criticized the dust hypothesis and presented arguments supporting the water-droplet theory. They also suggested that the surface of Venus is covered with an ocean of water. This seems highly unlikely in view of the high surface temperature (about 600° K).

Deirmendjian[25] analyzed microwave brightness determinations of Venus in the light of recent theoretical results dealing with light scattering and absorption by typical terrestrial clouds and precipitation. He states that existing data do not preclude the presence of large amounts of water vapor in the lower atmosphere of Venus, and that the microwave brightness distribution in the millimeter and centimeter region can be explained by a planet-wide, continuous, and thick water-cloud veil. He estimates the water content of such a veil to be 10 gm cm^{-2}.

Venus exhibits limb darkening in the infrared region (λ = 8 to 13μ). Pollack and Sagan[26] have proposed three general catagories of models to explain this darkening. In model A, darkening is attributed to the temperature gradient in an unknown absorber above the cloud deck. In B, darkening is caused by a combination of the temperature gradient and the angular dependence of the emissivity in multiple-scattering clouds. In C, the clouds coherently redistribute radiation reaching them from below. Only model C could be rejected.

The surface temperature of Venus has been determined from measurements of the microwave radiation from the surface of the planet. This temperature is considerably higher than the blackbody equilibrium temperature, which for an albedo of 0.76 is 229° K.[27] Several explanations have been suggested for the high surface temperatures. One of these is based on the "greenhouse effect." The glass roof of a greenhouse is transparent to visible light, which is absorbed by the floor and other objects in the greenhouse. This raises the temperature of these objects which increases their rate of radiation in the infrared. The infrared radiation cannot escape directly since the glass is opaque to this radiation. The result is the desired general increase in temperature within the greenhouse. Counterparts of the glass in the atmosphere of Venus are carbon dioxide, water vapor, and probably the clouds.

Öpik[28] rejects the greenhouse hypothesis. He proposes that the atmosphere below the visible clouds is dry and dusty, and is kept in motion by winds above the clouds. According to this model, which Öpik calls the aeolosphere model, little heat is lost from the surface by radiation because the suspended dust constitutes a nearly opaque screen, transparent only to electromagnetic radiation having wavelengths exceeding about 3 cm. The winds keep the dust in suspension and this dust is extremely fine because during millions of years the particles have ground together.

The difficulties with this model have been reviewed by Kellogg and Sagan.[7] For instance, Öpik suggests that calcium and magnesium carbonates, which have the required optical properties, are the main constituents of the dust. But it is questionable whether carbonates could have formed in the absence of liquid water. This model also conflicts with Deirmendjian's suggestion of the importance of a water-cloud veil, described above.

A third structure for the atmosphere of Venus is the ionosphere model proposed by Jones[29] and Sagan, Siegel, and Jones.[30] This model has an ionosphere containing a very high concentration of electrons which accordingly is opaque to long radio waves and transparent to shorter ones. The high temperature measured at centimeter wavelengths refers to the ionosphere, and the temperature at the surface is much lower, about $300°K$. Thus, the Venus surface temperature is comparable to that of Earth, and liquid water might accumulate on the surface.

The electron density required for such an ionosphere is probably about $10^9/cm^3$ to $10^{10}/cm^3$. It is very unlikely that the electron density exceeds $10^8/cm^3$.

The Mariner II spacecraft which passed within 34,800 km of Venus in 1962 carried equipment which permitted a distinction to be made between the greenhouse and aeolosphere models on one hand and the ionosphere model on the other. Centimeter-length microwave radiation originating at the surface would exhibit limb darkening since the radiation generated near the apparent edge (limb) would pass through and be partially absorbed by a greater amount of cold atmosphere than would the radiation originating near the center of the planetary disc. On the other hand, radiation originating in the ionosphere would exhibit limb brightening since radiation from the limb would be produced by a thicker ionospheric layer than that from the center of the disc. Mariner II carried a directional microwave radiometer which scanned the surface of Venus, measuring the 1.9 cm radiation. Limb darkening was found, which strongly indicates that the ionosphere model is inapplicable.

Another study undertaken with Mariner II of possible significance with respect to the nature of the particles in the atmosphere of Venus involved measuring the intensity of radiation of 1.35 cm wavelength, where water vapor absorbs, and comparing it with the intensity of the 1.9 cm radiation. There was very little difference, which indicates that there is very little water vapor in the atmosphere of Venus, perhaps about one-thousandth that in the Earth's atmosphere.[1]

Venus passed through inferior conjunction in June, 1964 and on June 19 it was only a little over 2° from the Sun as observed from Earth. The portion of Venus illuminated by the Sun was almost entirely hidden from view, and the visible portion was a crescent, somewhat like the new Moon. A peculiarity of this crescent was that instead of being the expected semicircle, it was an almost complete circle.[31] This appearance was attributed to scattering of sunlight by very fine dust in the upper atmosphere of Venus, above the ordinary cloud layer. The diameters of the particles were probably generally less than 2μ and their concentration decreased rapidly with decreasing distance above the cloud layer.

MERCURY

Mercury is the planet closest to the Sun and is unique in that its period of revolution around the Sun and its period of rotation on its axis appear to be identical, namely, 88 Earth days. Possibly Mercury once had a period of rotation greater than its period of revolution but tides slowed the former until the two periods almost coincide. Since the orbit of Mercury is highly elliptical, about three-eighths of the planet continually faces the sun, three-eights continuously faces away from the sun, and the remaining one-fourth has a day and night each equal to the length of 44 terrestrial days.

Rice[32] has pointed out that the situation on Mercury, if it has no atmosphere and the periods of revolution and rotation actually coincide, must be very different from that if there is no atmosphere, but the two periods do not exactly coincide. First consider the former case. The hot side would always have a temperature of about 400°C and the cold side near absolute zero. Probably no compounds would occur at or near the surface on the hot side and it would probably be covered with a layer of dust consisting of such nonvolatile elements as silicon, aluminum, iron, calcium, magnesium, and carbon. Very light elements, such as most of the gases in the Earth's atmosphere, would escape to interplanetary space, while those of intermediate volatility would distil to the cold side of Mercury and freeze out.

In the second case, if the difference in period is not great, Rice points out that a given point on the planet would alternately be heated to about 400°C and then cooled to very low temperatures. The elements of intermediate volatility would continuously distil around the planet. Impaction of meteoroids on the cold side of the planet would cause local heating which in turn could lead to chemical reactions. Free radicals and various stable compounds might be formed which would immediately freeze. This process, according to Rice, would produce a band of intense chemical activity around the planet.

Finally, there is the possibility that Mercury does have a very thin atmosphere. It cannot produce a surface pressure of more than a few mm Hg since no significant light refraction can be measured when Mercury makes a transit across the face of the Sun. The dark side of Mercury would have to have a temperature exceeding about 100°K to prevent condensation of the atmospheric gases, and temperature measurements with microwave techniques indicate the dark-side temperatures may exceed this value.[33] Kozyrev[34] has reported the results of spectroscopic measurements indicating the presence on Mercury of a hydrogen atmosphere of about 10^{16} particles/cm^3. He suggests that the solar proton flux replaces the hydrogen which escapes into space.

JUPITER AND THE OTHER MAJOR PLANETS

Jupiter is by far the largest of the planets, and its mass is nearly $2\frac{1}{2}$ times that of all the other planets added together. Its mean distance from the Sun is 778 million km but because of the orbital eccentricity the distance varies from 740 million km to 817 million km.

The inclination of Jupiter's equator to its orbital plane is very small. Peek[35] states that it is 3.07° and Glasstone[1] that it is 1.03°. In consequence, seasonal effects must be small and none have been observed. The length of the Jovian year is 11.86 terrestrial years. Its rotation period is about 9 hours 55 minutes. Since Jupiter and the other major planets (Saturn, Uranus, and Neptune) have orbits that lie beyond Earth's orbit, they exhibit only full and gibbous phases.

The surface of Jupiter is always obscured by clouds but the top of the cloud layer exhibits a number of unusual features (Figure 7-4). The most characteristic of these are the bands that are parallel to the equator and the large "red spot." These features have been used to determine the speed of rotation of the planet, but it is noteworthy that the red spot does not rotate at precisely the speed of the solid surface, sometimes lagging behind and at other times speeding ahead.

The light colored, yellowish bands are called zones and the dark ones are called belts. They are sufficiently permanent that the main ones have received names, such as the Equatorial Belt, the South Temperate Zone, etc. The intensities of the belts and zones, and irregularities in them, change markedly with time. Similarly, the red spot varies in an irregular manner and at times almost disappears.

The following is the composition of the atmosphere of Jupiter according to Öpik:[36]

Species	He	H$_2$	Ne	CH$_4$	Ar	NH$_3$
Mole %	97.2	2.3	0.39	0.063	0.042	0.0029

Figure 7-4. Jupiter in blue light, showing large red spot. Taken with 200-in. telescope. (*Photo: Mount Wilson and Palomar Observatories*)

He suggests that a solid hydrogen-helium model for Jupiter's internal structure is the only one consistent with observation and theory. He showed that a differentiation by condensation during the formation of Jupiter, especially "snowing out" of hydrogen, can explain an accumulation of hydrogen in the core of such a planet. A trace of water probably also exists in the Jovian atmosphere, and the amounts of ammonia and water are probably limited by their vapor pressures at the temperatures prevalent there. The temperature at the upper surface of the clouds has been estimated to be between 140° and 200°K.

Spinrad and Trafton,[37] on the basis of high-dispersion spectrograms they obtained, suggest a somewhat different H/He ratio than that proposed by Öpik:

Species	He	H_2	Ne	CH_4
Mole %	60	36	3	1

This, of course, ignores the low concentration of ammonia which, along with methane, has been identified spectroscopically in the atmosphere of Jupiter.

Methane and ammonia strongly absorb ultraviolet radiation. The absorption spectra consist of continua or diffuse bands and therefore these compounds must photolyze to form free radicals. Such free radicals and their reaction products may be responsible for certain features of the Jovian atmosphere. Urey and Brewer[38] have suggested that the fluorescence of ions and free radicals such as NH_2, N_2^+, CN, CH_2, CH^+, CH, and C_2 in ultraviolet light contribute to the brightness of Jupiter and that variations in the emission of ultraviolet light from the Sun may be responsible for variations in the brightness of Jupiter during the sunspot cycle. The clouds of Jupiter often exhibit many colors, and Rice[39] has suggested that the blue color results from the condensation of the radical NH and that the yellow color is produced by the condensed radical NH_2NH. Urey[40] has proposed that stable colored chemical compounds are formed as a result of free-radical reactions and suggests the compounds diazomethane, azomethane, and cuprene (yellow), and tetrazine (red) as possible constituents of Jovian clouds.

The clouds of Jupiter probably consist mainly of crystals of ammonia. However, there may also be particles consisting of organic compounds in addition to those mentioned above. The methane undergoes photolysis to form methylene and methyl radicals:

$$CH_4 \xrightarrow{h\nu} CH_2 + H_2 \tag{7.1}$$

$$CH_4 \xrightarrow{h\nu} CH_3 + H \tag{7.2}$$

Similarly, the ammonia undergoes photolysis:

$$NH_3 + h\nu \rightarrow NH_2 + H \tag{7.3}$$

These radicals can undergo a multitude of reactions such as

$$CH_3 + CH_3 + M \rightarrow C_2H_6 + M \tag{7.4}$$

$$CH_3 + C_2H_6 \rightarrow CH_4 + C_2H_5 \tag{7.5}$$

$$C_2H_5 + CH_3 \rightarrow C_3H_8 \tag{7.6}$$

$$CH_3 + H_2 \rightarrow CH_4 + H \tag{7.7}$$

$$CH_3 + NH_2 + M \rightarrow CH_3NH_2 + M \tag{7.8}$$

Such reactions can produce high molecular-weight compounds which condense from the atmosphere, producing or contributing to the clouds. Whether some of these reactions occur to an appreciable extent depends on the temperatures in the upper Jovian atmosphere. Hydrogen abstraction reactions such as 7.7 have an appreciable activation energy (5-15 kcal per mole) and will not occur to an appreciable extent if one of the lower estimates of the temperature at the top of the cloud layers is correct.

Either hydrogen abstraction reactions must occur or hydrogen itself must absorb ultraviolet radiation more strongly than is generally assumed. Otherwise methane and ammonia would have disappeared long ago from the Jovian atmosphere. Recent reexamination of early planetary temperature measurements indicates that the temperature at the top of the cloud layer exceeds 200°K, so perhaps the former explanation is correct.[41]

The solar radiation flux has been obtained with rocket-borne spectrometers, and absorption coefficients are known for both methane and ammonia. Therefore, it is possible to make very rough estimates of the rates of photolysis of methane and ammonia.[42] At depths where 50 per cent and 90 per cent of the Lyman alpha radiation have been removed by the methane, the rates of photolysis of methane have been estimated to be 1.1×10^4 and 7.4×10^3 molecules cm^{-3} sec^{-1}, respectively, and the rates of photolysis of ammonia have been estimated to be 1.2×10^4 and 4.3×10^4 molecules cm^{-3} sec^{-1}, respectively. Unfortunately, insufficient is known about Jovian atmospheric temperatures and about absorption coefficients of many of the compounds that may be produced in the Jovian atmosphere to calculate the steady-state concentrations of such compounds.

Almost nothing is known about the sizes or size distributions of the particles in the Jovian clouds. This is largely because the polarization curve for diffuse reflection by the cloud layer can be observed over only a few degrees. Some scattering of blue light occurs above the cloud layer, and this is probably by ammonia particles which are very much smaller than the wavelength of light. Such particles would scatter the light according to the laws of Rayleigh scattering.

Saturn, Neptune, and Uranus also have very thick atmospheres. Methane has been identified in the atmospheres of all three which almost certainly also contain very large amounts of hydrogen, helium, neon, and argon, and amounts of ammonia and water vapor limited by their vapor pressures at the temperatures in the planetary atmospheres. Saturn, like Jupiter, shows visible cloud changes which greatly influence its appearance, and studies of the light scattered by the atmospheres of Uranus and Neptune suggest that they also have a haze or cloud cover.

Saturn, of course, is particularly interesting because of its rings. There are three of these, designated A, B, and C in order of decreasing radius. The outer diameter of A is about 274,000 km. A and C are not so bright as B, and they are translucent, which demonstrates that they consist of particles rather than being continuous. Little is known of the nature of these particles. The infrared spectrum of the rings is much like the reflection spectrum of hoar frost,[8] so the particles may be crystals of ammonia. Our knowledge of Saturn up to 1962 has been reviewed by Alexander.[43]

PLUTO

Pluto is so far from the Sun, about 7.4×10^9 km, that its temperature must be very low. Any gases present would freeze and its atmosphere, if any, must be very tenuous. Thus stable clouds of any sort seem to be out of the question.

COMETS

The possible contribution of comets to the fine particles in the inter-planetary space of the solar system has been mentioned repeatedly. Therefore, it is appropriate to discuss their nature and the manner in which they produce particles.

Comets can be defined as objects in the solar system that have the ability to release relatively large amounts of dust and gas when heated by solar radiation, especially when relatively close to the Sun. Since the material emitted by the comet is never regained, the lifetimes of comets must be quite limited when compared with those of other major objects in the solar system.

Comets travel in a wide variety of orbits, some of which are indis-tinguishable from those of minor planets; the paths of others are highly eccentric and are greatly tilted with respect to the plane of the Earth's orbit. The orbits of some 566 comets have been determined, compared with more than 1600 minor planets.[44] Many comets have greatly elon-gated orbits and such orbits are specific to comets. Some of these travel distances from the Sun that are appreciable fractions of the distances to the nearest stars.

A fully developed comet has three characteristic parts. The nucleus resembles a star and almost certainly consists of solid material. The coma, or head, surrounds the nucleus and is more hazy in appearance than the nucleus, having no well-defined boundary. It probably consists largely of a mixture of solid particles, neutral molecules, and atoms. The tail of a comet may consist of both gas and dust. The spectrum of light from the tail consists of lines and bands superposed on a continuum. The lines and bands are due to emission from various excited species, principally ions, while the continuum is scattered sunlight and contains the Fraunhofer lines of the Sun. The tails usually extend away from the Sun but occasionally tails develop which seem to extend toward the Sun. A fairly recent example of a comet with a sunward tail or "spike" was Comet Arend-Roland which appeared in 1956 and was visible to the unaided eye. Two views of this comet are shown in Figures 7-5 and 7-6. Although it appears to have a tail directed toward the Sun, this is actually an illusion of perspective. The appearance was explained by Larsson-

Figure 7-5. Comet Arend-Roland (1956-h), showing apparent spike or sunward tail. (Courtesy Gunnar Larsson-Leander and *Arkiv för Astronomi*, **2**, No. 23, 259 (1958))

Leander[45] as resulting from cometary matter very strongly concentrated in the orbital plane. Nonetheless, some anomalous tails may actually extend toward the Sun.

The spectrum of the head and nucleus of a comet exhibits structure which has been identified as being produced by neutral atoms, molecules, and free radicals which appear only within the heads, and by various ions which are more characteristic of the tails. The former include[46] CN, C_2, C_3, NH, OH, NH_2, CH, Na, O, Fe, and Ni, while the latter include CO^+, N_2^+, and CH^+.

Figure 7-6. Comet Arend-Roland (1956-h). (Courtesy Gunnar Larsson-Leander and *Arkiv för Astronomi*, **2**, No. 23, 259 (1958))

The tails of comets may consist largely of dust particles or largely of ions. These differences in composition are responsible for differences in the acceleration away from the Sun and thus for differences in the appearance of the tails. Those composed largely of ionized gas are usually straight and narrow, while those whose spectra are largely that of scattered sunlight, and are presumably composed mainly of dust, tend to be wide and curved. The Comet Mrkos (1957-d) had two tails, one long and straight and having a discontinuous spectrum, and the other curved, rather short, and exhibiting a continuous spectrum (Figure 7-7). Apparently the former tail was gaseous and the latter consisted of dust.

Not all comets develop tails as they come near the Sun. About one-half of the tails that do develop consist of ions although these may be accompanied by dust tails as well.

Both the acceleration and shape of tails consisting of fine particles can be explained, at least in general terms, by radiation pressure. Radiation pressure cannot explain the behavior of tails composed of ions and electrons (plasma tails) and their features probably result from solar corpuscular radiation, the "solar wind." Little is known about the size of the dust particles. The theory of the mechanical behavior of the dust tails bears the name Bessel-Bredihhin, and has been reviewed by Wurm.[46] While this theory confirms the indications based on optical characteristics that such tails consist of fine particles rather than ions, it tells us little else about the particle size. If the particles ejected from comets, such as those in the tails, are the major constituent of the zodiacal cloud, we have a crude idea of their size distribution as described in Chapter 5. Liller[47] studied the color, brightness, polarization and configuration changes of

Figure 7-7. Comet Mrkos (1957-d), exhibiting two tails. The long one was gaseous and the short, curved one consisted largely of dust. (*Courtesy Professeur M. Dufay, Observatoire de Haute Provence*)

the particulate tails of Comets Arend-Roland (1956-h) and Mrkos (1957-d). Spectroscopic observations of the tails of both comets showed that most of the visible light was scattered by solid particles. The color was definitely redder than sunlight and established that the probable diameters were within the range 0.25 to 5μ. The polarization values are consistent with those which would be obtained if the particles were iron spheres with diameters near 0.6μ and masses about 8×10^{-13} gram. Liller states that this result is supported by studies of micrometeoroids collected at high altitudes which consisted of large numbers of small iron spheres. The particles were accelerated away from the comet nuclei at about 1 cm sec^{-2}. Calculations were made from these results of the rates of mass loss for the two comets and ultimately the comet masses. Measurements of surface brightnesses of the tails permitted estimates to be made of the masses of the tails. The results of these calculations are given in Table 7-1.

Two theories of the structure of the cometary nucleus have been widely accepted. One of these is the "sand-bank" model. According to this theory the nucleus consists of a loose aggregate of solid particles of various sizes accompanied by considerable gas. The particles are held together by gravitational forces, or possibly just because they maintain similar orbits about the Sun. The disintegration of comets is explained as being caused by solar heating or tide raising. The other theory may be called the icy conglomerate comet model. According to this model the nucleus was formed from interstellar material at temperatures between 10 and 100°K. The nucleus consists of a discrete solid mass. When the nucleus approaches the Sun, evaporation of the more volatile components releases the less volatile particles which produce the dusty tails.

TABLE 7-1. DATA LEADING TO THE MASSES OF THE COMETS[47]

	Comet 1956-h	Comet 1957-d
Date of observations on which results are based	April 30.2, 1957	August 23.2, 1957
Distance from nucleus at which observations were made	2.12×10^6 km	4.42×10^6 km
Average separation of scattering particles	4.2 meters	3.1 meters
Mean number density of scattering particles	1.35×10^{-8}/cm^3	3.4×10^{-8}/cm^3
Mean mass density of scattering particles	1.1×10^{-20}g/cm^3	2.5×10^{-20}g/cm^3
Assumed volume of tail	8×10^{33} cm^3	8×10^{33} cm^3
Mass of scattering particles in tail	9×10^{13}g	2×10^{14}g
Rate of mass loss of comet (scattering particles)	8×10^7g/sec	1×10^8g/sec
Mass of scattering particles lost by comet per revolution	5×10^{14}g	7×10^{15}g
Estimated lifetime of comet (number of revolutions)	100	100
Total scattering particle mass (1957)	5×10^{16}g	7×10^{17}g
Total mass (guess)	10^{18}g	10^{19}g

Unfortunately, the existence of discrete nuclei cannot be proved or disproved by direct observation. Some comets do not seem to have a nucleus, but this may be because the nucleus is too small to be apparent.

Whipple[48] has discussed the difficulties with the sand-bank model and they can be summarized as follows:

(a) The amount of gas lost from comets seems to be so large relative to the amount of solid that it is difficult to explain its being carried along by a swarm of small discrete particles.

(b) Judging from the area and mass estimates for the larger comets, the nuclei of such comets can consist of at most a few large particles.

(c) Both accelerations and decelerations of comets seem to occur.

(d) Some comets come very close to the Sun. For example, 1882 II came within one solar radius of the Sun's surface. At this distance heat from the Sun would have completely vaporized any particles smaller than about 30 cm in diameter. This comet did break into several parts following passage around the Sun and it has been suggested that it vaporized and later recondensed. Whipple[48] points out that this comet is one of a group of six with very small perihelion passages. This is strong evidence that a parent comet existed which survived a very close passage at least once and split up to form the six comets. Particles comprising any such sand-bank comet would have to be of the order of meters in diameter to survive. Whipple has also emphasized that a number of other comets have passed within 0.1 astronomical units of the Sun, close enough so that a cometary head made of very small particles would have vaporized.

(e) Comets at times undergo tremendous bursts of brightness, and the sand-bank model provides no explanation, although neither does any other model. One comet, the Schwassmann-Wachmann, undergoes bursts of several magnitudes periodically within a matter of hours. The suggestion has often been made that such bursts are the results of collisions between asteroids and the nuclei of comets, but the Schwassmann-Wachmann comet undergoes such bursts beyond Jupiter, where asteroid-like objects are rare.

A compact sand-bank model has also been proposed. While this seems to overcome some of the difficulties mentioned above, others remain, especially that of accounting for the large gas-to-solid ratio.

The theory of an icy nucleus seems to be more generally accepted than that of a sand-bank nucleus but it also has its difficulties. For example, the icy nucleus model has been criticized from the standpoint that if such a nucleus breaks up, a great deal of crushing would occur accompanied by a large increase in surface. This might be expected to be accompanied by an enormous burst of luminosity. Whipple,[48] however, argues that such a nucleus would "...just fade out without a burst." This would occur if an irregularly shaped icy nucleus disappears by sublimation and breaks up while rotating relatively slowly.

Possible major constituents of the ice of cometary nuclei are the clathrates. These are solids which have many of the properties of chemical compounds but actually consist of individual molecules of gases trapped in voids which are an integral part of the crystalline structure of certain solids. Thus, the binding is strictly physical rather than chemical. The solid "hydrate" of methane, $CH_4 \cdot 6H_2O$, is almost certainly this type of substance. The existence of this compound in the cometary nuclei could explain the presence of methane in the nuclei at relatively high temperatures.

According to the icy nucleus theory, the particles forming the tails are gradually liberated as the ice sublimes and are forced away from the Sun by radiation pressure. However, they are sometimes ejected sufficiently forcefully in other directions that anomalous tails are produced. The icy nucleus theory does not provide an explanation for cometary bursts. Possibly the nucleus in some way stores solar energy which reaches it as radiation and liberates it in bursts. Another possibility is that free radicals trapped within the icy nucleus are somehow freed to react and release the necessary energy. Possibly reaction occurs between free radicals and stable organic molecules such as acetylene. Whipple[48] has suggested that if the original deposition of matter in the nucleus is very irregular, there may be local high concentrations of very volatile material. Heating of such material as the comet approaches the Sun, and outer layers of the nucleus are removed by ablation, might produce a sudden blowout accompanied by outgassing. He also suggested that irregular sublimation from the surface of the nucleus might produce nonradial forces accompanied by large changes in rotation which in turn might produce disruption. Of course, it is possible that several such processes are operative, different ones occurring at different times.

It is not surprising that the origin of comets is even more of a mystery than their composition. Several theories have been proposed, none of them very satisfactory. For example, they may have been formed by condensation during much the same time that the planets were formed. It has also been suggested that whatever produced the asteroids simultaneously produced fragments moving in unstable orbits.[49] A third possibility is that they were formed of material captured by the solar system from interstellar space after the planets were formed.

Donn,[50,51] assuming that the solar system was once a supersaturated nebula that rather quickly condensed to form "primary" particles, concluded that a large fraction of these particles were long single crystals ("whiskers"). This agrees with Hibbs'[52] suggestion that the Moon is covered with such needles which originally were formed by condensation from a solar-system nebula. Donn suggests that while most of the grains became part of asteroids, satellites, or planets, many small accumulations formed in the vicinity of Jupiter and Saturn and eventually became comets. Isolated primary particles would not survive over the several billion years that have elapsed since they were formed. If so, cometary dust is probably the only source of relatively unchanged particles that condensed from the primordial solar nebula. Disintegration of cometary nuclei releases meteoroids, and the larger aggregates are the very low density "dust-ball" meteoroids.

Comets lose some of their mass on each pass near the Sun (perihelion) and can only survive a few hundred passes. Since comets still exist, a very large number must have been formed originally, unless it is assumed that they continue to be formed or that they are captured by the solar system. Oort[53] has proposed that a cloud of about 2×10^{11} comets was formed along with the rest of the solar system and moved to a distance of about 10^5 astronomical units from the Sun. Originally this cloud was much closer to the Sun. Perturbation of the orbits of one of these comets brings it into the planetary region at perihelion. In time, this comet will be captured by the huge mass of Jupiter, and changed from a long period comet to a short period one that is periodically visible from Earth.

Dauvillier,[49] on the other hand, believes that the comets are continually being formed from asteroids as they pass near Jupiter. According to this hypothesis, planetary systems which have no asteroids, that is, no broken planet, have no comets.

There are numerous arguments that make the idea that comets originate outside the solar system untenable. For example, in that case their orbits would be retrograde as often as direct, which is not so. Also, their orbits would often be highly hyperbolic instead of elliptic. A few comets do have weakly hyperbolic orbits, but these orbits seem to have been perturbed by the major planets.

GALACTIC DUST

The galaxy in which we live, the Milky Way, contains large amounts of interstellar dust, and galaxies in general are probably very dusty systems. The dust in our own galaxy can be observed as dark patches in the Milky Way. One of the best examples of such a dust cloud is the Coalrack, near the Southern Cross. The best example which can be seen from the northern hemisphere is probably the rift near the constellation Aquila.

The clouds are largely found in the spiral arms where they are a great nuisance to astronomers since they prevent observations of distant parts of the galaxy, such as its nucleus.

The scattering coefficient for the clouds increases with decreasing wavelength of the incident light. Judging from the characteristics of the scattered light, the particles are solid and the mean radius is less than about 0.3 micron.

Considerable information concerning the nature of galactic particles has been obtained by studying the polarization of light from distant stars, a phenomenon that was discovered independently by Hiltner[54] and by Hall.[55] The plane of vibration is perpendicular to the galactic plane. The light from a distant star is polarized only if it is reddened, and this polarization is independent of the physical properties of the star.[56,57] The polarization is most likely produced by the same particles that obscure stellar light. The results of the polarization measurements can be accounted for if the particles are elongated and oriented; such orientation requires a force, which may be provided by a magnetic field. There is considerable evidence that the required fields exist. For example, magnetic fields can be produced by turbulence in the interstellar gas, and Davis and Greenstein[58] have suggested that the lines of force must be oriented along the spirals of the galaxy.

Spitzer and Tukey[59] believe the grains are ferromagnetic and are composed mainly of iron, magnesium, and their compounds. They suggested that the particles responsible for the polarization are formed by collisions between other particles, and estimated that one out of every four particles is compound, consisting of ices of water, ammonia, and methane surrounding a dense nucleus. Davis and Greenstein[58] assume that the particles contain mainly compounds of hydrogen with about 12 per cent iron by weight. Their mechanism for orienting the particles, which they assume are spinning, is the small, non-conservative torque resulting from paramagnetic relaxation in material containing a few percent of iron. It is interesting to speculate concerning the possibility that the particles might be single-crystal whiskers such as those proposed for interplanetary space by Donn.[51]

Dauvillier[49] believes that galactic dust is produced by stellar explosions, that it thus requires the prior formation of atoms and celestial bodies, and that it is the end-product of a long and complex evolution. He points out that the particles must be positively charged as a result of their being irradiated with stellar ultraviolet light and states that this must prevent agglomeration.

The weight concentration of dust particles in the Milky Way has been estimated to be about 10^{-26} gm/cm^3. This is an average concentration, and local densities are undoubtedly higher.[1]

The presence of dust in galaxies other than our own would be expected, and there is considerable evidence that this is so. The Large Magellanic Cloud contains large amounts of dust, although the Small Magellanic Cloud contains very little. Dauvillier[49] reports that Elvius and Hall studied the polarization of light from a dozen galaxies. Considerable polarization was noted, the maximum being 15 per cent for M 82.

We can do little more than speculate concerning fine particles in inter-galactic space. A luminous background, perhaps consisting of both particles and gas, has been observed in large clusters of galaxies. The number concentration of galaxies near the center of a large cluster appears to be lower than near the edge of the cluster, and this may result from obscuration of central galaxies by a cloud of particles and gas. In our galaxy, dust seems to be concentrated toward the center. Perhaps it is gradually lost from the spiral arms to intergalactic space. If so, its ultimate fate becomes a problem in cosmology.

REFERENCES

1. Glasstone, S., "Sourcebook on the Space Sciences," New York, Van Nostrand, 1965.
2. Leighton, R. B., Murray, B. C., Sharp, R. P., Allen, J. D., and Sloan, R. K., *Science*, **149**, 627 (1965).
3. Anders, E., and Arnold, J. R., *Science*, **149**, 1494 (1965).
4. Witting, J., Narin, F., and Stone, C. A., *Science*, **149**, 1496 (1965).
5. Baldwin, R. B., *Science*, **149**, 1498 (1965).
6. Kliore, A., Cain, D. L., Levy, G. S., Eshleman, V. R., and Drake, F. D., *Science*, **149**, 1243 (1965).
7. Kellogg, W. W., and Sagan, C., "The Atmospheres of Mars and Venus," Publication No. 944 of the National Academy of Sciences-National Research Council, Washington, D.C., 1961.
8. Kuiper, G. P., in "The Atmospheres of the Earth and Planets," G. P. Kuiper, Ed., Chicago, Univ. of Chicago Press, 1952.
9. Spinrad, H., Munch, G., and Kaplan, L. D., *Astrophys. J.*, **137**, 1319 (1963).
10. Dunham, T., in "The Atmospheres of the Earth and Planets," G. P. Kuiper, Ed., Chicago, Univ. of Chicago Press, 1952.
11. Danielson, R. E., *American Scientist*, **51**, 375 (1963).
12. Dollfus, A., "Polarization studies of planets," in "The Solar System. III," G. P. Kuiper and B. M. Middlehurst, Eds., Chicago, Univ. of Chicago Press, 1961.
13. Dollfus, A., "Visual and photographic studies of planets at Pic du Midi," in "The Solar System. III," G. P. Kuiper and B. M. Middlehurst, Eds., Chicago, Univ. of Chicago Press, 1961.
14. Sagan, C., *Icarus*, **1**, 70 (1962).
15. de Valcouleurs, G., "Physics of the Planet Mars," London, Faber and Faber, 1954.
16. Palm, A., and Basu, B., *Icarus*, **4**, 111 (1965).
17. Link, F., *Bull. Astron. Inst. Czech.*, **2**, 1 (1950).

18. Bouska, J., and Svestka, Z., *Bull. Astron. Inst. Czech.*, **2**, 6 (1950).
19. Evans, D. C., *Science*, **149**, 969 (1965).
20. Hess, S. L., *Astrophys. J.*, **127**, 743 (1958).
21. Cameron, A. G. W., *Icarus*, **2**, 249 (1963).
22. Kuiper, G. P., *Communications of the Lunar and Planetary Laboratory*, 1, No. 15, 83 (1962).
23. Lyot, B., *Ann. Obs. Paris-Mendon*, **8**, 70 (1929).
24. Menzel, D. H., and Whipple, F. L., *Publ. Astron. Soc. Pacific*, **67**, 161 (1955).
25. Deirmendjian, D., *Icarus*, **3**, 109 (1964).
26. Pollack, J. B., and Sagan, C., *J. Geophys. Res.*, **70**, 4403 (1965).
27. Jastrow, R., and Rasool, S. I., *J. Geophys. Res.*, **67**, 1642 (1962).
28. Öpik, E. J., *J. Geophys. Res.*, **66**, 2807 (1961).
29. Jones, D. E., *Planetary and Space Science*, **5**, 166 (1961).
30. Sagan, C., Siegel, K. M., and Jones, D. E., *Astron. J.*, **66**, 52 (1961).
31. Dollfus, A., *Endeavour*, **24**, 87 (1965).
32. Rice, F. O., *Chem. Engr. News*, 89, Feb. 15, 1965.
33. Roberts, J. A., *Planetary and Space Science*, **11**, 221 (1963).
34. Kozyrev, N., *J. Brit. Astron. Assoc.*, **73**, 345 (1963).
35. Peek, B. M., "The Planet Jupiter," London, Faber and Faber, 1958.
36. Öpik, E. J., *Icarus*, **1**, 200 (1962).
37. Spinrad, H., and Trafton, L. M., *Icarus*, **2**, 19 (1963).
38. Urey, H. C., and Brewer, A. W., *Proc. Roy. Soc. (London)*, **241A**, 37 (1957).
39. Rice, F. O., *Sci. Amer.*, **194**, No. 6, 119 (1956).
40. Urey, H. C., "The Planets: Their Origin and Development," New Haven, Yale Univ. Press, 1952; "The atmospheres of the planets" in "Encyclopedia of Physics, Vol. L11," Berlin, Springer-Verlag, 1959.
41. Murray, B. C., *J. Geophys. Res.*, **67**, 1649 (1962).
42. Cadle, R. D., *J. of the Atmos. Sciences*, **19**, 281 (1962).
43. Alexander, A. F. O'D., "The Planet Saturn," New York, Macmillan, 1962.
44. Roemer, E., in "The Solar System, IV," B. M. Middlehurst and G. P. Kuiper, Eds., Chicago, Univ. of Chicago Press, 1963.
45. Larsson-Leander, G., *Arkiv för Astronomi*, **2**, 259 (1958).
46. Wurm, K., in "The Solar System, IV," B. M. Middlehurst and G. P. Kuiper, Eds., Chicago, Univ. of Chicago Press, 1963.
47. Liller, W., *Astrophys. J.*, **132**, 867 (1960).
48. Whipple, F. L., in "The Solar System, IV," B. M. Middlehurst and G. P. Kuiper, Eds., Chicago, Univ. of Chicago Press, 1963.
49. Dauvillier, A., "Cosmic Dust," New York, Philosophical Library, 1964.
50. Donn, B., in "Cosmic Dust," H. E. Whipple, Ed., New York, New York Academy of Sciences, 1964.
51. Donn, B., *Icarus*, **2**, 396 (1963).
52. Hibbs, A. R., *Icarus*, **2**, 181 (1963).
53. Oort, J. H., *Bull. Astron. Inst. Ned.*, **11**, 91 (1950).
54. Hiltner, W. A., *Science*, **109**, 165 (1949); *Nature*, **163**, 283 (1949).
55. Hall, J. S., *Science*, **109**, 166 (1949).
56. Hiltner, W. A., *Astrophys. J.*, **109**, 471 (1949).
57. Hall, J. S., and Mikesell, A. H., *Astron. J.*, **54**, 187 (1949).
58. Davis, L., and Greenstein, J. L., *Astrophys. J.*, **114**, 206 (1951).
59. Spitzer, L., Jr., and Tukey, J. W., *Astrophys. J.*, **114**, 187 (1951).

Author Index

Subject Index